Poverty of Democracy

Pitt Latin American Series

John Charles Chasteen and Catherine M. Conaghan, Editors

POVERTY OF DEMOCRACY

The Institutional Roots of Political Participation in Mexico

□ □ □ □ □ □ □

CLAUDIO A. HOLZNER

University of Pittsburgh Press

Published by the University of Pittsburgh Press, Pittsburgh, Pa., 15260
Copyright © 2010, University of Pittsburgh Press
All rights reserved
Manufactured in the United States of America
Printed on acid-free paper
10 9 8 7 6 5 4 3 2 1

Library of Congress Cataloging-in-Publication Data
Holzner, Claudio A.
    Poverty of democracy : the institutional roots of political
participation in Mexico / Claudio A. Holzner.
        p.   cm. — (Pitt Latin American series)
    Includes bibliographical references and index.
    ISBN 978-0-8229-6078-2 (pbk. : alk. paper)
    1. Mexico—Economic policy—21st century. 2. Free
enterprise—Mexico. 3. Political participation—Mexico. 4.
Democracy—Mexico.   I. Title.
    HC135.H65 2010
    323'.0420972—dc22   2010020951

For Sarah, with love

Contents

Figures

Tables

Preface

I became interested in the poor's political participation when I was a senior in college studying Latin American politics. Between 1982 and 1990 almost all countries in the region abandoned authoritarianism in favor of multi-party democracies, democracies that almost universally implemented strict austerity programs and structural reforms designed to shrink the state's role in the economy and promote free trade, deregulation of industries, privatization of businesses, a reduction of subsidies, and an emphasis on economic growth and macroeconomic stability rather than on poverty reduction or eliminating income inequalities. I wondered, if the poor made up a majority of the population in such countries as Bolivia, Peru, and Mexico, why didn't they take advantage of democratic politics to mount more electoral resistance to the implementation of neoliberal reforms?

The conventional answers from the academic literature—that the poor participate less in politics precisely because they are poor and undereducated, or that they participate primarily in protests, social movements, and rebellions—were not very satisfying. The poor experiment constantly with different strategies—political and nonpolitical, formal and informal, collective and individual, peaceful and violent—to satisfy their most immediate needs and to improve the situation of their families. If one set of strategies fails or becomes impractical, they quickly shift to a different mode with greater promise. Sometimes this means temporarily exiting the political system. But such quiescence is usually transitory and ends once new opportunities arise in the political system that make political action worthwhile again. Thus studies that emphasize the quiescence of the poor, or that focus exclusively on social movements and resistance politics, miss much of what is interesting and powerful about lower-class activism.

I set out to study how Mexico's poor were adjusting their political strategies to the massive institutional changes Mexico had experienced between 1990 and 2000. These changes included the fall from power of the Partido Revolucionario Institucional (PRI), the world's longest-ruling party at the time, the emergence of a multiparty democracy, and the implementation of neoliberal reforms that radically altered the relationship between the state and its citizens. What I found confirmed what many political scientists already know but tend to ignore when studying political participation: "Individuals live and operate in a world of institutions. Our opportunities and prospects depend crucially on what institutions exist and how they function" (Sen 1999, 142).

Unfortunately, Mexico's imperfect democracy has not offered the poor many political opportunities or bright prospects. Neoliberal reforms raised the costs, decreased the benefits, and narrowed the choices the poor had for political action, making it much more difficult for them to mount individual or collective challenges to the policies they opposed. Free, fair, and competitive elections have also failed to offer adequate choices at the ballot box or freedom from the clientelist pressures that had silenced their voices in the past. The cumulative result has been a slow exodus from formal politics, which seemed to suit Mexico's technocratic elite just fine.

Declining political participation among the poor is troubling, however. The success of democracy in Mexico and other Latin American countries ultimately depends on the public's participation in the political process and the system's responsiveness to popular demands. Of particular concern in Latin America is the extent to which the poor—who make up as much as 50 percent of the population in some countries—are able to voice their preferences and influence the decisions of policymakers in meaningful ways. Despite the promise that neoliberal economic policies would bring rapid economic growth and generalized prosperity to Latin America, poverty levels have not improved significantly in the region and the gap between the richest and the poorest in these countries has widened. Massive income inequalities polarize political issues and make democratic compromises among political elites and popular groups more difficult. Widespread poverty and perceptions of social injustice can provoke violent protests and popular insurgencies that destabilize the political system and lead to a hardening of political regimes. Moreover, whether Latin American countries consolidate their democratic institutions and practices or slip back to more authoritarian forms of government depends, at least in part, on integrating the poor into the political system and strengthening their stake in the democratic process. If their economic marginalization translates into political marginalization, the poor are less likely to defend young democracies from authoritarian backsliding.

Mexico's political future is uncertain. The rule of law and human rights are under siege, robust and steady economic growth remains elusive, and for better or worse the PRI is once again on the rise. If we are to understand the direction that political change will take in the future, we need to pay attention to what these transformations look like from the ground up, from the point of view of average men and women.

I have incurred many debts in writing this book, most of which I will never be able to repay. I am grateful to the women and men in Mexico who invited me into their homes, offered me food and hospitality, and who answered my questions patiently, thoughtfully, and candidly—sometimes enduring several hours of my prodding and prying. I arrived in the field armed with social science theories and two decades of formal education; but it was these people, most of whom never studied beyond the sixth grade, who taught me the most about politics in Mexico. I have tried to faithfully reproduce their voices so that others might learn from their experiences as well.

I have been interested in the broad subject of the poor's political participation for a long time. Gary Wynia oversaw my undergraduate thesis at Carleton College and guided me through early attempts to shape my ideas on the subject. Daniel Levine has been a model scholar and mentor, giving me sage advice throughout the project, always encouraging me to look for the general in the particular. I benefited greatly from Pradeep Chhibber's careful scrutiny of my arguments, and my conversations with him have left a mark on my thinking that extend well beyond this project. Jonathan Fox provided a great deal of intellectual inspiration and much advice and helpful criticism. At the University of Michigan I benefited greatly from contacts with many wonderful mentors and scholars, including Ronald Inglehart, Ann Lin, Robert Pahre, Jeffrey Paige, and Jennifer Widner.

The greatest help, support, and intellectual stimulation in graduate school often comes from one's friends and colleagues. I was fortunate enough to be surrounded by some of the smartest, most humble, and unselfish people I have ever met. Devra Coren, Amaney Jamal, Darcy Leach, Irfan Nooruddin, and Paula Pickering patiently read numerous drafts and provided steadfast support during the most difficult times. I want to thank Ravi Bhavnani, Brian Hoe, Ryan Hudson, José Raúl Perales, Dulcey Simpkins, and Marek Steedman for their loyalty, friendship, and support throughout our graduate careers.

I received financial support for my research from several institutions. The National Science Foundation provided a Dissertation Improvement Grant (SBR-9810237) that made my extended research in Mexico possible. The Latin American and Caribbean Studies program and the International Institute, both at the University of Michigan, provided financing for initial field studies. Additional funding for transcription costs and research assistance was generously provided by the Political Science Department and by the Horace H. Rackham School of Graduate Studies of the University of Michigan. At the University of Utah the Tanner Humanities Center supported a semesterlong leave from teaching, and the College of Social and Behavioral Science and the Political Science Department offered additional financial assistance.

I also want to thank Ronald Inglehart, the World Values Survey, the Comparative Studies of Electoral Systems (CSES), the library at the Centro de Investigación y Docencia Económica (CIDE) and Latin American Public Opinion Project (LAPOP) and its major supporters (the U.S. Agency for International Development, the United Nations Development Program, the Inter-American Development Bank, and Vanderbilt University) for making their data available.

In Mexico, Federico Estévez provided me with office space and institutional support at the Instituto Tecnológico Autónomo de México (ITAM) during my research stay in Mexico City. I also benefited immensely from the help of Alejandro Moreno, Enrique Cabrero, Alberto Díaz-Cayeros, Fausto Diaz Gómez, Manuel Marroquín, Paola Martorelli, Beatríz Magaloni, Eugenia Mata García, Victor Gabriel Muro, Luis Miguel Rionda Ramírez, Alain de Remes, Allison Rowland, and Ana Vásquez Colmenares, who allowed me to share my ideas with them and gave me valuable advice during initial phases of my research.

The field research was made vastly more productive and enjoyable by the assistance of numerous activists and organizations in Mexico, including Centro Mexicano de Filantropía (CEMEFI), Fundación VAMOS, Fundación DEMOS, Semillas-Sociedad Mexicana Pro-Derechos de la Mujer, and the staff at Equipo Pueblo in Mexico City; Adriana Cortés Jímenez of the Fundación Comunitaria del Bajío, the Poli-Asociación Para Desarrollo Integral Comunitario (PADIC), Araceli Cabrera Alcaraz and Francisco Javier Sentíes Laborde at the Coordinación General Para el Desarrollo Regional (CO-DEREG) in Guanajuato; and in Oaxaca the Centro de Apoyo al Movimiento Popular Oaxaqueño (CAMPO), Marcos Leyva at EDUCA (Servicios para una Educación Alternativa), Servicio al Pueblo Mixe (SER), and Casa de la Mujer Rosario Castellanos. My debt to Othón Cuevas and the staff at Centéotl is deep and deserves special mention. They unselfishly opened the doors of their organization and aided my research in countless ways.

I am grateful to Rosa Roldan Teixeira and Angeles Cerrillo Vida from Palermo, and Vicente de Juan Morales and Adriana Figueroa in Ann Arbor, for their help transcribing interviews. Thanks to Saul Alarcón, who helped with charts, tables, and data analysis. I am grateful to Melissa Goldsmith, who dedicated large amounts of time to managing, coding, and analyzing large and complicated datasets. Her expert skills not only made this book possible, they also made it better. At the University of Pittsburgh Press, Devin Fromm and Joshua Shanholtzer provided encouragement and ushered the manuscript patiently and efficiently through the publication process. Copyeditor Amy Smith Bell's careful editing improved the text immensely.

I have never thanked my parents, Anna and Volkmar Holzner, enough for their love, support, and encouragement. The sacrifices they made for my education and well-being were often invisible to me but nonetheless considerable. Throughout the research and writing phases of this project, I have stopped to ponder how I could ever thank my wife, Sarah, for all that she has meant and contributed to the enterprise. She was at times therapist, counselor, adviser, critic, supporter, research partner, and mentor. She accompanied me to Mexico, assisted with interviews, and read more chapters and papers related to this topic than should be required of loved ones. No words can capture the deep influence on me, on my ideas, and ultimately on the person I have become as a result of sharing these experience with her. How can I properly acknowledge all that she has contributed? Her answer to this question when I posed it to her reflects her wonderful giving spirit and sense of partnership that makes every day with her a joy: "A simple thank you will do. It's part of the deal." Sarah, thank you.

Poverty of Democracy

CHAPTER I

THE RETURN OF INSTITUTIONS

Political Opportunities and
Political Participation

Mexico's political system was once hailed as the "perfect dictatorship," characterized by regular elections, widespread legitimacy, and uninterrupted rule by the same political party (the Partido Revolucionario Institucional, or PRI) for seventy years. One of the distinguishing characteristics of Mexico's brand of authoritarianism was its relative openness to political activity from ordinary citizens and social groups. There was little that was free or fair about this political activism, however. During the PRI's long reign, political participation was encouraged only when it provided support for the ruling party, tolerated when it was aimed at securing limited material benefits, and violently repressed when its goals were significant political change. This changed after 1990, when a series of sweeping political reforms opened up the political system, encouraged opposition parties to challenge the PRI's electoral hegemony at the polls, and created significant new opportunities for Mexican citizens to engage in political activities. This combination of political reforms, real electoral competition, and citizen activism worked together to steadily erode the PRI's power. By the 2000 presidential elections the democratic transformation was complete, as voters finally toppled the PRI from power in elections that were universally regarded as free, fair, and competitive. After a lengthy democratic transition, Mexican citizens were now largely free to vote for whom they pleased, protest when they liked, and make large and small demands on the system.[1]

There is a dark side to Mexico's democratic transition, however. Evidence from public opinion surveys shows that the poor, who make up as much as 50 percent of Mexico's population, participate in many fewer political activities than more affluent Mexicans. This is true for almost any kind of political activity, whether voting, protesting, contacting politicians, signing petitions, or working on political campaigns. Not only are the poor participating less, they are on the whole less interested in politics, more skeptical about the ability of elections to give them power over their leaders, and seem resigned to having little say in the political process. Curiously, the participation gap between the rich and the poor widened during the democratic transition, peaking in 2000, when the consolidation of democratic practices should have created incentives and opportunities for all citizens to become more involved in politics.

Mexico is not alone. A growing number of studies have revealed the shallowness of Latin American democracies, where deep socioeconomic inequalities are increasingly mirrored in political practice (Agüero and Stark 1998; Chalmers et al. 1997; Holzner 2007a and 2007b; Huber and Solt 2004; Kurtz 2004; Levine and Molina 2007; Oxhorn and Ducatenzeiler 1998a and 1998b; Posner 2008; and Weyland 2004).[2] This stratification of political participation by income is troubling for any democracy, since it undermines the core principle of political equality—that the interests and preferences of all will be given equal consideration in the decision-making process. But in Mexico and other Latin American countries, where levels of poverty and income inequality are among the worst in the world, the overlap between socioeconomic and political inequalities has added political significance. It may beget democratic systems that are not representative, responsive, or accountable to more than half of the population.

This book seeks to understand how Mexico's stratified pattern of political participation emerged. Stated simply, why do the poor in Mexico participate less than the rich? I examine the political activity of citizens from all income levels, paying special attention to the political activity of the poor who, despite the promises of industrialization and free trade, still make up half of the country's population. To many this disparity in participation rates will not seem like a puzzle, since the finding that the poor participate less than the rich is so common in the literature (at least in research that focuses on the United States as a single case), it has become an axiom of politics. The conventional answer places the participatory burden on individuals, who choose to participate or abstain according to their personal motivation or individual resource endowments (see Milbrath and Goel 1977; Verba, Nie, and Kim 1971; Verba, Schlozman, and Brady 1995; and Wolfinger and Rosenstone 1980). Other political scientists have explored the impact that people's experiences in schools, churches, organizations, and other nonpolitical institutions have on political participation (see Burns, Schlozman, and Verba 2001; Rosenstone and Hansen 1993; and Verba, Nie, and Kim 1978). But these conventional explanations have ignored the powerful influence political institutions and the activities of the state have on patterns of political behavior. Although there is little doubt that personal characteristics matter for political activism, and organizations certainly do much of the work in mobilizing people into politics, individuals must also have incentives and opportunities to become involved. If political activity is too costly, too risky, or unlikely to produce the desired outcome, people—no matter their income level or organizational involvement—will choose nonpolitical activities to achieve their ends.

I have placed politics—public policies, the activities of the state, features of the party system, and the rules and practices that govern the political process—squarely at the center of explanations of political participation. These variables make up the institutional environment that has had powerful direct and indirect effects on people's decisions about whether, when, and how to become involved in politics. The institutional environment influences political behavior directly by shaping the incentives and opportunities (or obstacles) for political action. In Mexico political opportunities and incentives are not distributed equally, and this inequality explains much of the difference in political activity between the poor and the rich. Political institutions and opportunities also impact behavior indirectly through their effect on political attitudes and levels of political engagement, which are themselves powerful predictors of political activity. In Mexico the poor are much less interested in politics and have lower levels of political efficacy than higher-income groups. This book traces the cynical and apathetic attitudes of the poor back to their direct experiences with the state, the political system, and a democratic process that has left them disenchanted with politics.

Because of the massive institutional changes Mexico experienced between 1990 and 2000, the country is an ideal place to explore the institutional roots of political participation. During this decade Mexicans lived through a dramatic transformation from a one-party authoritarian regime to a multiparty competitive democracy. The citizens experienced just as radical a transformation from a state-led development model to a free-market model emphasizing free trade, reduced government spending, and diminished state regulation over the economy. The decline in political activity among ordinary Mexicans, particularly the poor, and the stratification of political participation that emerged after 2000, are closely related to these big structural reforms implemented during the same decade. Privatization, elimination of trade barriers, cutbacks of subsidies for basic food stuffs and agricultural inputs, and especially a shift to targeted poverty-alleviation programs such as Oportunidades have raised the costs, reduced the benefits, and narrowed access to decision makers; these changes have affected the poor more than the middle and upper classes.

Democratization has had a mixed effect on political participation. Its effect has been more varied because the spread of democratic practices has been uneven throughout Mexico. Where elections are truly clean and fair, where leftist parties compete effectively, and where state and local governments govern democratically, political activity is bolstered; where authoritarian practices and rulers persist, citizens (unless they are captured by clientelist organizations) often see little reason to become politically involved. Because authoritarian enclaves are strongest in Mexico's poorest states, cities, and neighborhoods, the poor are much more likely to experience this authoritarian and demobilizing side of the Mexican political system.

This focus on institutions helps reframe core questions. Rather than asking simply why the poor participate less than the rich, the proper question becomes, Under what conditions do the poor participate less than the rich, and under what conditions can participation rates become more equal? What is the state's role in stimulating or constraining citizen participation? Are there specific state structures and policies that enhance the participatory capacity and motivation for some groups while diminishing it for others? Is it possible that democratic systems, where the participatory gap is large, create greater participatory obstacles for the poor or demand resources they have in least supply? Is it possible that the actions of the state and not the attributes of individuals are truly behind this participatory gap? The answers give us a deeper understanding of the connections between individual-level factors, political institutions, and political participation that should be relevant beyond Mexico.

Political Participation under Authoritarianism

It may seem strange to talk about political participation in an authoritarian regime, which we often associate with repressive governments that crack down on any kind of independent political activity. In truth, most authoritarian regimes experience, if not actually tolerate and encourage, a fair amount of political activity from their citizens, whether in the form of periodic protests or strikes, voting in rigged elections, militancy in officially recognized political parties or organizations, or contacting and lobbying of local officials. Mexico's brand of populist one-party authoritarianism was particularly open to citizen political activity, and in fact depended on it to enhance its legitimacy and democratic credentials. Elections at all levels of government occurred regularly and often, and were usually contested by more than one party. Outside of the electoral arena, protests, marches, and strikes were relatively common occurrences that were usually tolerated as long as they did not explicitly challenge the legitimacy of the ruling party. Political contacting of government officials was also a common strategy, especially among the urban and rural poor, who relied on personal connections and clientelist networks to secure a share of government patronage and petition for public works and services.

Although the PRI liked to claim it ruled Mexico democratically, and could point to regular elections with high turnouts as proof of this claim, most of those elections had been marred by fraud and by clientelist mobilization that guaranteed overwhelming PRI victories in almost all local, state, and national elections through the mid-1990s. Thus political participation was a double-edged sword. On the one hand it provided citizens, especially the poor, with opportunities to voice their concerns and lobby for a share of government spending. Through membership in formal organizations many of them became politicized and learned how to participate in politics. On the other hand most political action was channeled through the PRI's corporatist organizations, whose primary function was not to represent the interests of its members but to control political activity and so limit the demands on the regime coming from below.[3] Moreover, the primary function of elections and political campaigns was not to choose a government but to legitimate the PRI in power. Indeed, a great deal of political activity was largely symbolic, mobilized by elites through clientelist networks and limited to ritualistic regime-supporting activities (Cornelius 1975 and Eckstein 1977). So great was the PRI's control over political institutions and organizations that critics and opponents of the PRI often abstained from voting, soiled their ballots, or simply dropped out of politics altogether, realizing that a small but ineffective opposition did more to legitimate the PRI's claim to power than to undermine it. Thus Mexico's authoritarian political system—particularly the links between the state, the party, and the poor—produced both mobilized activism and learned apathy among the poor.[4]

Because of the regime's authoritarian character, most students of Mexican politics saw political participation as having little importance for deciding who would govern. Consequently, there are few independent studies of political participation before 1990.[5] Even official numbers are suspect. For example, turnout rates for presidential elections during the 1950s, 1960s, and 1970s were very high—often above 80 percent—but it is now well understood that those figures were inflated by the government to make their victories seem all the more impressive. What studies do exist document a relatively high level of political activism by the urban and rural poor, especially if they were members of organizations affiliated with the ruling party. Although much of this political activity was not strictly voluntary because it was coerced or cajoled through clientelist organizations, the poor did have strong incentives to be active in public life. For starters, their access to the political patronage doled out by the state through PRI organizations depended on their willingness to participate when called upon. More to the point, given the state's rapid expansion under the import-substitution-industrialization (ISI) development model, its control over enormous resources, its predilection for large-scale and comprehensive poverty-alleviation projects, and the scarcity of private sources for credit, input, and jobs, the poor had clear incentives to pay attention to politics and to target the state when seeking solutions to their most pressing needs. As a result, voting, attending rallies for PRI candidates, political demand making, petitioning, and protesting government officials were routine strategies for both the urban and rural poor during this period.[6]

Data are not available to tell us whether political participation, constrained as it was, was stratified by income before 1990. Evidence from early studies suggests that overall Mexicans with more education were more engaged with politics and felt more efficacious about their activity (Almond and Verba 1963; and Nie, Bingham Powell, and Prewitt 1969a and 1969b). The earliest wave of the World Values Survey carried out in Mexico in 1981 shows a small but statistically significant difference in the political participation rates between low- and high-income groups.[7] However, among members of organizations the pattern may have been reversed. Norman Nie, G. Bingham Powell, and Kenneth Prewitt (1969b) showed that in Mexico low-status individuals with high organizational involvement outparticipated all other groups, including high-status individuals who also were active in organizations.

Political Participation during and after the Democratic Transition

After the 1988 presidential elections, in which the PRI's candidate, Carlos Salinas de Gortari, won a dubious victory and millions of Mexicans took to the streets to protest electoral fraud, analysts of Mexican politics began paying more consistent attention to political participation, giving us a clearer picture of who participates and how much. The World Values Surveys, carried out approximately every five years in Mexico, provide the best information about changing patterns of political participation between 1990 and 2000, albeit for a limited number of political activities. Table 1.1 shows the average level of political activism for low-, medium-, and high-income Mexicans from 1990 through 2005. Using 1990 participation rates as the baseline, two patterns are evident. First, the data confirm that during the decade there was a consistent gap in political participation across income groups. However, the gap widened after the democratic transition and became statistically significant starting in 2000, suggesting that the stratification of political participation got worse as the decade progressed. Second, political participation rates underwent a rather remarkable decline between 1990 and 2000, before recovering again in 2005. The decline happened for all income groups and for essentially all political acts.

Data from the 2000 wave of the Comparative Studies of Electoral Systems (CSES) survey allow us to examine political participation rates in more detail, since it collected information about many more political activities, in-

Table 1.1. Political Participation during Mexico's Democratic Transition

	Low income	Medium income	High income	Significance
1990	0.66	0.72	0.82	
1995	0.55	0.59	0.65	
2000	0.20	0.26	0.37	***
2005	0.41	0.47	0.64	***

Source: World Values Survey 1981–2005.
Notes: Values indicate the mean number of political acts calculated from a six-point scale (0–5) that includes protests, strikes, boycotts, sit-ins, and signing petitions. The 2005 survey only asked four of the five political participation questions (protest, petition, boycott, and other), so values for that year are based on a five-point scale.

The symbols *** indicate that the difference across income groups is statistically significant at 0.01.

See Appendix A. Survey Questions and Variables for an explanation of how the income categories were constructed.

cluding voting, participation in political campaigns, and contacting federal representatives. Figure 1.1 breaks down the average level of political activity across eight income categories using an index of political activism based on nine distinct political acts.[8] This gives a clear picture of just how stratified political participation had become in Mexico by 2000. With the exception of the most affluent Mexicans, political engagement increases monotonically with income, so that compared to the poor, the most affluent Mexicans participate on average in nearly one additional political act.

Political acts are not equal in their consequences for the political process. Some activities communicate a lot of specific information to government officials, such as personal contacting or signing petitions; other political acts, like voting, are rather blunt instruments for communicating preferences. Voting is also impossible to multiply—each person should be able to vote only once in each election—whereas the volume of other activities—like donating money, time spent working or volunteering for a campaign, or the number of times someone contacts a public official—can be more easily

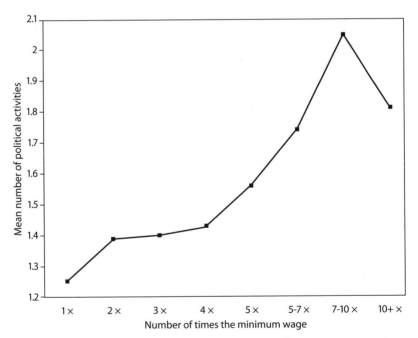

Figure 1.1. Overall Political Participation by Income. The income categories are multiples of the monthly minimum wage, which in 2000 was $1,128 pesos per month, or approximately US$110. *Source*: CSES-CIDE 2000.

multiplied to increase the potential influence over decision makers. Electoral acts have their greatest influence on the selection of government representatives, but relatively little influence on what they do once in power. Government-directed activities, however, have a more direct influence on the actual decisions and actions of officials already in power. Although on average there is a large difference in levels of activism across income groups, it is worth knowing whether the disparity is large, small, or whether it even exists for different kinds of political acts. Are there political activities for which the disparity in participation is lower or even reversed? Is the gap larger for electoral activities such as voting and volunteering for campaigns than for government-directed acts such as protesting and petitioning?

Figure 1.2 uses data from three national-level surveys to compare political activism by income group across a wide variety of political activities. It is evident that for almost all activities, the poor participate less than the most affluent and usually less than all other income groups. For some activities, such as signing petitions, talking about politics, and contacting government representatives, the differences are large and statistically significant. For other activities, such as protesting, donating money to political campaigns, or joining a political party, the differences are very small. The participatory gap is widest for government-directed activities, which communicate the most information to government officials and have the greatest potential effect on public policies. On average, the poor participate about half as often in these kinds of acts than the most affluent. The gap is smaller for electoral activities, but when we aggregate across electoral activities, the income gap is noticeable and statistically significant.

Voting is by far the most common political activity for Mexicans regardless of their income level and has received the most consistent attention in studies of political participation.[9] Election turnout has always been high in Mexico, almost always exceeding 50 percent even for midterm elections. It peaked at 78 percent in the 1994 presidential elections, which was also the first election administered by the newly created Instituto Federal Electoral (IFE). Curiously, turnout rates have declined steadily since then, reaching 64 percent in 2000 and only 58 percent in 2006, even though those were the two most competitive elections in modern Mexican history. Not only has turnout declined, it has also become increasingly stratified by income. Scholars studying electoral participation in Mexico during the 1960s and 1970s documented very high turnout rates in rural and poor regions, usually much higher than in urban and more affluent regions (Ames 1970; González Casanova 1985; Nie, Powell, and Prewitt 1969a and 1969b). More

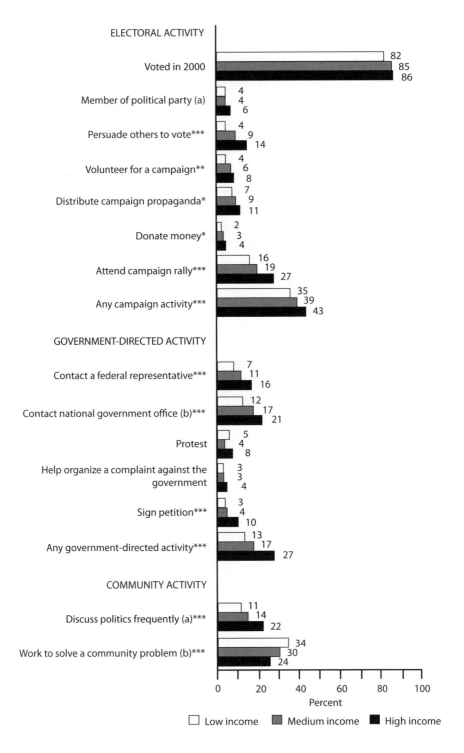

recently, Joseph Klesner and Chappell Lawson showed that up until the 1980s, district-level electoral participation was negatively correlated with levels of education and local economic development (Klesner and Lawson 2000; and Lawson and Klesner 2004). However, according to these authors, by 1991 the relationship became strong and positive, so that "Mexico's more affluent and politically engaged citizens are now more likely to participate than the poorer, less informed and rural voters" (Klesner and Lawson 2000, 19).

The poor participate more often than middle- and high-income individuals in only one activity: working together with neighbors to solve community problems. Besides voting, this is the most common political activity undertaken by low-income Mexicans. There is some debate about whether community problem solving is actually a form of political participation. For some, this kind of community activity is a form of exit from politics because it does not target the state, affect the selection of government representatives, or allow citizens to communicate their preferences to political leaders (Dietz 1998).[10] Either way, the implication is clear: when faced with a collective problem, the poor are more likely to seek solutions through informal activities that do not give them much voice among decision makers.

Although the focus here is on understanding Mexico's stratified pattern of political participation around the time of the democratic transition, it is worth noting that the income gap persists. Figure 1.3 shows overall levels of political activism across different demographic groups for 2006. In Mexico, as in most other countries, there is a close relationship between income and education levels, and resource-based theories generally argue that education levels are the single most important factor in explaining income gaps in political activity. In Mexico, however, low levels of education do not seem to be the source of the income gap in participation, because Mexicans with less than a sixth-grade education participate just as much or more than those who graduated from high school. This finding challenges a common stereotype about low-income Mexicans: that they are too uneducated or ignorant to be politically engaged. The data also calls into question the stereotype that

---

Figure 1.2. *(opposite)* Political Participation by Income. The value for "any campaign activity" includes all electoral activities except voting and being a member of a political party. The value for "any government-directed activity" excludes only contacting a national government office. Here *, **, and *** indicate that the difference between low-income and medium- to high-income individuals is statistically significant at 0.1, 0.05, and 0.01 levels respectively. *Source*: CSES-CIDE 2000; (a) World Values Survey 2000; and (b) LAPOP 2004.

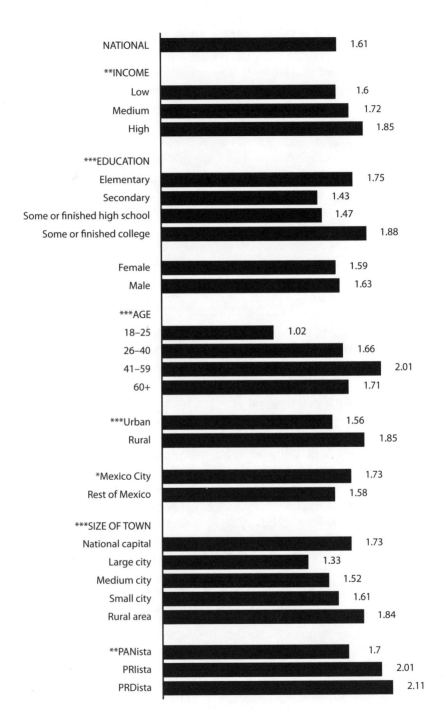

NATIONAL	1.61
**INCOME	
Low	1.6
Medium	1.72
High	1.85
***EDUCATION	
Elementary	1.75
Secondary	1.43
Some or finished high school	1.47
Some or finished college	1.88
Female	1.59
Male	1.63
***AGE	
18–25	1.02
26–40	1.66
41–59	2.01
60+	1.71
***Urban	1.56
Rural	1.85
*Mexico City	1.73
Rest of Mexico	1.58
***SIZE OF TOWN	
National capital	1.73
Large city	1.33
Medium city	1.52
Small city	1.61
Rural area	1.84
**PANista	1.7
PRIista	2.01
PRDista	2.11

rural residents are more apathetic about politics than urban ones. With the exception of Mexico City residents, the opposite seems to be the case: residents of medium-sized and large cities participate on average in the fewest number of political activities. These results are hints that something besides socioeconomic variables are behind the income gap in political participation.

The Institutional Roots of Political Participation

There is another way to think about political participation that makes better sense of the variations across time and locales in the political activity of ordinary citizens. This approach places political and institutional variables (such as party systems, state-society links, and the actions of the state) at the center of explanations of how, when, and why individuals become active in politics. This emphasis on the power of institutions to shape individual behavior is commonplace in sociology and economics and is at the core of rational-choice institutionalism and historical institutionalism within political science. One of the core insights is that understanding individual needs, predispositions, resources, and preferences is not enough to explain political behavior. Rather, all human behavior, including political activity, occurs within institutional constraints that shape actors' choices of possible activities and influence the incentives they have for undertaking them.

An important advantage of an institutional approach is that it forces scholars to take seriously the obstacles citizens face when attempting political activities even within well-established democracies. Too often, explanations of political participation, particularly survey-based models, assume that political activity takes place in a frictionless environment where actors are free to choose from a wide range of political acts constrained only by their abilities and motivations. Attention to institutional constraints forces us to abandon these naïve assumptions about democratic politics, allowing us to see old patterns in a new way. For example, in the United States there is a strong positive relationship between socioeconomic status and political

Figure 1.3. *(opposite)* Who Participates in Mexico: Mean Number of Acts, 2006. The figure reflects the mean number of activities calculated on the basis of an additive scale of eight different kinds of political activities: voting in presidential elections, working for a political party or candidate, persuading others to vote for a party, attending meetings of a political party, attending city council meetings, participating in a protest or march, contacting a federal representative, and participating in solving a community problem. Here ** and *** indicate that the differences across categories are significant at 0.05 and 0.01. *Source:* LAPOP 2006.

participation. Instead of placing the blame on the poor for their inactivity, as conventional theories do, it could very well be that the poor participate less because the rules of the political process restrict their access to decision makers while government policies make politics less relevant to them.

Jim Crow laws are an obvious and extreme example of how laws and government policies can disenfranchise whole groups of people. But other more subtle forms of exclusion are more common and pervasive. For example, studies by G. Bingham Powell Jr. (1986, 36) and by Steven Rosenstone and Raymond Wolfinger (1978) have argued that voter registration laws in the United States depressed the turnout of low socioeconomic status individuals much more than that of other groups and probably account for the unusual degree to which education and other socioeconomic resources are directly related to voter turnout. Andrea Louise Campbell (2003) has also shown that differences in government programs, such as Social Security and welfare programs, can explain both the activism of the elderly and the apathy of the poor. The lesson is that resources matter in the United States because the opportunities for political participation are structured in such a way as to make resources matter. Where the political process is more permissive, where the state subsidizes political participation, and where the poor feel like they have access to decision makers, resources matter less.[11]

Despite the central place that political institutions have in other areas of political science, and despite the obvious fact that political participation occurs within well-regulated and -defined institutional environments, the role of the state and other political institutions is still underappreciated within the political participation literature.[12] Numerous comparative studies of political participation—whether comparing participation across countries (Verba, Nie, and Kim 1978) or across time within the same polity (Dietz 1998; and Rosenstone and Hansen 1993)—have consistently shown that for most kinds of political activity, institutional factors are as or more important than socioeconomic status and attitudes for explaining variation in political activity by individuals. Social movement theories in particular have moved far beyond individual and psychological factors, recognizing the central importance of political opportunities in explaining the ebb and flow of protests and social movements. Despite this compelling evidence, research into the institutional determinants of political participation remains fragmented and sporadic and does not yet constitute an integrated approach to explaining political behavior. This book seeks to contribute to an understanding of citizen activism by developing an explanation of citizen activism that privileges institutional factors instead of individual ones.

Methods, Cases, and Research Design

Research into the determinants of political participation shows how theories, methods, and research designs can reinforce each other over time, blinding researchers to the influence of certain variables that are important for explaining political action. Ever since the publication of Angus Campbell, Philip Converse, Warren Miller, and Donald Stokes's *The American Voter* in 1960 and Gabriel Almond and Sidney Verba's *The Civic Culture* in 1963, individual-level factors (such as attitudes, values, and resources) have dominated theorizing about the causes of political participation. In turn, surveys have by far been the preferred method for studying political participation, since their strength lies precisely in uncovering relationships between the attributes of individuals and their behavior. However, because surveys are essentially snapshots of reality, and because the vast majority of survey studies of political participation have been carried out in a single case (the United States), our understanding of the factors that shape political participation is heavily influenced by research that studies a single case at single points in time. Thus most studies of political participation hold institutional factors constant, rendering invisible their impact on political activities.

In contrast, whenever research designs have allowed institutional contexts to vary, whether across space or over time, the findings affirm the significance of political institutions as explanatory factors. But truly comparative institutional studies of political participation—like the classic studies by Sidney Verba, Norman Nie, and Jae-On Kim (1978); G. Bingham Powell Jr. (1986); and Steven Rosenstone and John Mark Hansen (1993)—are still few and far between. The emphasis on individual-level variables exists therefore not because individual factors are theoretically more important. It exists because they are more amenable to measurement by the dominant method and because most studies fail to incorporate variation in institutional context into their research designs, inhibiting the development of a comparative theory of institutional effects on political participation.

Although I focus on a single country in this book, Mexico provides ample opportunities to carry out a truly comparative study of political participation. In the span of a single decade, between 1990 and 2000, neoliberal economic and democratic political reforms in Mexico produced radical transformations in state structures, in the role of the state in society, and in its capacities to control participatory activities. In terms of economic policy, Mexico has been among the most consistent countries in Latin America in its implementation of free-market and free-trade reforms, transforming not just its economic policies, but also the scope of state activities and the links between state and society. In ten short years Mexico witnessed the end of a one-party autocracy, the emergence of competitive elections at the local and national levels, electoral reform that eliminated most fraud and totally transformed how elections are organized, the erosion of the vast powers of the presidency, and the alternation of parties in power in both the executive and legislative branches. Because citizens of Mexico have had to adjust their political behavior to the new rules of the political game, these rapid and sweeping institutional changes provide an excellent opportunity to study the impact of institutional variation on political participation.

In addition, the impact of national policy initiatives and major structural reforms have been filtered through state and local institutions, creating a diversity of local political environments that differ significantly one from another. In fact, democratization and the decentralization of state power has occurred very unevenly in Mexico, creating a "patchwork quilt" in which open and democratic local governments and institutions exist side by side with highly authoritarian and sometimes coercive ones (Beer 2003; Fox 2000; and Snyder 1999). This irregularity with which national-level economic and political reforms have taken root locally also means that state-society links and political practices vary significantly from town to town and even neighborhood to neighborhood. This variation in local political contexts creates additional opportunities to design a comparative study. Thus, although the book focuses on a single country, I carry out a comparative study of political participation by taking advantage of both longitudinal and cross-sectional variation in institutional environments within Mexico.

My strategy is to exploit the advantages of qualitative and quantitative methodologies, which have offsetting strengths and weaknesses that together allow for greater insights and understanding. I use national-level surveys carried out between 1990 and 2000 to describe patterns of political participation and to test various models of political participation. However, the quantitative analysis came only after years of ethnographic fieldwork and analysis of large amounts of qualitative data. Although existing theories provided some guidance in choosing variables to include in the statistical models, the interviews and case studies pointed me to independent variables and relationships I would never have thought to explore or that were not contemplated in the existing literature.

But my fieldwork did much more than suggest hypotheses to test. By carrying out dozens of lengthy interviews, participating in the activities of local organizations, and living in the communities I studied, I came to appreciate the powerful ways in which the institutional context shapes the political activities of ordinary citizens independently of their particular resource endowments. Indeed, it was by analyzing the qualitative evidence collected that I was able identify the causal mechanisms that linked institutional contexts with political behavior and develop an institutional theory of political participation. Although I am confident that the causal mechanisms identified accurately described processes occurring elsewhere, it is always wise, if possible, to test a theory using cases that were not used to generate the theory. The regression analysis of national-level survey data allowed me to do just that.

I carried out the bulk of my fieldwork during a fifteen-month period between 1998 and 2000 in four communities in the southeastern state of Oaxaca, one of Mexico's poorest and most diverse states.[13] Patron-client relationships are still very strong in many parts of the state, making local politics among the most restrictive and least democratic in all of Mexico. Nonetheless, political and electoral reforms begun in the early 1980s have given local governments greater fiscal autonomy and administrative responsibility. They have made some local political systems competitive and democratic, and overall they have begun to transform municipalities into increasingly important arenas of political participation. Oaxaca has a history of organizational activism linked to progressive elements of the Catholic Church, and more recently the state has been targeted by government- and NGO-sponsored development projects. As a result of these conflicting pressures, democratic local governments and practices have spread unevenly across the state—much as they have across the rest of Mexico—creating a complex mix of pluralist enclaves coexisting with authoritarian strongholds and semi-democratic subnational regimes.

Much of my time in the field was spent observing and participating in the activities of six grassroots organizations in three rural towns—La Ciénega, Teotitlán del Valle, and Zimatlán—and in Nezacubi, a squatter settlement located in the state's capital. This selection represents a variation across local party systems, political parties in power at the municipal level, urban and rural settings, and the structure, size, and political affiliation of organizations.[14] Although it would be possible (albeit much more costly) to examine the impact of political institutions and opportunities cross-nationally, the strength of this subnational comparative design is that it achieves variation on a number of core factors while maintaining constant most variables—such as national regime type, national institutions, electoral laws, and national economic and social policies—that would confound any cross-national analysis.

Because my principal theoretical interest is in how contextual variables impact individual political behavior, the bulk of my qualitative evidence comes from more than sixty in-depth interviews with members of the grass-roots organizations I studied.[15] The questionnaire I developed asked some standard questions about political attitudes, demographic background, and political experience. But the core consisted of a set of open-ended questions designed to collect political life histories of these individuals to relate differences in political behavior (over time and across individuals) to changes in organizational membership and the local political environment. By listening to the poor in this way, I uncovered and traced the complex links between big structural changes and individual decisions about what kind of political strategies to pursue. In particular, because economic and institutional reforms associated with the shift from an ISI to a free-market model of development occurred at the same time as democratic reforms, I needed to isolate the impact of neoliberal reforms from democratic ones. In-depth interviews were especially useful in this task because they allowed citizens to describe which institutional changes—those associated with increased political competition or those associated with the structure and action of the state—were foremost on their minds when thinking about protesting, petitioning, or otherwise trying to influence the state. Thus the interviews were essential in building an institutional theory of political participation: it was actors themselves who taught me which institutions mattered most and how they mattered.

I then developed a number of hypotheses and expectations based on my theory and tested them against other explanations of political participation using data from the Mexico waves of the Comparative Study of Electoral Systems (CSES) surveys. Although survey research is becoming standard practice in Mexico, there are still relatively few surveys that ask about political activities outside of voting. The CSES surveys are a particularly rich source of data to test my hypotheses because they collected information about a large number of political activities *and* about institutional factors, and because the two surveys I rely on most were carried out in 2000 and 2003—precisely the period of time during which I carried out my interviews.[16] To the extent that results of the statistical analysis are consistent (or inconsistent) with observable implications of my argument, they also provide evidence in support for (or alternatively that undermine) the overall argument.

I should make one more note about the research design of this study. My interviews and much of my statistical analysis focused exclusively on the political activity of low-income individuals. Such a research design has at least two advantages for theory building. First, it compels researchers to acknowledge the diversity of poor people's political participation while challenging assumptions about the relative passivity of the poor. Second, holding socioeconomic status essentially constant forces us to look beyond individual attributes such as education and income to explain variations in political behavior. Thus it was by interviewing only low-income Mexicans that I was able to see more clearly the impact of institutions on citizen activism. I also carried out separate regression analysis for low- and high-income individuals. It is standard in statistical studies of political participation to include all income groups in the same regression equation. That is a valid strategy if we assume that the social and political processes that influence people's level of political activism are the same for all income classes. However, one of the main arguments of this book is that public policies and political institutions—and the opportunities and obstacles they create for political activity—affect the poor differently than higher-income individuals. The logic of this argument requires separate regression equations so that we can examine whether the same political institutions have different effects on the poor and the wealthy.[17]

CHAPTER 2

TOWARD AN INSTITUTIONAL THEORY
OF POLITICAL PARTICIPATION

Since the late 1980s, citizens of Mexico have lived through a period of extraordinary political, social, and economic transformations. Politically they have witnessed the fall from power of the world's longest-ruling party, a transition to a multiparty democracy, and a newly vibrant political arena that offers them many innovative ways to express their opinions at the local, state, and national levels. Economically they have endured the implementation of severe austerity programs, deep economic crises, and neoliberal reforms that have sharply reduced the scope of state activity and altered the links between the state and society. A close look at how the poor have adapted their political participation to these unprecedented changes in the institutional context reveals a wide range of responses that belies the image often portrayed of the poor as quiescent and constrained by the poverty that envelops them.

The residents of Nezacubi, a squatter community established in 1992 on the hills above the city of Oaxaca, have been experimenting with a variety of strategies in response to the shifting institutional context to satisfy their pressing need for basic services, more consistent police patrols, and of course legal titles to their land. Their struggles to get water service to the neighborhood exemplifies the diverse repertoires of action they have used over the years, both in the formal political arena and through self-help strategies. During the initial period of the settlement, all of the residents got their water from a stream, carrying it in buckets back to their shacks to cook and wash clothes. Later, some of the residents adapted by pooling their money to hire a truck to fill the neighborhood's cisterns twice a week.[1] Other residents continued to get water from the creek or purchased it illegally from neighbors who were connected to the city's system. Until 1995 the city, state, and national governments were still controlled by the PRI, so early on residents established a neighborhood committee and dutifully aligned themselves with the ruling party, hoping that their loyalty and the personal connections of their leader would yield quick results. However, efforts to petition the city and state governments for water service through established corporatist channels failed. Additional infrastructure projects were too expensive for the city to undertake by itself. ADOSAPACO (Administración Directa de Obras y Servicios de Agua Potable y Alcantarillado de la Ciudad de Oaxaca), the state-level water utility, refused to provide squatters with water service because they did not have legal titles to the land and there was no way to collect service fees.[2]

Residents then added new activities to their repertoire. Small groups of them staged regular protests at the offices of the state water utility; larger groups organized communitywide meetings with city officials to negotiate the terms under which they would be allowed to purchase the titles to their plots. During the 1994 presidential election some residents organized to attend campaign rallies and vote for the PRI, recognizing that elections are a unique opportunity to pry some benefits from governments. This did not work, so in 1995 a majority of neighbors broke free from the PRI to create a new neighborhood committee. They threw their support behind the pro-business PAN (the Partido de Acción Nacional) in that year's mayoral elections, hoping that increased democracy, transparency, and governmental accountability would do the trick. This was an unlikely alliance to be sure, but their gamble seemed to pay off when the PAN defeated the PRI for the first time in the city's history and retained control of the city's government in 1998.

The new administration rewarded Nezacubi for its electoral support by installing water and sewage pipes in the neighborhood within months of taking office. Although the city could provide the infrastructure, they could not actually provide the water, which was controlled by the state government. Indeed, because the PRI remained firmly in control at the state level, residents' local-level activism was ineffective and sometimes even counterproductive. ADOSAPACO connected all of the neighborhoods surrounding

Nezacubi to the city's water grid but continued to deny Nezacubi access to the service as punishment for defecting to the opposition. It was clear that as long as the PRI had control over the state government, little would change in the neighborhood.

By 2000 many of the most active residents had dropped out of formal politics, disenchanted and disillusioned with the powerlessness of the local administration and the lack of responsiveness of the state government. This does not mean they ceased to be politically involved, just that they shifted their activism away from the formal political arena. The most important activity in the neighborhood was increasingly becoming the weekly *tequio*, a self-help tradition of voluntary community service through which settlers provide for themselves the public goods and services that they need. Another important local institution in Nezacubi (and in neighborhoods across Mexico) is the regular community assembly (*asamblea*), where neighbors debate options and make important decisions affecting the neighborhood. Self-help strategies like *asambleas* and *tequios* have become more important and more necessary as public financing for infrastructure projects has dried up.

The story does not end there, however. In 2004 the three main opposition parties formed an electoral coalition to challenge the PRI in the statewide elections. The prospect of finally ousting the PRI from power at the state level seduced many residents of the neighborhood into public life again; they attended campaign rallies for the opposition, distributed propaganda, and turned out at the polls in large numbers. The election results were a punch in the stomach: the PRI won with a plurality of the votes (47.6 percent to 44.4 percent) amid widespread allegations of fraud, vote buying, and even manipulation of the computerized vote-counting system. A few months later the PRI won the mayoral elections in the city for the first time since 1992 amid widespread voter apathy and low turnouts. Despite hundreds of opposition-party victories in Oaxaca and elsewhere in Mexico, democratization had not brought much change for the residents of Nezacubi. To this day, nearly two decades after their initial settlement, none of the houses in the neighborhood have running water or indoor plumbing. The vast majority of families use latrines that they have dug behind their houses.[3]

Most studies of lower-class activism seek to explain why the poor move from quiescence to activism, usually defined as participation in social movements or other forms of collective action. But the preceding discussion makes it clear that this is the wrong question to ask because it presumes that when the poor are not protesting or participating in some sort of a social movement, they do not behave in politically relevant ways. In fact, the poor experiment constantly with different strategies—political and nonpolitical, formal and informal, collective and individual—to satisfy their most immediate needs and to improve the situation of their families. If one set of strategies fails or becomes impractical, they quickly shift to a different mode with greater promise. Sometimes this means temporarily exiting the political system, but such quiescence is usually transitory and ends once new opportunities arise in the political system that make political action worthwhile again. Thus studies that emphasize quiescence or that focus exclusively on social movements and resistance politics miss much of what is interesting and powerful about poor people's activism. The appropriate puzzle is not to explain why the poor move from quiescence to activism. Rather it is to explain how they choose among the multitude of strategies available to them—including exit—and how these choices differ across contexts, over time, and across individuals.

In trying to understand how Mexico's stratified pattern of political participation emerged, we should not be satisfied with a theory that can only explain why the poor sometimes participate politically less often than the rich. Any explanation should be able to provide an answer to the following four questions:

1. Why do the poor sometimes participate more than individuals with larger personal resource endowments? A theory that can account for poor people's apathy as well as their activism is better than a theory that can only explain why they do not participate.
2. Why do actors choose the political activities that they do? Actors have a wide variety of political activities from which to choose, but even in the most democratic systems, they rarely choose to participate in more than two or three of these. Why do they pick one set of activities over another? Why do they choose different activities at different points in time and in different locations?
3. Why do people move in and out of the political arena over time? Habitual voters do not always vote; people who never protested sometimes decide to join others in contentious activities; and activists sometimes drop out of politics altogether. A theory of political participation should be able to account for the fluid nature of political participation.
4. Why do overall levels of political participation in a country increase or decrease over time?

Unfortunately, none of the main theories of political participation can adequately answer all four of these questions. Survey-based explanations of citizen activism dominate the political participation research in the United States and increasingly also in emerging democracies as public opinion polling becomes more common. These studies place such individual-level variables as attitudes, values, political skills, and socioeconomic status, including income and education, at the center of explanations of political participation. But these variables do a poor job of explaining the ebb and flow of political participation, such as why individuals move in and out of the political arena, why overall levels of political participation change, or why they differ across contexts. The literature on voter choice and electoral turnout, which has paid close attention to legal and institutional factors in addition to individual-level factors, does a better job at explaining variation in turnout across cases and over time, but only for voting activity.

Similarly, social movement theories that focus on such contentious political activities as strikes and protests have moved decisively beyond individual and psychological factors, recognizing the central importance of factors like the availability of organizational resources, the openness of the political system, the structure and actions of the state, and the framing strategies used by social movement leaders (see Clemens 1996; Gamson and Meyer 1996; Jenkins 1983; McAdam 1982; McAdam, McCarthy, and Zald 1996; Snow and Benford 1992; Snow et al. 1986; Tarrow 1998; and Tilly 1978). These theories can account for many of the most dynamic elements of social movements and protests, explaining why movements arise when and where they do, why they grow and end, and even what kind of strategies movement activists pursue. However, the social movement literature focuses on a relatively uncommon set of activities.[4] We need a theory that explains not just protest activity or voting but also more common everyday forms of political participation.

Drawing on a variety of literatures from sociology and political science, I articulate an institutional framework of political participation that explains changing patterns of political participation in Mexico as well as who participates and how in other settings, both democratic and authoritarian. In seeking causal connections between structural factors and individual decisions, I do not ignore the individual resource constraints that weigh heavily on the participatory options of citizens. But the thrust of my argument is institutional in its emphasis, privileging structural factors and resources that are *external* to individuals. By emphasizing the importance of the political opportunities over individual-level factors, I am deliberately attempting to shift the analytical emphasis of theories of political participation away from individual "resource-mobilization," which places the burden of action, and hence the blame for inaction, on individuals while ignoring the powerful ways in which political opportunities and the political process constrain individual behavior.

Resources, Attitudes, and Political Participation

The so-called standard model of political participation has dominated explanations of political participation since the 1960s (see Leighley 1995 and Verba, Nie, and Kim 1978). According to this model, individual socioeconomic status (SES) and political attitudes are the main determinants of political participation. Although this research tradition has yielded important insights, its narrow emphasis on individual and psychological factors has important limitations. Political attitudes and values are so close to what we are trying to explain, and the direction of causation is ambiguous enough, that theorizing in this vein easily becomes circular. Models that emphasize actors' resource constraints—including the civic voluntarism model developed by Sidney Verba, Kay Lehman Schlozman, and Henry Brady (1995)— improve on attitudinal explanations, but they still have trouble accounting for rapid fluctuations in the political activity of individuals, or for the high level of political involvement of lower-class groups in certain contexts. Moreover, although SES models and attitudinal models do a good job of explaining who participates in the United States, the strong correlation between individual-level factors and political activity is often not replicated elsewhere.[5] Despite these and other problems with individual-level models, they continue to have a central place in the American politics literature and are exerting a powerful influence on political participation research in emerging democracies.[6]

Socioeconomic status and resource constraint theories of political participation trace activism to the resource stockpiles of individuals—their education, income, and the degree to which they have acquired politically relevant skills.[7] The logic behind SES and resource-constraint models is straightforward and intuitively appealing: all else being equal, actors who possess more politically relevant resources can afford to participate in more activities more often than individuals with fewer resources (Verba, Schlozman, and Brady 1995; and Wolfinger and Rosenstone 1980). Indeed, some costly and challenging activities (such as donating money to campaigns or writing letters to representatives) may only be available to actors with abundant socioeconomic and civic resources.

Although proponents of SES and resource explanations claim that the strength of these models lies in their empirical power to predict political activity, SES models are actually weak predictors of activism in many contexts. A glance at comparative studies of political participation reveals that resources provide little guidance for understanding why political participation varies over time, across cases, and among individuals.[8] First, SES models of political participation are generally pessimistic about the participatory potential of the poor and consistently underpredict their levels of activism. Comparative evidence from the United States, Latin America, India, and other regions shows that the poor draw on a rich array of repertoires of action in their efforts to influence the decisions of government officials or to secure access to public goods. Numerous studies outside of the United States have shown that they frequently outparticipate groups and individuals with much higher income and educational levels (see, among many others, Booth and Seligson 1978; Cornelius 1975; Dietz 1998; Eckstein 1989a; Eldersveld and Ahmed 1978; Gaventa 1980; McAdam 1982; Nelson 1994; Oxhorn 1991; Schneider 1995; Scott 1985; and Verba, Nie, and Kim 1978). Conversely, the United States has the ignoble distinction of having by far one of the lowest turnout rates among established democracies, despite having one of the wealthiest and most educated populations.

In a similar vein, although factors like skills, income, and educational levels certainly matter, once they exist, they are relatively constant and cannot explain why patterns of participation can change quite dramatically in short periods of time, or why individuals move in and out of politics. For example, political activism in the United States has been declining steadily since the 1970s at the same time that incomes and education levels have increased. In *Mobilization, Participation, and Democracy in America*, coauthors Steven Rosenstone and John Hansen (1993) used longitudinal data for the United States to show that citizen activism fluctuates not just from election year to election year, but also from month to month in between elections. Neither SES nor civic skills, resources that once acquired and not easily lost, can explain such rapid fluctuation in citizen activism. More to the point of this book, SES and resource models cannot explain key empirical variations observed in Mexico: why the poor sometimes participate more than the rich, why overall levels of participation have declined since the 1990s, and why the poor participated less *after* democratic reforms were implemented.

These empirical problems have their roots in pluralist assumptions inherent in SES and survey models that ignore the powerful ways that political institutions condition and constrain the behavior of individuals. These explanations of political participation assume that the democratic political arena is a frictionless environment with no institutional interference on political activities so that all individuals are free to choose from a wide range of political activities, limited only by their own desire and ability to do so. These explanations place the burden of action on the shoulders of individuals, ignoring the powerful ways in which unequal access to government officials, income inequalities, state policies, the mobilization strategies of political parties, and other structural features of local and national political contexts constrain the choices for action available to them.

A great deal of research has shown that these pluralist assumptions are simply wrong (see Bacharach and Baratz 1962; Gaventa 1980; Piven and Cloward 1979 and 1997b; Schattschneider 1960; and Verba, Nie, and Kim 1978). All political systems—democracies included—set up opportunities and barriers to participation that have different effects on the capacity and willingness of people from different income groups to engage in politics. This is true for established democracies and is especially true in emerging democracies like Mexico's, where authoritarian enclaves and practices endure. For example, in the past poll taxes in new democracies (like England and the United States) set up barriers to participation that denied lower classes the right to vote but did not affect the landed elite at all. Today, laws that regulate the size and frequency of campaign contributions, that regulate who can register to vote, that restrict the number and kind of political parties that can compete in elections, or that weaken or strengthen labor unions affect the affluent and the poor differently. Neoliberal reforms severely narrowed the range of issues that were discussed and debated in Mexico and changed the rules of the game in ways that made it more difficult for the poor and working classes in Mexico to participate effectively. By establishing barriers to participation that were hardest for the poor to overcome, these reforms and the new rules of the game created a mobilization of bias in which the poor and their issues were systematically excluded from the decision-making arena.

Thus institutions do not simply interfere with the ability of individuals to convert socioeconomic resources into activism, as Verba, Nie, and Kim (1978) have observed. They also determine which resources and skills matter and how much they matter for political activism. From an institutionalist perspective the stratification of political participation by socioeconomic status is not only due to the unequal distribution of resources in societies, but also to specific institutional constraints that make income and education matter more for participation. Therefore, when the poor participate less frequently in politics than the rich, we should investigate what about the political system discourages them from exercising their political voice.

In addition to resources, standard explanations of political participation also emphasize the importance of political engagement and political attitudes—the factors that shape people's motivations to take part in political life. Typically measures of political engagement include questions about people's interest in politics, how important politics is in their daily lives, whether they think their political activity has any impact, and the strength of partisan feelings. Decades of research have confirmed a strong and positive relationship between political engagement and political activity, so these variables have become staples of political participation research. To be truly useful, however, attitudinal explanations need to explain where these attitudes and values come from and why they change. By and large, the political participation literature treats political engagement as a property of individuals, as a set of preferences or psychological orientations toward politics that were developed over relatively long periods of time through early socialization experiences in school or within families or with experiences in such adult institutions as church, the workplace, civic organizations, or in the neighborhood context.[9] Other studies, noting that the poor are on average much less engaged with politics than more affluent groups, have attributed differences in political attitudes to their level of education or income, both of which give individuals the capacity and motivation to become politically active.[10] This insistence that political engagement develops independently of people's experiences with politics is intuitively unsatisfying and theoretically problematic, but ultimately it is deemed necessary to avoid issues of reciprocal causation.[11]

What if preferences for politics were not just the product of a lifetime of socialization experiences, but also shaped by people's direct and recent political experiences? What if instead it is levels of party competition, the actions of the state, the performance of government, and the policies it implements that shape people's preferences for politics, their feelings of political efficacy, their levels of partisanship, and support for democracy? If this were the case, then rather than thinking about political engagement as an attribute of individuals, we could think of engagement as measures of how the political system actually works.[12] This is an important practical and theoretical distinction. Theoretically, if political engagement is shaped by the rules that govern politics and by the actual responsiveness of elected officials to different groups of people, then lower levels of political engagement and political efficacy among the poor would be evidence not that they are uninterested in politics or apathetic. Rather, it would be evidence that they have had different experiences—likely more negative ones—with political institutions and with the political process than middle- and upper-class individuals. From a practical perspective, if political efficacy and political engagement measures really do tap into how political systems work, these widely used measures can be used as proxy variables for institutional performance that make it relatively easy to study the impact of some institutional factors on the political participation of different social groups. If we can establish that political attitudes have some of their origins in political institutions, and in turn, that these attitudes affect political participation, we will have a much better understanding of the mechanisms through which political institutions affect political participation.

A great deal of research from a variety of literatures gives us good reason to think that political attitudes do depend on the institutional availability of opportunities to participate in local and national politics. First, research has shown that political engagement and political participation are reciprocally related, so that political activism is both a cause and a consequence of political interest and efficacy (Almond and Verba 1989, Finkel 1985 and 1987, and Pateman 1970). If institutions influence who participates and how much, institutions will also impact levels of political engagement. So, for example, if a political system systematically depresses the political activity of the poor and working classes, we should not be surprised to find that poor and working-class individuals are also less engaged with politics (Gaventa 1980). Conversely, if low-income groups or otherwise marginal groups have privileged access to the state, as was the case for unionized workers in Western Europe (Verba, Nie, and Kim 1978) or for African Americans living in U.S. cities governed by an African American mayor (Bobo and Gilliam Jr. 1990), we should see higher rates of political participation than we would expect from their socioeconomic status alone and higher levels of trust in government, efficacy, and interest in and knowledge of politics.[13]

Nancy Burns, Kay Lehman Schlozman, and Sidney Verba (2001) have also noted the importance of political opportunities for explaining gendered differences in political participation. They discovered that although women in the United States participate less often than men, and are less likely to be psychologically involved with politics than men, the root of this differential engagement cannot be traced to women's pre-adult experiences in school and with their families, nor in their adult experiences at work, in church, or in other nonpolitical organizations. Instead, the researchers found the source of women's lower levels of political interest, political knowledge, and efficacy in the number of women who vie for or hold important political offices in the respondent's congressional district or state.[14] The more visible women are in positions of power, the more likely female respondents are to be involved in politics (ibid., 342–49). In other words, the underlying factor explaining why women participate less than men is not psychological engagement but politics—in this case the gendered political environment.[15]

Case studies of labor movement activism and urban squatters movements in countries as diverse as Chile, Mexico, and Peru have also shown that poor people's efficacy, trust in government, and political activism depends mostly on the structure of state-society links that open and close channels of access to state resources and decision makers, and create fluctuating incentives for participation for different social groups (Cornelius 1975, Dietz 1998, Eckstein 1977, Oxhorn 1995, Schneider 1995, and Stokes 1995). When a group's access is high—for example, that of organized labor during Peron's presidency in Argentina or in the first few decades of the PRI's rule in Mexico—its efficacy and participation in politics surpass that of higher-income groups. However, these drop dramatically when opportunities for access close (Cook 1996, Craig and Cornelius 1980, Davis 1983, Houtzager and Kurtz 2000, and Middlebrook 1995).

A recent study by Roderic Ai Camp has taken advantage of binational survey data to compare the attitudes and political participation of Mexicans living in Mexico with the attitudes of recent Mexican migrants to the United States. Camp (2003) found that Mexican Americans begin to adopt the American definition of democracy (liberty over equality) after having resided in the United States for only a year. This innovative research design allows him to show rather conclusively that political attitudes and values, even apparently deeply held values about the meaning of democracy and citizenship, are not fixed attributes of individuals or of social or national groups. Rather, they can change very quickly if the political context changes (or if individuals leave one context for another).

From such an institutionalist perspective, therefore, if the poor feel less efficacious or alienated from the political system, and so participate less, it probably is not because they are ignorant or incompetent, but because they understand all too well that the odds in the local or national political game are stacked against them.[16] According to Frances Fox Piven and Richard Cloward (1997a, 276), "It does not seem reasonable . . . to ascribe the low level of participation among the poor to lack of political interest or lack of political will. It is more likely due to a lack of political power. The syndrome among the poor that some call apathy is not simply a state of resignation; it is a definite pattern of motivated inaction impelled by objective circumstances. People who know they cannot win do not often try."

The connection between the concept of political efficacy and political opportunities is not just empirical and theoretical but conceptual as well. If we pay attention to how political scientists construct measures of political engagement, it is apparent that these factors may not measure citizens' acquired sense of competence or their inherent interest in political matters; rather, they measure the political opportunities that individuals from different social groups have to access the state and political leaders to express their preferences or grievances (Balch 1974; Craig and Maggiotto 1982; Craig, Niemi, and Silver 1990; Finkel 1985; Morrell 2003; Niemi, Craig, and Mattei 1991; and Pollock III 1983). Consider measures of political efficacy. Although initially conceptualized as a single concept that reflected an individual's belief in his or her own capacity to participate and to influence the political system, conventional measures used in most survey studies actually tap into two separate concepts: internal efficacy and external efficacy. Internal efficacy is rooted in an image of the self—namely, in self-perceptions that the individual is capable of understanding politics and competent enough to participate and influence politics. External efficacy, however, taps into features of the political system—namely, an individual's belief that government officials will be responsive to political pressure from citizens. Although this distinction between internal efficacy and external efficacy is generally acknowledged, in practice most studies still use measures of external efficacy to explore the relationship between individual attributes and behavior.

All of these findings point to the same conclusion: that measures of political attitudes tell us more about how respondents think the political system works than about beliefs in their own abilities. Individuals are not efficacious or inefficacious, engaged or detached in any absolute sense. Rather, feelings and expressions of efficacy are rooted in the concrete experiences people have with issues, government offices, and officials, and so they change as their political experiences change. If this is true, the correlation between efficacy, socioeconomic status, and political participation is not a given but should vary depending on how institutional ties and access to the state are distributed among social groups. If low-income groups have privileged access to the state—or conversely, if the middle class is shut out of politics by an authoritarian regime—we would expect the correlation between efficacy, socioeconomic status, and participation to be weak or negative. Similarly, if within the same country the opportunities for access changed over time (for example, as a result of a democratic transition or the election of a populist leader), we should see changes in both the efficacy and political participation of the most affected groups. Thus, although attitudes are not the main causal factor behind political participation, they are one of the mechanisms through which politics affects behavior.

Rational Choice, Political Participation, and Institutions

The core assumption of rational-choice approaches is that actors are utility maximizers who choose activities that are the most likely to provide them with the greatest net benefit. According to basic choice models of political behavior, when contemplating political activities, actors enter the political arena with fixed and stable preferences over *outcomes*, then choose actions to achieve the most desired one. Typically the basic choice model for a political act (represented by the subscript $_a$) is represented by an equation with the following form: $U_a = p(B_a) - C_a$. In this equation, U_a is the expected utility of choosing act "a," B_a is the actual benefit obtained from the outcome, "p" is the probability of the outcome happening by choosing act "a," and C_a represents the costs associated with carrying out the act.[17] Based on this equation, the expected utility of an act depends not just on the size of the benefits relative to the costs, but also on the likelihood of the political activity influencing the outcome.

The most common critique of rational-choice models of this kind is that they severely underpredict actual political activities, whether they are individual activities like voting or collective ones like protests. Basically, the benefits of the activity and the probability the activity will make a difference are too small and the costs too high to motivate anyone to act. In most scenarios predicted by this model, abstention is the dominant strategy because actors will enjoy the benefits of election victories or policy decisions whether or not they actually do anything politically to influence the outcome. In short, most of the time for most people, it is simply irrational to attempt political activities.

One way political scientists have tried to improve the predictive power of this basic model is by adding a term that represents the selective or consumption benefits individuals derive from political participation, benefits they can only enjoy by engaging in the activity and which they enjoy regardless of the outcome (Downs 1957; and Riker and Ordershook 1969). These selective incentives are usually represented with the letter D, where D_a represents the selective incentives an actor receives from undertaking act "a." Adding this term to the previous equation, we get a new model: $U_a = p(B_a) + D_a - C_a$. We can think of this D term as the preference or "taste" individuals have for politics, akin to common measures of political engagement.[18] People who are more interested in politics, who are strong partisans, or who feel a duty to participate will presumably derive a greater benefit from doing so, and thus will bear the costs more willingly. Although this modification improves the predictive power of the model, it does so at the risk of becoming tautological and unfalsifiable: to say that people vote or protest because they want to is really not very useful.[19] Moreover, it begs a prior theoretical question similar to the question raised by attitudinal models of political participation: Where do people's tastes for politics come from?

Rational actor models of political participation share some of the core theoretical problems of SES and attitudinal problems—namely, their emphasis on individual resources and preferences, with little or no consideration of how institutions constrain behavior. In a rather bold statement, John Aldrich (1993, 247) declared that "virtually all scholars agree with . . . the 'fundamental equation' of political behavior, which is that preferences (attitudes, beliefs, values) determine behavior. Rational-choice theory is about just how those preferences determine behavior." This is simply wrong, however. It ignores the voluminous literatures in economics, sociology, and political science that not only see institutional constraints on choice as much more important and useful explanations of behavior than preferences alone, but also recognize the power of institutional contexts for shaping actors' preference for politics (see Druckman and Lupia 2000, North 1981, and Wildavsky 1987).

This emphasis on preferences to explain behavior is perplexing because even the basic choice model hints at the importance of institutions for motivating and shaping political action. Although rational-choice models conceptualize the benefits (B) and costs (C) of actions in terms of individual preferences, in fact, the rules of the political game, the actions of political elites and of the state largely determine the benefits possible from political action (for example, in the form of policies) as well as how costly political activity will be. The term p, which represents the probability an action will produce the desired outcome, also contains a lot of information about how the political system works. For example, individuals contemplating protesting new legislation that will limit the right of workers to strike will be very attentive to features of the political environment that influence the likelihood of success, including whether a leftist party is in power, the relative power of the executive versus the legislative branch, how fractionalized the party system is, whether elections are imminent, and, not least, the repressive capacity of the state. All of these institutional factors are outside the control of individual actors but nonetheless weigh heavily on their calculations about whether and how to act.

Several rational-choice models incorporate institutions and contextual factors into their models, exploring how they affect the B, C, D, and "p" terms, but much of this theorizing has focused narrowly on voting behavior and turnout and still ignores other powerful ways that institutions constrain choice and shape political action (Aldrich 1993, Cox and Munger 1989, Finkel and Muller 1998, Goodwin and Mitchell 1982, Kato 1996, Teixeira 1992, Uhlaner 1989, and Whiteley 1995). Nonetheless, this attention to *political* factors is a useful step forward that improves upon narrow rational-choice models and validates the importance of studying both institutions and preferences when explaining political behavior.

Organizations and Political Mobilization

Standard SES and attitudinal models can sometimes explain who participates and how, but not when they participate. Rational-choice models can explain why people sometimes choose not to participate, but cannot adequately explain why people bother to vote, protest, or attempt most kinds of political activities even though the likelihood of making a difference is usually negligible. Mobilizational approaches to political participation—akin to resource mobilization (Jenkins 1983; and McCarthy and Zald 1977) and political process approaches from social movement theory (McAdam 1982 and Tarrow 1998)—overcome many of these empirical and theoretical problems by shifting the emphasis from individual-level factors to the role of organizations and political leaders in mobilizing people into politics. These approaches—epitomized by Verba, Nie, and Kim's *Participation and Political Equality* (1978), Rosenstone and Hansen's *Mobilization, Participation, and Democracy in America* (1993), and Piven and Cloward (1979, 1997a, and 2000) in various publications—do not attempt to replace SES, attitudinal, and rational-choice explanations of political participation. Rather, they build on them by emphasizing the powerful independent effect that organizations and the dynamics of the political process have on political participation.[20]

Organizations—whether voluntary associations, interest groups, or political parties—do much of the work of mobilizing people in and out of politics. They accomplish this in several ways. Organizations, particularly interest groups and political parties, deliberately mobilize political activity by canvassing potential voters, organizing a petition drive, or coordinating a letter-writing campaign, for example. People are more likely to participate if someone asks them to, and they are more likely to be asked if they are members of an organization.[21] But asking people to become involved is perhaps the least powerful way organizations stimulate citizen participation. Organizations also provide a social solution to the individual collective action dilemma by lowering the costs and increasing the benefits of participation. Through the social networks they cultivate and draw upon, organizations provide potential participants with information about issues, policies, candidates, and procedures; members may also provide a helping hand when it comes to voting or contacting a city official, and suggest effective ways to participate. In these and other ways, organizations subsidize the costs of participation, a factor that may be most important for resource-poor citizens. Organizations also contribute to the benefits side of actors' calculations by providing selective rewards to participants and costs to those who do not participate. Individuals acting alone may derive some purposive benefits—that is, intrinsic rewards that derive from the act of participation itself (see Rosenstone and Hansen 1993, 16)—but organizations can provide much larger and more consistent benefits to participants.

In addition to purposive benefits, organizations and leaders can reward active members with status and recognition within an organization and with such selective material rewards as government jobs, a larger share of government patronage, or more frequent distribution of material benefits like credits. Organizations can also impose selective costs on members to discourage apathy. According to Rosenstone and Hansen (ibid., 24), "because [social networks] can distinguish participants from pikers, they can also selectively reward the one and sanction the other." This latter insight is important because rational-choice explanations generally assume that nonparticipation is costless, making activism irrational. However, if organizations and social networks are strong enough to identify and punish nonparticipants, it may not be rational to abstain, particularly for low-cost activities like voting.

Participation that arises from group contexts may also be more common because members can reasonably expect that their coordinated activism will have a greater impact than if they acted alone. Using the language of the standard model of participation, individual political efficacy is likely to be greater among members of organizations, and from the perspective of rational-choice models, the probability ("p") of the activity having the desired effect will be higher, making political participation more likely. Moreover, in certain contexts, especially clientelistic ones, group leaders and members have strong incentives to participate frequently and in concert to secure particularistic benefits in the form of patronage, policy benefits, or targeted public works projects for a neighborhood. In these cases the aim of political participation is not to swing an election (an unlikely occurrence anyway) or to sway a legislative policy debate, but to demonstrate loyalty to secure material rewards for oneself or one's group (Uhlaner 1989). Organizations may also suppress or bar members from certain kinds of activities. Strong party systems are most likely to have this effect, but strong corporatist organizations can use their power to suppress or discourage participation, particularly certain kinds of participation, like protests or strikes (Verba, Nie, and Kim 1978). For example in Mexico, corporatist organizations encouraged members to vote (for the ruling party) and petition political leaders and the state for material benefits, but they generally discouraged protests and other kinds of autonomous and regime-challenging activities (Cornelius 1975 and Davis 1983).

In addition to organizations, the mobilization strategies employed by elites are another key independent variable of mobilizational approaches that help explain who participates and how. Political participation does not just happen within organizations in civil society; rather, it is mobilized by political parties, political leaders, and politicians who have their own interests in mobilizing people into politics. The mobilization efforts of political leaders create the very opportunities for citizens to participate, opportunities they may not otherwise have had (Rosenstone and Hansen 1993, 26). However, as Piven and Cloward have reminded us, political leaders do not try to mobilize everybody all of the time. Indeed, politicians and political parties have little interest in citizen activism per se. They promote public involvement only when it helps achieve other ends (win elections, pass bills, influence policies, receive campaign donations) that enhance their personal or political standing. They may actually discourage citizen involvement if it does not fit with their self-interested objectives (Piven and Cloward 1997b and 2000). For example, because political parties, especially in majoritarian systems, strive to maintain the broadest possible coalition of supporters, they will often avoid issues of most interest to the poor, which tend to be divisive and risk alienating other groups the party relies on to win elections (Piven and Cloward 1997b, 281–82). Thus the strategic calculations of political leaders determine a lot about who participates, and can explain why the poor and marginalized often participate less than, but sometimes more than, more affluent individuals.

The mobilizational approach does not supplant SES, attitudinal, and rational-choice explanations but builds on them to provide an account of political participation that is more powerful empirically and richer theoretically. Empirically, it is strong where individual-level theories are weak: it does a better job of explaining the ebb and flow of political participation, both at the individual level and at the aggregate level; it can explain why the poor sometimes participate more often than the affluent, while still explaining why they usually do not; and it helps explain why people attempt political acts even though according to narrow rational-choice approaches it is irrational for them to do so. In short, mobilizational theories explain everything individualist accounts do and more, exactly the condition under which we should abandon an old theory in favor of a new one.

Another important advantage of the mobilizational approach is that it reminds us that political activism rarely arises spontaneously, even among the most affluent and educated. Instead, actual participation depends heavily on the opportunities and costs imposed by the political process, which are outside of the control of individuals. Thus it recognizes that both political apathy and political activism are a product of the opportunities and constraints the political process provides for meaningful voice. This shift in emphasis from the individual to the institutional is immensely important. It brings the political participation literature closer in line with useful theoretical developments in political science and sociology, including social movement theories, that underscore how institutional constraints affect actors' ability to turn preferences into actions. It takes seriously the political and social context within which decisions to become politically active are made; it has alerted many researchers to the seemingly obvious fact that politics matters for political participation. Perhaps most importantly and fruitfully, by raising our gaze up from the individual and broadening our analysis to include the political context in which actors find themselves, the mobilizational approach allows us to see familiar patterns in new ways. In the words of Rosenstone and Hansen (1993, 234),

The withdrawal of citizens from electoral politics is not wholly of their own choosing, is neither the product of satisfaction or despair. The influx of citizens into governmental politics is likewise not wholly of their own choosing, is neither the product of enthusiasm nor cynicism. . . . Once we take political participation out of the realm of the attitudinal and place it in the sphere of the political, once we find its causes not only in individuals but also in the political system, the meaning of citizen participation in a democracy changes dramatically. By itself, citizen involvement implies neither legitimacy nor vigilance, neither contentment nor estrangement, neither virtue nor indifference. Instead, political participation tells us more about a political system than about its citizens.

The principal weakness of mobilizational explanations of political participation is that they stop short in their search for institutional influences on political participation by leaving the state out of their analysis. Although the activities of organizations and their interactions with political parties and elites certainly matter, they are not the only and usually not the most important sources of opportunities and constraints for citizen political action. The state also has enormous influence on who participates and how they do so.

That is not to say that there has been no attention paid to the ways in which public policies, the breadth of state activity, and the receptivity of political institutions to citizen input influence political participation. For example, Andrea Campbell (2003) has shown how the Social Security program in the United States is primarily responsible for high levels of activism among the elderly, and Henry Dietz (1998) has used longitudinal evidence to show how the political activity of urban residents in Peru is very sensitive to changes in the state's activities and capacities.[22] Many other studies have focused on the state's role in producing myriad related outcomes including interest group activity, elite bargaining, and changes in popular political culture and citizen attitudes.[23] Despite the central place the state has in the study of many political phenomena, and despite the obvious fact that the goal of political participation is to influence the state's activities, studies like those carried out by Campbell and Dietz are still rare and do not yet constitute an alternative approach.

Toward an Institutional Approach

An institutionalist approach for studying political participation places features of the political process *and* of the state at the center of explanations of who participates, when, and how. Evaluation of theories of political participation suggests several ways that the political process influences people's decisions about whether to attempt political activity. The political opportunity structure approach within the social movement literature goes further, specifying political and social institutions that are likely to be the most powerful determinants of political action, while the rationalist and historical institutional schools outline in detail the mechanisms through which political institutions shape the behavior of individuals. Although each of these bodies of literature are well developed, their insights are rarely used to understand noncontentious political activities by ordinary citizens. Instead, they focus on the behavior of elites, legislators, bureaucrats, market actors, or collective movements.[24] Yet there is no reason these perspectives cannot be generalized to all forms of political activity. After all, political participation involves people's interaction with the state and other political institutions that shapes their ability and desire to participate in politics and determines what kinds of political activities they can choose from.

The first task is to specify which institutions matter most for citizen activism. Social movement theories provide a useful starting point by highlighting the importance of "political opportunity structures" for understanding movement dynamics within and across political settings (Jenkins and Klandermans 1995; McAdam, McCarthy, and Zald 1996; and Tarrow 1998). Political opportunities are commonly defined as "consistent—though not necessarily formal or permanent—dimensions of the political environment that provide incentives for action by affecting people's expectations for success or failure" (Tarrow 1998, 77). Political opportunities arise when political space opens up that gives citizens greater access to decision-making arenas and broadens the menu of tactics or actions they can choose from. The actual configuration of political institutions that are relevant for political participation will likely differ across political systems—voter registration laws may matter in one setting but not in another, for example. Nonetheless, the social movement literature identifies two sets of factors that should influence citizen political activity: (1) the state and the policies it implements and (2) the system of representation, including electoral rules, the characteristics of the party system, and the competitiveness of elections.

Many studies that consider the influence of the state on political participation have focused narrowly on authoritarian settings, where the state uses its monopoly over coercive force openly and deliberately to tightly regulate citizen political activity. Studies of political participation in democratic settings, however, have rarely addressed the powerful role of the state in stimulating or hindering political participation.[25] Instead, they assume, more or less implicitly, that states in democratic systems impose few if any restrictions on participation, at least no restrictions that meaningfully affect overall patterns of activism. Even the mobilizational approaches focus on the opportunities and constraints for participation that arise from the actions of political parties and politicians, bracketing altogether the question of the state's influence on political behavior.

This is puzzling since the state, more than any other institution, has immense power to motivate, shape, and suppress political action. The state's basic activities—taxation, public works projects, enforcement of laws, maintaining order—and its control over resources create enormous incentives for citizens to target the state to satisfy their needs. States also organize the political environment in which political participation takes place, determining and enforcing (or sometimes not enforcing) the rules of the political game, regulating systems of representation, and determining which political activities are legal or illegal. Because the state never wields this power with complete impartiality, it creates opportunities for certain kinds of participation and for certain groups in society while discouraging other kinds of action and groups. Although the state's activities are usually not designed to influence patterns of participation, they inevitably do, whether directly by creating opportunities or constraints for action or indirectly by shaping citizens' political attitudes and beliefs.

Not all state activities affect all modes of political participation equally. Social movement scholars emphasize the willingness and capacity of states to use repression in dealing with protests, but this dimension is not as important for less contentious forms of political action.[26] Similarly, though voter registration laws exert a powerful influence on voter turnout, there is little reason to expect they have much effect on the frequency of letter-writing, making direct contact, or protesting. Perhaps the most important activities of states for overall activism are the public policies they implement, whether they be macroeconomic policies, funding for social-spending programs, tax laws, environmental policies, regulation of business, or decisions to go to war. Not only do these activities create immense incentives for people with interests in the policies to try to influence their formulation and implementation, but once implemented, they also create entrenched interests that keep people involved in politics, creating long-term habits of participation that spill over into other arenas and endure even after the initial stimulus is gone. Generally, the greater the scope of state activities—or more precisely, the greater the relevance of the activities of the state for individuals—the greater the incentives they will have to pursue political activity over other strategies that are also available to them. Therefore "activist" states that have the capacity and willingness to provide a large number of services and programs, and which take a larger role in the domestic economy, should stimulate more participation by a broader set of individuals. Minimalist states that have little capacity or desire to regulate the economy, provide public services, retirement programs for the elderly, or safety nets for the poor should encourage much less activism.[27]

In addition to the implementation of policy, other state activities that matter are related to its willingness and capacity to enforce the rule of law, particularly regarding electoral law, political and civil rights, and the rules that govern the political process. Emerging democracies often exist in poor countries with weak states that cannot reliably enforce electoral rules, particularly rules that prohibit fraud, limit campaign spending, or crack down on corruption.[28] Where elections are not clean, ruling parties use the state's resources for electoral advantage. Where civil liberties are not protected, turnout is likely to be much lower, although the incidence of protest might be higher. Moreover, in such situations government supporters likely vote more and protest less, while opposition supporters do the opposite.

The level of formal and informal access ordinary citizens have to political institutions and important decision makers is also important for political participation and depends in part on the state's formal structures. Frequent elections, abundant opportunities to directly influence policy decisions (through referenda, for example), and the decentralization of authority to local and state governments are formal and fairly stable features of political systems that create numerous points of access for citizen input. But where policymaking decisions are centralized in a few ministries or bureaucracies, based on technocratic criteria with few opportunities for lawmakers to influence the specifics of the policy, citizens have little incentive to engage in political activity to influence the content of policy decisions.

Access to decision makers does not depend only on the state. Less formal and more fluid configurations of the political system, such as the receptivity of parties and politicians to input from individuals and groups in civil society and the availability of sympathetic allies in positions of power, also influence who has more access and therefore more incentives to participate. There has not been much research done on this topic, but we might expect political systems based on proportional representation to be less open to citizens making direct contact compared with majoritarian systems where each legislator represents and is accountable to a specific geographic constituency. In proportional representation systems, affiliation with organizations and especially with political parties is likely to be a prerequisite for many kinds of political activity, while majoritarian systems are more open to individual and unorganized pressures. Similarly, people living in cities governed by directly elected mayors have more reason, incentives, and opportunities to contact city officials than people living in towns where local leaders are appointed by the president or which are governed by hired managers (Macedo et al. 2005).

The characteristics of the party system—which includes the number of parties, the distribution of power among parties, and the variety of ideological positions represented by parties in government—should also matter for political participation (Kriesi 1995). The poor are more likely be active in politics when the relative power of parties on the left is high. Although it may sometimes be enough for the left to be competitive in elections to stimulate political activity among the poor, it is more important for leftist parties or populist candidates to actually win elections for the participatory potential of popular groups to be maximized. This is more likely in proportional representation systems, where the threshold for gaining representation in government is relatively low compared with majoritarian systems. In Mexico, for example, the left-of-center PRD has typically been the least powerful among the three main parties, with little or no organizational presence in hundreds of municipalities across the country. Its inability to win elections, and sometimes to even field credible candidates, reduces the opportunities for the poor to be active in politics. This does much less damage to the political activity of middle and upper classes.

The competitiveness of elections should also matter for political participation beyond voting. Where multiple parties compete in closely contested elections, citizens usually have more points of access to decision makers, if for no other reason than politicians have more incentives to respond to the demands of constituents and pressure groups in between elections. Thus, to ensure reelection, incumbents are more open to direct-contacting activities by citizens and groups, may visit their home district more often, seek out the support of large organizations, and are generally more responsive to citizen activism. More parties also means that a wider variety of issues is represented in policy debates and election campaigns, giving individuals more choices that approximate their policy preferences. This should raise their interest in politics, their level of political efficacy, and their overall engagement with politics—all of which have the effect of boosting participation in a variety of political acts.

Finally, the rhythms of the political process determine a lot about when people are mobilized and which activities they are more likely to pursue. The frequency of elections, the cyclical and seasonal calendars of legislatures, the issues that are placed on the political agenda, and similar features of the political process all send signals to potential actors about when to act and what kind of activities to pursue (Rosenstone and Hansen 1993). Although every political system is different, and provides different incentives for different groups to participate, some general expectations suggest themselves. Participation is greater when important decisions are pending and when the outcomes are not foregone conclusions. Thus we would expect more participation close to election time, and more still if the outcome of the elections were uncertain. Similarly, we should expect more contacting, protesting, and letter-writing when important decisions are scheduled in parliaments and the greatest amount of activity by those most affected by the decisions. In addition, because bureaucracies are less open to political pressure than legislatures, we should expect less political mobilization and political participation when decisions are made by technocrats or by apolitical formulas than when they are made by elected leaders. Similarly, we should expect less participation when policymaking power is heavily concentrated in national-level bodies than when this power is shared by state and local governments, which participants can target at a lower cost (ibid., 34–36).

The next task is to specify how political institutions affect individuals' political activity. I borrow core insights from rational and historical institutional approaches, the two main schools of institutionalist research within political science, in addition to insights from the mainstream political participation literature, about how institutions shape behavior. Institutions shape the *incentives* that actors face when contemplating political activity. From this perspective, political activity is more likely when political opportunities open that increase the benefits, reduce the risk, or increase the likelihood of success of a specific political act. This expectation is similar to the core expectation of choice theoretic models of political behavior, with one subtle difference.

Whereas narrow rational-choice models tend to be apolitical, looking for the source of costs and benefits of political activities in individuals' attitudes, beliefs, and values (such as feelings of internal efficacy, partisanship, or feelings of political duty), from an institutionalist perspective the state, the actions of parties and elites, and the specific characteristics of the political system are the *primary* source of costs and benefits of political activity. They thus weigh heavily on individual decisions about whether to participate or abstain (Aldrich 1993). The poor are especially sensitive to changes in this calculus of participation resulting from institutional obstacles to participation because they have substantially lower thresholds before participation becomes too costly (Wolfinger and Rosenstone 1980). They also tend to discount future benefits from elections and policy decisions much more heavily than more affluent actors.

In Peru, for example, the state—whether controlled by authoritarian or democratic governments—has been incapable of generating adequate resources for its citizenry, especially its poor, and of distributing these insufficient resources efficiently and equitably. According to Henry Dietz, under such macro-political conditions, the poor recognized that the state could not or would not provide for them, so they stopped petitioning the state. It became apparent that as a source of assistance, the state had become "tragically irrelevant to the poor, just as the needs of the poor for assistance were becoming increasingly desperate because of economic breakdown and deepening poverty" (Dietz 1998, 236).[29]

Institutions also shape behavior by *constraining* people's choice over possible modes of political action. Most models of political participation assume that individuals are free to choose from a wide array of political acts, constrained only by their own resources, abilities, and desire. But this assumption is unrealistic because it ignores the powerful ways that institutional arrangements and the political process—democratic or otherwise—constrain the range of activities from which actors can realistically choose. Registration laws, campaign finance laws, the timing of elections and legislative sessions, labor policy, fiscal and economic policy, the vicinity of government offices, the repressive capacity of the state, protection (or lack thereof) for political and civil liberties, and other features of the political environment determine which political acts are available to individuals and groups at any given time. In Mexico it is relatively easy to register to vote, but other constraints affect the choices low-income citizens have. For example, democratic reforms have done a lot to protect the political rights of individuals, but the Mexican state continues to suppress and repress political mobilizations from low-income and working-class actors, often with a great deal of violence. This narrows the choice they have for political influence. The choice at the ballot box is also limited because left-of-center parties are not competitive in many local and state elections and because fraud is still prevalent in many areas, particularly in poorer states and areas where local autocratic rulers still dominate.

Institutions impact behavior by shaping people's *preferences* and their ideas about what is politically desirable and possible (Kato 1996, Koelble 1995, and Wildavsky 1987). Expanding opportunities that decrease the costs of action and increase the likelihood of success sparks political activity, generates an interest in politics, and creates a sense among citizens that they can influence the behavior of political leaders. Narrowing opportunities reduce engagement, efficacy, and interest in politics—but only among those individuals facing these constraints. In addition to these relatively short-term effects on people's political attitudes, if structural opportunities or constraints persist over time, actors may move from a "logic of interests" (in which actors act on the basis of their preferences over outcomes) to a "logic of appropriateness" (in which political activism or apathy becomes habitual) so that actors develop preferences over the actions themselves (March and Olsen 1984). For example, Andrea Campbell (2003) has found that over the course of the existence of the Social Security program in the United States, the expansive opportunities for participation it created cultivated a participatory ethic among the elderly so that voting and political contacting is not just something they do to accomplish an objective: it is one of the ends they value.

In Mexico, poor people's acceptance and use of corporatist and clientelist political strategies was initially motivated by strategic decisions about which political strategies would produce the greatest good. The stability of the Mexican regime, the longevity of the PRI, and the pervasiveness of clientelistic relationships at all levels of the power structure gave clientelist practices time to become institutionalized into commonsense understandings of how politics "works." What began as strategic behavior over time took on more characteristics of habitual or norm-driven behavior: it became routinized in everyday life, people expressed a preference for it, and they found it difficult to imagine another way of doing things.[30]

The state, the policies it implements, and the features of the political process impact political participation directly by shaping the incentives and choices actors have for becoming involved in public life and indirectly by influencing their political attitudes, preferences, and engagement with politics. Together these direct and indirect effects work powerfully to shape patterns of political participation. This framework does not dismiss the importance of personal resource endowments for political action, but it recognizes that deficiencies in resources can be overcome when organizations and political leaders mobilize low-income citizens or when the state creates incentives for them to target state and governmental institutions. It also agrees with rational-choice models that political participation is based on rational individual decisions, but emphasize that these individual decisions cannot be understood on the basis of individual preferences alone. Preferences and resources create the potential for action, but cannot tell us when it will happen or what means actors will employ to achieve their ends. For that we also need to understand how particular institutions shape their motivations for attempting (or eschewing) political activities.

Comparisons across Time, Space, and Social Groups

Ultimately the value of this institutionalist framework lies in its ability to answer the four questions posed at the beginning of this chapter. Unlike SES, attitudinal, and rational-choice models, a focus on institutions allows us to explain why the poor sometimes participate more, but usually less, than more affluent groups. Specific institutional environments do not distribute political opportunities equally; rather, they create opportunities for some and constraints for others.[31] When important policy decisions are made by distant and impermeable bureaucracies, participation by ordinary citizens in these decisions is nearly impossible. But well-organized interest groups or corporations that have the resources and expertise to navigate through complex bureaucracies may not be discouraged. In general, political arrangements that raise the costs of political activity stifle the activism of resource-poor actors more than that of actors with larger resource endowments. Conversely, in places where leftist parties govern or where pro-poor policies are common, the political activity of low-income actors may exceed that of more affluent groups.

By influencing the relative benefits and costs of different activities, and even more powerfully by constraining the menu of political activities available to individuals, political institutions also influence actors' decisions about which activities to pursue. Variation in electoral laws, in party systems, and the size and scope of spending programs all determine which activities have the greatest potential for influencing the decisions of government officials and which activities, if any, are available to which groups. For example, where electoral fraud is prevalent, turnout may drop but protest activities by opponents of the regime may be more common than in localities where elections are more or less free and fair.

Attention to institutions and how they constrain actors' choices also allows us to explain why people sometimes exit politics. When deciding to participate in politics, people are not just choosing whether to vote, join an organization, or coordinate on community projects with their neighbors. They are also thinking about private means to achieve their ends, such as migration, dedicating more time to their job or education, or even crime. Whether formal or informal, political participation only makes sense if political activities are actually available as realistic choices and if people believe they can best achieve their objectives through political activism. Samuel Huntington and Joan Nelson (1976, 17) have stated this clearly: Certain issues—such as the effects of a drought, neighborhood infrastructure problems, promoting individual family and welfare, "may or may not prompt individuals or groups to turn to governmental action, depending on the perceived availability and effectiveness of this course of action compared with alternative means. . . . If nonpolitical means are as promising as, or more promising than, political channels, people may be expected to invest their time and energy accordingly."

An institutionalist framework can also help us account for the ebb and flow of citizen activism and differences in political activity across contexts.

Some aspects of the opportunity structure are stable and deeply embedded in political institutions and culture. These stable dimensions are useful in comparisons across space, explaining differences in political participation in different countries, states, cities, or even neighborhoods. Examples of stable political opportunities include electoral laws, centralization of political institutions and government decision making, state strength and repressive capacity, state strategies and capacities for social control, and perhaps even property rights and the distribution of resources in society (Fish 1995 and Tilly 1978). However, even these stable elements are not completely static, and in some countries they change with frustrating frequency. Since the early 1990s, neoliberal and democratic reforms in Mexico and Latin America have produced tremendous transformations in state structures, in the role of the state in society, and in its capacities to control participatory activities. Another example is Venezuela, which not too long ago was one of the most stable democracies in Latin America. But since 1992 it has seen two attempted military coups, the decay of its two-party system, the emergence of numerous new political parties at both the municipal and national levels, a flip-flopping between neoliberal reforms and more protectionist economic policy, and the ratification of a brand-new constitution. Such transformations in core structures can open important fresh opportunities for participation for some groups or close previously existing channels of access for others.

Other political opportunities, particularly those associated with systems of representation, are inherently dynamic, even volatile, shifting with events, policies, and political actors. These fluid dimensions of political opportunities can tell us a lot about why the level, form, and intensity of participation vary over time. Some dynamic dimensions of political opportunities include changes in access to government officials, the emergence of new political parties or movements, the appearance of influential allies or splits among the elite, changes in social and economic policy, and the emergence and strength of new local or regional organizations (Dietz 1998; McAdam 1982; McAdam, McCarthy, and Zald 1996; Tarrow 1998; and Tilly 1978).

Attention to institutional factors also enables (and encourages) within-country comparisons, allowing researchers to explain variations in who participates and how across local contexts. The strength and capacity of local governments to carry out infrastructure projects, the differences in the competitiveness of local party systems, variation in levels of fraud and authoritarian practices, the strength of local- and state-level autocracies, the uneven distribution of benefits from antipoverty programs, and the density and strength of organizations in local civil society are all important for understanding differences in levels of political participation across towns and cities within the same country.

The State, Democratic Reforms, and Political Participation in Mexico

Given this discussion, what can we expect about the relationship between political change and political participation in Mexico? The massive transformations of state-society relations resulting from neoliberal and democratic reforms in Mexico and across Latin America have created a new and very different strategic context for political participation that unsettled political habits developed under previous regimes. It is likely that neoliberal reforms have had class-specific impacts, discouraging the participation of lower-income citizens much more than that of the affluent. A number of researchers have noted a closing of access to public spaces in Latin American countries as a result of neoliberal reforms, a narrowing of access that affects the poor more than the middle class and the rich (see Holzner 2007a, Houtzager and Kurtz 2000, Kurtz 2004, Oxhorn and Ducatenzeiler 1998b, Roberts 1999, Teichman 2001, and Weyland 1996 and 2004). Repeated austerity programs that gutted federal spending programs and eliminated subsidies for basic foodstuffs, a decline in the spending and scope of rural development programs, and a general shrinking of state budgets have made the state less relevant for the poor. This reinforces a perception among popular groups that the state cannot or will not provide for them.

A particularly damaging aspect of these reforms was the centralization of economic decision making in a few ministries in Mexico City, taking policy decisions out of the hands of elected leaders and putting them in the hands of nonelected technocrats. Given the reduced discretionary power of elected officials over policy matters, and the difficulty of targeting technocrats in faraway ministries, the expected utility of contacting representatives or of organizing protests are now much lower. In addition, the shift from a state-centered to a free-market development model resulted in sharp cutbacks in state subsidies to the poor, reformed labor laws to favor businesses over unions, and altered social-spending programs in ways that depoliticized how funds are distributed—all of which made the state less relevant in the lives of the poor. Given these changes, we should not be surprised to note that the poor feel less efficacious and less engaged in politics than the more affluent, and less engaged than they did in the past. What is more worrisome is that if these exclusionary policies persist long enough—and they have been in place since the early 1990s in some countries—the poor will come to value political participation less and less, seeing it as inappropriate or inherently ineffective.[32]

Mexico's democratic transition will probably have a more mixed effect across activities and groups. During the initial period of the democratic transition, roughly between 1990 and 1997, Mexico saw sharp reductions in electoral fraud, increases in the competitiveness and fairness of elections, and hundreds of victories by opposition parties in local, state, and national elections. All of these transformations created new opportunities for Mexicans from all walks of life to become interested and engaged in politics. However, the spread of democratic practices has been very uneven in Mexico, producing a mosaic of democratic and authoritarian subnational regimes. Many of the most stubborn and powerful authoritarian enclaves endure in relatively poor states, towns, and neighborhoods, so that overall the poor continue to face more institutional constraints to their participation. In addition, state repression of popular organizations and parties on the left was common during the 1990s and even during Vicente Fox's presidency, creating additional obstacles to participation faced primarily by lower-class groups. In short, the end of PRI hegemony and the uneven process of democratization in Mexico has created an unequal distribution of participatory opportunities that tend to discourage the poor from activism.

The mobilization strategies of Mexico's major parties should also provides clues about why the poor participate much less than other groups. Between 1940 and 1980 the PRI had strong incentives to mobilize the poor into regime-supportive activities, in part to consolidate their power, in part to legitimize their revolutionary credentials, and in part to preempt electoral challenges from the left. After the economic crises of the 1980s and the 1990s, Mexico's political leaders were forced to implement austerity and structural reform programs that were deeply unpopular. Consequently, the PRI's dominant technocratic faction was much less interested in stimulating popular mobilization, particularly among the poor, outside of elections (Grindle 1995). Of course, opposition parties did have strong incentives to mobilize potential and actual partisans. However, Mexico's second-largest party during the decade, the pro-business PAN, had little interest in mobilizing the poor, while the leftist PRD suffered from a dysfunctional internal organization and could not mobilize voters outside of a few regional strongholds (Bruhn 1997). As a consequence, during the decade when democratic reforms were implemented most aggressively and most successfully in Mexico, the efforts of parties and politicians to strategically mobilize support magnified the class bias in political participation.

This changed in 2006 when the PRD, led by its presidential candidate Andrés Manuel López Obrador, had its best showing ever in federal elections, coming within a few hundred thousand votes of winning the presidency. Reversing previous patterns of declining participation, political participation spiked during the campaign as millions of rural and urban poor were galvanized by López Obrador's campaign. However, this election was the exception that proved the rule: outside of this unique event, wherever the PRD was not competitive in elections and voters' choice was limited to PRI or PAN candidates, the political participation of the poor suffered.

Given the importance of organizations and of political mobilization for political participation, any explanation of who participates and how in Mexico needs to pay attention to the impact that neoliberal and democratic reforms have had on the strength and number of interest groups and civil society organizations, particularly organizations that target the poor. Although there has been a proliferation of autonomous organizations in Mexican civil society, they tend to be small and weak, with limited power to mobilize members into political activity. In addition, democratization and neoliberalism have failed to eliminate clientelist organizations and practices in Mexico, which remain strong although not as closely aligned with the PRI as before. Ironically, where the spread of independent grassroots organizations successfully undermined the power of local patrons and allowed the poor to exit clientelist networks, participation rates among these newly autonomous citizens frequently declines. The reason is simple: clientelist organizations have strong incentives and powerful means to mobilize members into politics; once individuals exit these strong networks, they are less likely to be asked or forced to participate in politics. With fewer inducements and stimuli coming from the state and political parties, many people simply choose not to get involved.

□ □ □ □ **CHAPTER 3** □ □ □ □

NEOLIBERAL REFORMS, THE STATE, AND OPPORTUNITIES FOR POLITICAL PARTICIPATION

One of the difficulties of developing and applying an institutional framework is identifying which institutions matter most for citizen political activism. This problem is particularly acute in the case of Mexico because so much changed between 1990 and 2000. Reforms that opened the political system will certainly impact people's political activity, but it is much less clear whether and to what extent neoliberal reforms like the privatization of state-owned enterprises, cutbacks in state spending, free-trade agreements, and a shift to targeted poverty-alleviation programs matter for political participation. Existing research provides some guidance, but much of the terrain remains unmapped (see Kurtz 2004, Posner 2008, and Shefner 2008). I asked people directly about their experiences with neoliberal reforms and how those massive institutional changes impacted their desire and their ability to become politically involved. By listening to the poor, we can uncover and trace the complex links between big structural changes and individual decisions about what kind of political strategies (if any) to pursue. In-depth interviews allow people to describe which institutional changes— those associated with increased political competition or with the structure and action of the state—are foremost on their minds when thinking about protesting, petitioning, or otherwise trying to influence the state. In this way

51

I tease out the effects of structural reforms associated with neoliberal policies from the effects of reforms associated with democratization.

This shift in development models involved much more than a change in macroeconomic and spending policies. It also required a radical transformation of the institutions of the state, reshaping the ways in which it interacted with individuals and groups in society. My interviews point to several mechanisms through which reforms of the state discouraged Mexico's poor from participating in democratic politics. During the decade when neoliberal reforms were first implemented and consolidated, the incomes of most Mexicans declined, with some of the steepest declines occurring among the lower classes. Although most people suffered through this period, declines in income matter more for the poor because they have so little to spare. Even apparently trivial declines in resources are enough to make many kinds of political activity impossible for the poor. Consequently, despite significant improvements in political liberties and party competition, the poor with whom I spoke found it increasingly difficult to muster the material resources necessary to participate in Mexico's more open political process.

The combination of free-market reforms and the government's practice of dividing and weakening popular organizations had a devastating effect on the organizational resources available to the poor, since many of the traditional organizations that had mobilized the poor into politics lost resources, membership, and access to policymakers. Although Mexico experienced a revitalization of civil society during the 1990s, much of the new organizational energy was the domain of the middle class, with few interest groups able to aggregate the interests of the poor. Those that did seek to organize the poor suffered from small memberships, small budgets, and little capacity to access policymakers.

The declining relevance of government policy in the lives of the poor has perhaps been the most damaging to lower-class political mobilization. The switch from a development strategy characterized by heavy state intervention in the economy to a free-market model brought about important changes in the structure and the activities of the state. These changes—which centralized policymaking decisions in a few ministries in Mexico City, institutionalized the use of predetermined formulas to determine spending levels for education, health care, and poverty-alleviation programs, and reduced the size and scope of state activities—decreased the potential benefits of political action. At one point it made sense for people in Mexico to turn to politics to satisfy needs as diverse as affordable housing, better pay, lower prices for food for consumers and subsidies for inputs for farmers, for land, for jobs, for health care, for titles to land, for water, sewage and other services, and so on. But now, because the state has dismantled most of its subsidy and poverty-alleviation programs, the poor simply have less stake in the political system and fewer reasons to target the state to satisfy their needs.

My ethnographic research strategies help us understand why the poor might participate less than the rich but cannot tell us whether these dynamics hold across Mexico or what impact they have on overall levels of political participation. We should be especially cautious about generalizing to the rest of Mexico because the state of Oaxaca is unique in many ways. Nonetheless, the political, economic, and social consequences of neoliberal reforms are acutely felt and debated by its residents. I would expect their experiences to be very similar to those living in rural areas and regional capitals elsewhere. It is best to be sure, however. Chapter 4 tests whether the same factors and processes I identify in Oaxaca are at work elsewhere in Mexico, and whether their cumulative effect can account for the gap in political participation across income groups.

Whether free-market reforms have contributed to or detracted from the process of democratization in Latin America has been a controversial question (see Teichman 2001, 5–10). Politicians and analysts have worried about the negative short-term effects of radical economic reforms on the stability of Latin America's young democracies (Haggard and Kaufman 1992 and 1995). Many have also agreed that in the long-term, free markets and democratic reforms reinforce each other by reducing corruption, increasing accountability, freeing citizens from clientelist relationships, and laying the foundations for future economic growth (Samstad 2002, Teichman 1997 and 2001, and Wise 2003). After all, the experience of Western Europe and the United States suggests that stable democracies are most likely to survive in capitalist economic systems with a large degree of private ownership (Lindbloom 1977).

However, other researchers have warned that stabilization and structural adjustment reforms tend to weaken democracy where they are implemented. Adam Przeworski (1991) warned that economic stabilization and free-market reforms weaken democratic governance because they require governments to actively suppress political participation by weakening trade unions, leftist parties, and other social organizations that advocate for redistributive social and economic policies. More recently, a number of political scientists have pointed to the technocratic nature of reforms in Mexico and other Latin American countries that insulate policymakers from popular pressures while providing privileged access to powerful business interests and international funding agencies such as the World Bank (Shadlen 2000 and 2002 and Teichman 2004).

The empirical evidence from Latin America is mounting in favor of the second position, suggesting that while neoliberal policies may have stabilized democratic politics in the region, they did so at the expense of political participation, representation, and government responsiveness (Levine and Molina 2007, Roberts 1999, and Weyland 2004). Although politicians might court the popular vote with campaigns that promised generous spending policies, increased wages, and wealth redistribution, once in office they face considerable pressure not to diverge from market reforms (Stokes 2001). Case studies have shown that neoliberal reforms have a devastating effect on the ability of popular groups to mobilize by atomizing workers and peasants, weakening their ability to organize, and closing off access to key allies and government ministries (Houtzager and Kurtz 2000, Kurtz 2004, and Weyland 1996). Recent cross-national empirical studies confirm these impressions, showing that countries that pursued market reforms most aggressively incurred significant costs in the quality of democracy (Huber and Solt 2004).

Poverty and Declining Resources for Participation

Institutions matter in part because they influence how resources are distributed in a society. Economic policies (distributive social policies in particular) have profound and immediate effects on poverty levels, income inequalities, and the distribution of politically relevant resources among citizens. The distribution of income changed between 1990 and 2000, the period during which neoliberal reforms were consolidated and deepened in Mexico. This increasing stratification of income contributed to the stratification of political participation. Income levels matter for political participation in part because all political acts impose a minimum resource threshold on potential participants. Although voting is a relatively low-cost activity, many other political acts (such as writing letters, attending community meetings, contacting government officials, or protesting) are quite costly. Acts like donating money to campaigns require precisely the kind of resources that the poor have in least supply. Because the wealthy have more discretionary income and resources, they "can simply afford to do more—of everything—than citizens with little money" (Rosenstone and Hansen 1993, 12).

The logic of this argument suggests that marginal changes in income levels should be much more important for the political activism of the poor than the relatively affluent. While apparently trivial additions to the cost of participation will not affect the political participation of citizens with some discretionary income or savings, they may be enough to raise the burden of participation above the threshold for the poor.[1] Similarly, even small declines in income matter more for the poor because they have so little income to spare.[2] Any increase in the burden of participation or a decline in real income may be enough to turn resource-poor participants into nonparticipants, independently of other factors such as levels of engagement, civic skills, or membership in organizations.

Figure 3.1 shows how poverty levels have changed in Mexico since 1950 using three different methods for calculating poverty. One striking feature is that poverty changed little during the early period of neoliberal adjustment (1987–92) but got much worse between 1994 and 1998, before improving again to roughly the levels that existed before 1982.[3] This does not mean that neoliberal policies are to blame for this lack of improvement in the living standards of poor Mexicans.[4] It does mean, however, that policies like free trade, privatization, and the implementation of ambitious social spending and poverty-alleviation programs did little to put more money in the pockets of the poor. On the contrary, after the peso had declined during the 1960s and 1970s and stabilized during the 1980s, the 1994 peso crisis decimated the incomes of the millions of lower-middle and middle-class Mexicans, driving many of them into poverty. During the 1990s the structure of poverty changed, with the number of people living in extreme poverty increasing more rapidly than the overall poverty level (Boltvinik 2003).[5]

Low and declining real wages are an important cause of poverty in Mexico. According to data by Kevin Middlebrook (1995, 214–15), the real value of the minimum wage in Mexico City declined from an indexed value of 123.2 in 1982 to only 48 in 1993, a third of what it was in 1976 at the peak of ISI policies. More generally, real wages in manufacturing suffered a sharp decline, dropping 30 percent in real terms between 1982 and 1989. They staged a recovery under the Salinas administration (1988–1994), but nearly all these gains were lost in the aftermath of the 1995 economic crisis (Pastor and Wise 2003; and Salas and Zepeda 2003). Alejandro Portes and Kelly Hoffman (2003, 65) conclude that neoliberal policies exacerbated "what was already a gulf in the economic condition and life chances of the wealthy and the poor. More than ever, the fact was reaffirmed that, in Latin America, it is not necessary to be unemployed to be poor. The vast majority of the working population receives wages that would condemn them to poverty, in part because of the generalized underdevelopment of their national economies, but also because of the highly skewed distribution of the economic pie."

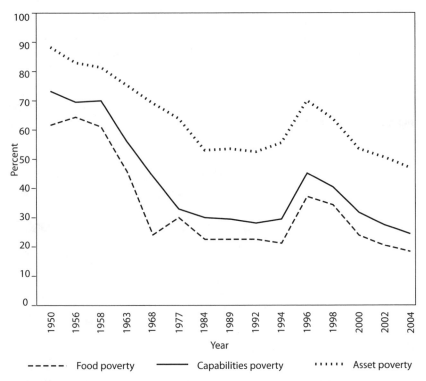

Figure 3.1. Evolution of Poverty in Mexico, 1950–2004. "Food poverty" is defined as the proportion of the population that has a per capita monthly income that is insufficient to purchase a basic and essential food basket. The thresholds were 739.6 pesos per person for urban areas and 548.17 pesos for rural areas (2004 prices, approximately US$66 and US$49 per month). "Capabilities poverty" is set at 909.71 pesos (US$81) per person per month for urban areas and 651.77 pesos (US$58) for rural areas (2004 prices). It measures the proportion of the population that can acquire a minimum necessary food basket but does not have enough income to acquire minimum acceptable levels of health and education. "Asset poverty" is set at 1487.34 pesos (US$132) and 1000.4 pesos (US$89) per person per month for urban and rural areas respectively (2004 prices). It is defined as the minimum level of per capita income necessary to cover minimum nutritional, health, and education needs but not enough to acquire minimum levels of shelter, clothing, and transportation for all household members. *Source*: Székely 2005, 12–16.

Although political scientists focus on income and education to gauge people's capacity to engage in political activity, individual opportunities and constraints for political participation are only partially related to these socio-economic resources. Other dimensions of poverty (such as access to health care, adequate housing, or the quality of local infrastructure) also weigh heavily on political activity. This is true not only because material wants suggest the specific needs around which the poor might mobilize for political action, but also because these wants create powerful constraints on the choices of political activities available to the poor. To give but one example, millions of Mexico's rural poor live in relatively isolated communities that lack access to basic transportation and communications infrastructure. A trip to a medical clinic, the regional market, or to the local government offices might require a walk of several hours, whereas a round trip to the state capital to visit the government's agricultural extension offices could easily take several days. This puts many opportunities for political action beyond the reach of those living in marginal communities.

For our purposes, this poverty of choices and opportunities is more relevant than the poverty of income, for it translates directly into the poor's diminished capacity to participate as equals in the democratic process.[6] It is worthwhile to analyze changes in the Index of Marginalization (IM), a measure of poverty used by Mexico's National Population Council (Consejo Nacional de Pobación, CONAPO) that recognizes multiple factors that contribute to poverty and which has the added advantage of being available for all states and municipalities in Mexico, thus providing a truer sense of how poverty is distributed across Mexico.[7] The index differentiates between five categories of marginalization, ranging from "very high" to "very low."[8] Although the index takes income levels into account, it also measures eight other basic dimensions of poverty and deprivation, including a lack of access to water and sanitation services, a lack of basic education, the quality of available housing, and the availability of basic infrastructure. High marginality scores signal the residents experience high levels of poverty, precarious living conditions, and a lack of basic opportunities for social advancement. Given the importance of literacy, income, and access to infrastructure for political action, high marginality rates also imply a reduced set of opportunities to become involved in public life.

Have Mexico's economic policies improved people's access to such opportunities for social and political participation? According to evaluations by the Mexican government, between 1990 and 2000, eleven of thirty-two states showed marked improvement in marginalization levels, but fourteen

Table 3.1. Socioeconomic Conditions in Oaxaca

Name of municipality	Population	Percentage of population 15 and over that is illiterate	Percentage of working population earning less than two times minimum wage	Percentage of houses without				IM score[a] 1995	IM score[a] 2000	IM score[a] 2005
				Indoor plumbing	Electricity	Concrete floors	Sewage and toilet			
Oaxaca	256,130	5.31	41.46	9.31	1.87	10.64	1.67	-1.34	-1.67	-1.56
Zimatlán	16,801	14.91	69.00	21.06	4.53	47.04	22.51	-0.11	-0.24	-0.18
La Ciénega	2,942	15.92	83.96	1.88	0.62	40.05	5.02	-0.07	-0.14	-0.35
Teotitlán del Valle	5,562	15.82	80.76	6.01	2.45	39.5	33.32	0.09	0.15	0.32
Oaxaca state	3,438,765	21.50	71.93	26.95	12.54	41.60	18.07	1.85	2.08	2.13
Mexico	97,483,412	9.46	50.99	4.23	4.79	14.79	9.90	n/a	n/a	n/a

Source: INEGI 1995; and CONAPO 1998, 2001, and 2005.

[a] "IM score" refers to the Index of Marginality score from CONAPO.

In 1995, CONAPO classified the city of Oaxaca as having "very low" levels of marginality; Zimatlán, La Ciénega, and Teotitlán del Valle as having "moderate" levels of marginality; and the state as a whole as having "very high" levels of marginality.

of thirty-two got worse. It is significant that most of the improvements happened in states that were already relatively well off, such as Baja California, Coahuila, and Nuevo León, whereas poor states like Chiapas, Guerrero, Oaxaca, and Tabasco fared much worse. At the municipal level, fewer than 9 percent of municipalities improved conditions for residents sufficiently to be reclassified into a lower marginality category, while 16 percent of municipalities worsened their classification. Here, too, most of the municipalities that improved (113 of 197) were already relatively well off, moving from conditions of low to very low marginality. Only 5 percent of municipalities (84 of 1,615) scoring medium to very high levels of marginalization managed to improve living conditions enough to graduate to a lower category (CONAPO 2004).

Between 1990 and 2000 the most significant improvements at the national level occurred in the provision of basic service infrastructure, such as electricity, water, and sewage services; by comparison, improvements in educational levels were relatively small.[9] Changes in measures of income and wages were the most discouraging: the percentage of workers whose salary was less than two times the minimum wage was essentially the same in 2000 (51 percent) as it was thirty years earlier (54.6 percent) (ibid., 37). This indicator actually worsened in Chiapas, Guerrero, Mexico City, Sinaloa, Tabasco, and Veracruz. Minimum wage lagged inflation during this period, which means that workers are earning much less today in real terms than they have in the past.

The state of Oaxaca and its municipalities were among those where social and economic opportunities did not improve significantly or in fact deteriorated during the period of neoliberal adjustment. Statewide marginality scores worsened from 1.85 in 1995 to 2.08 in 2000 and 2.13 in 2005 (table 3.1). Some individual towns fared better, but here, too, improvements were concentrated in communities that already enjoyed access to basic infrastructure and services. Conditions improved between 1995 and 2000 in three of the four towns where I carried out interviews—La Ciénega, Oaxaca, and Zimatlán; only Teotitlán del Valle, the poorest of the four communities, scored higher on the marginality index in 2000 compared with 1995. Table 3.1 summarizes the socioeconomic conditions for the four towns and compares them to averages for the state and the country as a whole. The four towns enjoy better-than-average access to services and socioeconomic opportunities than most towns in the state. In particular, the city of Oaxaca enjoys very low levels of marginalization on the whole, while the other towns have moderate to low levels of marginality.[10] However, compared with Mexico as a whole, the three rural towns have much lower levels of infrastructure and services. Only the capital city of Oaxaca compares favorably with national averages.

What can we conclude from this data about changes in people's income and other resources for political participation in Mexico? The period between 1980 and 1990 is often referred to as Latin America's "lost decade" because the economies of most countries in the region experienced minimal if not negative growth during that period. From the perspective of Mexico's poor, the period between 1990 and 2000 was also a lost decade, characterized by declining wages, sharp increases in poverty levels, and a significant redistribution of power-conferring resources from the poor and the middle class to the wealthy. Although absolute conditions in Mexico did not necessarily get worse during this decade, the benefits of the economic growth brought about by macroeconomic reforms during the 1990s were concentrated in places where people were already relatively well off. For the most part, they bypassed towns where social and economic deprivations were most severe.

My intention is not to argue that neoliberal reforms caused worsening poverty and income levels during the decade.[11] That argument cannot be made on the basis of macroeconomic statistics alone, and for my purposes it is largely beside the point. What matters for political participation is that incomes declined for the poorest segments of the population during the neoliberal adjustment, that access to resources became more stratified, and that people *thought* the government's policies were the cause of their economic hardship. The last point is important because it created among the poor a perception that the government had abandoned its traditional (if symbolic) role as caretaker of the poor and created strong feelings of pessimism, resentment, and resignation about their ability to affect in any meaningful way the political process.

This aggregate poverty data gives us a sense of the debilitating effect economic policies had on the lives of the poor and on their capacity to participate in politics. However, it cannot tell us whether or how these policies affected their actual political behavior. Interviews and conversations with low-income people experiencing the effects of these reforms are much more valuable for this purpose. The vast majority of people with whom I spoke were critical of free-market policies that, from their perspective, were making them worse off than before. Peasants and urban squatters alike complained about declining subsidies, rising inflation, unemployment, and unabated corruption by local and national leaders—all of which they associated with neoliberal reforms implemented since the 1990s. The following quotations are typical of the responses I received to the open-ended question: "What is the biggest problem facing your town or your country today?"

The biggest problem in Zimatlán is that the countryside is suffering. We get some support (*apoyos*) from the government, but they are very few now. And there are no jobs for people here, there is a lot of unemployment, but there are no factories, no *maquiladoras* to give people jobs.

—LILIANA, ZIMATLÁN

Well, poverty, which is so common. Money doesn't buy anything anymore. There's no employment, there is no business to help you, there's no work.

—FORTINA, ZIMATLÁN

The economy and poverty. Also unemployment and rising prices. With prices always going up, there is less money left over for food. For example, I can't buy meat as often as I used to because prices are too high.

—HUGO, TEOTITLÁN DEL VALLE

For some time now what poor people like me complain about is the rising prices, about things becoming so expensive. So I think that if the poor had enough money to buy the things they need to support themselves, they wouldn't have to steal, so crime would also go down.

—OSCAR, NEZACUBI

This focus on inflation is somewhat perplexing. Because Mexico had brought inflation under control by the mid-1990s, I hardly expected rising prices to be such a salient issue.[12] However, inflation tends to affect the poor more than the affluent, since low-income consumers spend a greater proportion of their income on basic food and are less able to protect their savings and income from devaluation.[13] This concern with inflation also becomes less perplexing by noting that the poor, especially the urban poor, receive almost all of their income from wages.[14] However, limiting wage increases was a key component of the government's economic stabilization strategy during the 1980s, while opening Mexico's domestic markets to international competition further limited wage increases in the 1990s. The outcome of economic stabilization and neoliberal reforms was to keep wage increases extremely modest during the entire decade, so that real wages did not keep pace even with historically low inflation rates. The poor understand this relationship between inflation and wages all too well, as Tomás, a resident of the capital city explained to me: "What's the use of raising wages without protecting prices. It is no use to improve salaries if things double in price."

Although free-market reforms have made many of the specific material needs of the urban and rural poor more pressing—for better wages, better prices for their products, for access to credits and government subsidies—these same reforms have weakened the capacity of Mexico's poor to do anything politically to improve their situation. Consider petitioning and political contacting. Petitioning party and government officials for assistance has been one of the most common and meaningful forms of participation for Mexico's poor. Although it is a strategy that reflects the clientelist relationship between political leaders and the poor, and as such it tends to reinforce power asymmetries, the poor still view it as necessary to secure their share of government patronage (Holzner 2004). Contacting government officials is a costly strategy, requiring a significant investment in time, money, and lost wages. Declining incomes mean that the opportunity cost of political participation is higher now than during the prereform era, discouraging the poor from attempting political contacting on their own.

Beatriz's situation is typical. She is the mother of seven, lives in a squatter settlement in the state capital, and has been loyal to the PRI for years. Her husband has a stable job with the municipal police, but his salary is not enough to lift the family out of poverty. "What we worry about the most is work to support our children," she said, "to buy them clothes, shoes, and to build a house out of solid material. But we have to work every day. If we miss one day that means we won't have anything to eat." Together with twenty of her neighbors, Beatriz has been petitioning the local and state PRI delegations to secure land titles. After giving $1,200 pesos toward their titles and visiting PRI offices for several months to put pressure on party officials, Beatriz decided to cut her losses and simply gave up trying to contact her local representative or PRI officials. It simply became too expensive. "We don't try to petition anymore," she explained. "Every time we go [to the PRI offices] we have to pay the bus fare, I lose time from work, and I have to find someone to take care of my two children that don't go to school. We just can't afford it anymore."

Declining incomes affect people living in the countryside even more because they face greater costs than residents of the state capital who do not have to take as much time off or travel as far to petition government offices. From La Ciénega, Norma, the vice president of a women's organization in rural La Ciénega affiliated with the PRI's CNC (Confederación Nacional Campesina, the National Peasant Confederation), has been making the sixty-minute trip to the city of Oaxaca for years. She petitioned the PRI and local branches of federal ministries for fertilizer, seeds, and credit for herself and members of her organization. Over time, as the state cut back on rural subsidies, as PRI organizations had fewer resources to distribute to loyal members, and as the prices for corn, beans, and other goods her family grows dropped, it became increasingly difficult for her to make the trip to Oaxaca. Not only was it a waste of time and money, she said: it was a waste of money she did not have to spare: "What should we do? Yes, we could go to a government office, but how do we go about asking money from the government if they don't show their faces to us? You go with your petition and nobody is there to take care of you. I'm telling you that we don't even have money to go to Zimatlán regularly, how are we supposed to go to Oaxaca? And of course those who have money can write up petitions and send them, but they have money! And if it's not accepted, well, they have money to send another. But how am I going to write up a petition if I don't have anything? So there is nothing for us to do because we are poor. So we just sit here dying, waiting."

In addition, declining incomes push people away from political activities, where benefits take a long time to materialize, to more immediately lucrative activities such as taking on a second (or third) job, sending additional family members (including children) into the labor force, migration, or joining a local NGO that promises credit or income-generating opportunities.[15] We can think of these kinds of activities as exit strategies that help the poor satisfy their most pressing needs but do not enhance their political voice or lead to future political activism (Hirschman 1970). These exit strategies tend to substitute for rather than supplement political activities, further depressing poor people's engagement with the formal political process (Dietz 1998).

Organizations and Declining Opportunities for Mobilization

Organizations are key institutions for mobilizing citizens into all kinds of political activity—from voting to contacting politicians to protesting. This is especially true for resource-poor actors who depend more than others on organizations to subsidize the costs of political participation (Rosenstone and Hansen 1993 and Verba, Nie, and Kim 1978). Organizations can be a powerful source of political equality if enough of them seek to mobilize the poor; alternatively, they can contribute to more unequal levels of political participation if the affluent have more organizational opportunities than the poor. Contrary to pluralist assumptions about democratic systems, socioeconomic stratification by class and income are often mirrored in civil society. This creates divisions and power struggles that can produce undemocratic outcomes that exclude weaker actors from access to decision makers (Gaventa 1980 and Shefner 2008). In fact, the more likely outcome in electoral democracies is for the middle class and the affluent to have more organizational opportunities than the poor, since political parties and political entrepreneurs tend to direct their mobilization efforts toward high-status individuals. This in turn creates mobilizational forces that compound inequalities in participation (Piven and Cloward 1979 and 1997b; Rosenstone and Hansen 1993; and Verba, Nie, and Kim 1978).

In Mexico the state has had a powerful influence on the availability and distribution of organizational opportunities. During the period in which the ISI model of development and the PRI were dominant (roughly 1940 through 1982), much of the political activity of popular groups was mobilized and subsidized by state-sponsored corporatist organizations (Eckstein 1977, Hamilton 1982, Levy and Székely 1987, and Middlebrook 1995). Mexico's state-led development model created institutional links between the state and groups in society that encouraged groups to target the state directly. Given the huge scope of the state's activities, this development model also provided resources, access, subsidies, and protection from repression for loyal groups (Grindle 1986, Hamilton 1982, Houtzager and Kurtz 2000, Middlebrook 1986 and 1995, and Samstad 2002). In Mexico this meant that from 1950 through 1980, the political participation of labor, peasants, and urban popular groups was almost completely determined by organizational membership in official organizations (Nie, Powell, and Prewitt 1969a and 1969b). Although this meant that the political activity of the poor was tightly controlled, designed to deliver votes and organizational support to PRI candidates, it also meant that popular groups had the incentives, resources, and the encouragement to become involved in politics.[16]

Data on organizational involvement from the World Values Surveys shows that opportunities for membership in labor unions and political parties was fairly evenly distributed across social classes until 1990 (table 3.2). However, during the decade of neoliberal adjustment, opportunities to join organizations like labor unions and political parties—organizations that deliberately and explicitly mobilize members' political activity—became much more stratified by income. This stratification of membership likely contributed to increasing inequalities in political participation. Why did organizational opportunities become more stratified during this decade? In a pattern repeated across Latin America, Mexico's decisive shift away from the ISI model of development to a neoliberal one had a profoundly negative effect on the capacity of organizations to mobilize the poor into the political arena (Houtzager and Kurtz 2000, Kurtz 2004, Roberts 1999, and Wey-

Table 3.2. Membership in Unions and Political Parties by Income, 1990–2000

	Union membership		Political party membership	
	1990	2000**	1990	2000
Low income	3.4%	4.6%	6.0%	3.8%
Medium income	5.6%	7.6%	5.7%	4.0%
High income	2.5%	9.7%	4.4%	6.1%

Source: World Values Survey 1990 and 2000.
Notes: ** indicates that differences across income groups are significant at 0.05 level.
The table indicates the percentage of people who reported being members of either labor unions or political parties.

land 1996). Policies designed to create a more open and outward-oriented economy along with a greater emphasis on market relations in more arenas altered the class structure in ways that atomized workers and peasants. This made it much more difficult for them to organize effectively (Oxhorn 1998).[17] Particularly damaging has been the decline in formal-sector jobs and a proliferation of microenterprises and informal-sector employment during the period of neoliberal adjustment.[18]

Informal-sector workers are significantly disadvantaged compared with their formal-sector counterparts, because they must make a living through unregulated employment or direct subsistence activities, in the least profitable and productive enterprises and without any kind of government benefits or protection. They are marginal not only to the modern economy but also to the political system, since their precarious status and atomized working conditions make it difficult for them to organize. Similarly, as agricultural production became increasingly privatized, peasants and peasant organizations faced increased fragmentation, atomization, and demobilization (Houtzager and Kurtz 2000 and Kurtz 2004). Unlike workers in the formal sector, neither peasants nor the informal proletariat had a party they could call their own under neoliberalism.[19] Opening domestic markets to external competition, the creation of free-trade zones, plant closures, deregulation of key industries, and legislation designed to ensure labor market flexibility—all components of the neoliberal development model—have eroded the political power of unions, their ability to organize new members, and their capacity to mobilize workers. Consequently, union density in Mexico has declined steadily since 1984 in all industries and economic sectors, from about 30 percent to less than 20 percent in 2000 (Fairris and Levine 2004).

The technocratic turn in policymaking associated with the neoliberal model marginalized and weakened Mexico's corporatist organizations that had been responsible for mobilizing low-income Mexicans into the political process. As Mexico shifted away from a state-led development model, the Confederación de Trabajadores Mexicanos (CTM), the Confederación Nacional de Organizaciones Populares (CNOP), and the Confederación Nacional Campesina (CNC)—the PRI's corporatist organizations that grouped together labor unions, popular urban groups, and peasants respectively—fell into disfavor within the party and were increasingly marginalized from the policymaking process. Most trade unions during the de la Madrid (1982–1988) and Salinas (1988–1994) administrations, rather than organizing collective challenges to free-market reforms, chose to acquiesce to the government's macroeconomic stabilization and neoliberal reforms. They did so to the point of accepting wage freezes and other damaging compromises to preserve their institutional sources of political power (Samstad 2002, 11).[20] As a result, during the first phase of market reforms, the technocratic elite inside the Mexican state were able to implement trade liberalization, privatization, and constitutional reforms without interference or input from groups in civil society (Teichman 2004, 46).

Peasant organizations were among the hardest hit by neoliberal reforms and the withdrawal of the state from rural economic life. During the 1970s the state increased its involvement in rural areas by providing credits and subsidies for key inputs such as fertilizer, seeds, and crop insurance; by increasing the rate at which it distributed land; and by providing distribution channels with guaranteed prices (Grindle 1986, Kurtz 2004, and Myhre 1998). According to Marcus Kurtz (2004), this enhanced the role of the CNC as a mediator and a channel for dissent and public participation. But "as the wave of privatization crashed over the rural sector, the very institutions that had been expanded or created in the 1970s and 1980s to promote development and incorporate dissent ceased to exist or functioned at a dramatically reduced level" (ibid., 171).

To cite an example, peasant organizations were completely excluded from the decision-making process that led to one of the most important and controversial reforms carried out by the Salinas administration: the reform of Article 27 of the Constitution that privatized the *ejido* sector. Merilee Grindle's (1995) description of the way in which this decision was made highlights the closed-door nature of the process. A small group of technocrats, in consultation with President Salinas, decided on national policy: "There was virtually no discussion with those who would be affected most directly by the change, the *ejidatarios*, and only limited consultation with organizations representing the peasants; the peasants' confederation (the CNC) and the PRI were directly informed of the government's intentions only after they had been decided upon. . . . The change was the work of a small group of technocrats who were able to count on the political support of a highly technocratic and bureaucratized administration" (ibid., 47–48).

It is possible to argue that this decline in traditional corporatist organizations was not all bad, since it also opened up space for new, more independent organizations to form and grow. During President Ernesto Zedillo's administration (1994–2000), Mexico's political system became more competitive and opposition parties and labor organizations became more assertive. Independent trade unions took advantage of political openings to carve out greater independence from the state and pressure the government from outside of traditional corporatist arrangements (Samstad 2002). They were instrumental in blocking privatization of the energy sector and demanding more spending on social programs. Organizations in civil society also became more diverse and competitive in the 1990s as new organizations began to fill the vacuum left by retreating corporatist organizations. Important and innovative movements and organizations emerged during this period, such as the El Barzón debtor's movement, Alianza Cívica, as well as important NGO networks (Olvera 2004).

However, Mexico's more plural and independent civil society faces the same narrowing of political opportunities that weakened traditional corporatist organizations. The example of independent labor unions is instructive of the challenges new organizations face in mobilizing members and influencing policies. Plant closures, antiunion legislation, exclusionary policymaking processes, and a growing army of unemployed and underemployed workers pose serious challenges to all labor organizations, not just corporatist ones. Moreover, the Fox administration was quite unfriendly to all unions regardless of their party affiliation, implementing the Federal Labor Law in ways that perpetuated past limitations on workers' freedom of association, organization, and right to strike. The administration also put forth strategies designed to divide labor unions and co-opt their leaders (Meyer 2005). The result, according to Philip Oxhorn (1998, 205), is that the new state-labor relationship has shifted from one of controlled inclusion to one characterized more than ever by political exclusion.

Data on strikes and worker participation in strikes tells the story of declining labor union activism during this period.[21] Figure 3.2 shows the number of strikes per year in Mexico between 1975 and 2005, along with the number of workers involved in those strikes. After rising consistently during the presidency of Lopez Portillo (1976–1982) and peaking in 1982 at nearly two thousand strikes, the number of strikes declined precipitously as soon as Miguel de la Madrid took power, despite the severe austerity measures implemented by his administration.[22] The number of strikes continued to trend downward throughout the period of neoliberal adjustment and consolidation, averaging only twenty-four per year between 2000 and 2005 and mobilizing fewer than sixteen thousand workers annually. The number of workers mobilized follows a slightly different pattern, seemingly more sensitive to significant political events than economic ones. The number of workers mobilized increased steadily during the early period of economic stabilization policies (1982–1987) that restricted wage increases despite rampant inflation. Labor still showed some independence from the PRI as hundreds of thousands of workers mobilized between 1987 and 1988 to support Cuahutémoc Cárdenas, who defected from the PRI and ran against the PRI's neoliberal candidate, Carlos Salinas de Gortari, in the 1988 presidential elections.[23]

The mobilizations continued in the aftermath of the contested elections as millions of Mexicans protested widespread fraud and called for the annulment of the election results. However, this energy dissipated quickly as presidents Salinas (1988–1994) and Zedillo moved quickly to implement and consolidate neoliberal reforms. Indeed, neither the implementation of NAFTA in 1994, the Zapatista uprising in Chiapas in the same year, nor the economic collapse in 1995 elicited much of a response from labor. Despite a small peak in mobilization around the 2000 presidential election, the overall the number of workers mobilized declined between 1990 and 2000 (and into the Fox presidency after 2000).

New organizations in civil society, which experienced a period of dynamism after 1985, also suffered from declining political opportunities after 1990. Although the number of independent civil society organizations grew during this period, many of the new ones were small and resource-poor, with few if any links to local or national governments. As a result, growing pluralism occurred without growing political empowerment as civil society failed to gain any influence over public policies. Political elites were thus allowed to act with relative autonomy.[24] Oxhorn (1998) has described this kind of system of representation as "neopluralism," characterized by a weakening of organized interests, a fragmented civil society, the persistence of cli-

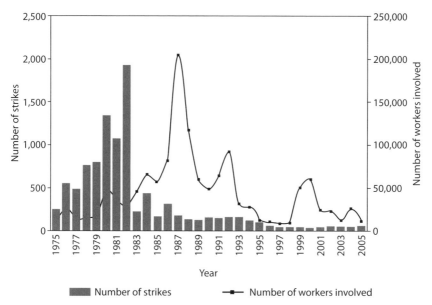

Figure 3.2. Number of Strikes and Number of Workers Involved, 1975–2005. The axes show the number of strikes per year and the number of workers involved per year. *Source:* ILO, author's calculations.

entelist forms of organization, technocratic elements in the government's dealings with individuals and groups, and the channeling of political participation into a narrow set of activities that does not effectively convey interests or affect policy.

Although neopluralist systems can appear democratic, they have distinct elitist tendencies that advantage resource-rich actors who are the only ones able to organize and lobby at the highest levels of government where policy is increasingly made. "In this context," Alberto Olvera (2004, 423) wrote, "parties and elections assumed an even more central place in the public sphere as the only means of articulating political action. In contrast, civic actors could only attract public and media attention if the staged demonstrations [were] of such magnitude that the media were forced to give them priority coverage." However, such costly activities are beyond the capacity of most popular organizations, which remain small, resource-poor, and unable to establish links either to the state or to broader movements and organizations. This results in a growing exclusion of citizens' voices from the political process despite growing organizational pluralism.

Organizational Pluralism in Oaxaca

By paying close attention to ordinary people's decisions about whether and when to join organizations, we can see how neoliberalism and the neopluralist system of representation it fosters affects people's ability and desire to attempt political activities. Although Oaxaca, with its large rural population and indigenous traditions, is somewhat of a special case in Mexico when it comes to organizational activity, it experienced a similar paradoxical combination of growing organizational pluralism without significant increase in citizen empowerment.[25] For example, La Ciénega, a town of fewer than three thousand people, had at least fourteen distinct organizations ranging from the *ejido* group, a peasant women's group affiliated with the CNC, several independent savings cooperatives, and at least six groups that managed local irrigation systems. Many individuals I spoke with had overlapping memberships in three or even four organizations and appeared to be quite active in each one. Teotitlán del Valle, a Zapotec village of roughly the same size, has twenty weaving cooperatives, in addition to dozens of committees that form part of the town's self-governing system.[26] In the capital city almost every *colonia* had at least one neighborhood organization; there were at least six distinct human rights organizations, several women's organizations, and countless church groups, sports clubs, and cultural associations.

Why so many organizations? Part of the answer, of course, has to do with the liberalization of the political system that allowed independent organizations to appear and survive. But neoliberal reforms, changes in state spending, economic crises, and new policy initiatives also created a strong demand for organizations that could help the poor gain access to essential material resources. At the height of PRI power and of the state-led development model, membership in a single organization—for example, the local CNC group—might have been enough to secure access to such key resources as credits, fertilizer, and markets. However, austerity programs that decreased government spending caused much of the government's assistance to dry up. Multiple organizational memberships have thus become a core survival strategy for the rural poor in Mexico.

On the supply side, the state's retreat from many of its functions, a mandate by the World Bank to channel development funds to local and community organizations, and the availability of funding from international foundations opened opportunities for NGOs to proliferate in Mexico and to take on increasingly important roles in the lives of the poor (Reygadas 1998). Traditionally, NGO activities in Mexico have centered around educational activities or on charitable social services targeting such specific groups as senior citizens, the disabled, and youths. Flush with money from international sources, NGOs began to sponsor larger and larger programs during the 1990s, often working with budgets larger than the resources available to local governments they assisted.[27] Some of these activities include the provision of such essential resources and services as education, health care, credits, and infrastructure development that were once the exclusive domain of the state.

In Oaxaca this financing vacuum was filled by a growing number of development-oriented NGOs that funded small-scale and local income-generating projects, producing an explosion of microorganizations across the countryside. For example, in Teotitlán del Valle, a town of artisans that specialize in weaving rugs and tapestries, a group of thirty women created their own weaving cooperative in 1992 to gain access to government credits and direct access to markets, the first of its kind in the village.[28] One interviewee, Blanca, explained the goals of the organization to me: "If we succeed in organizing ourselves, to register ourselves as an official organization, we could go to the governmental institutions and ask for *apoyos* [assistance]; and if we accomplish that, then we can buy our own looms and make our own rugs. That is why I joined, so I could have my own loom, to make my own rugs which I could then sell directly to customers." The women were initially quite successful in securing financial assistance from La Casa de La Mujer Rosario Castellanos and Semillas, NGOs in Oaxaca and Mexico City, respectively, that work on women's issues. A group of men followed the women's example two years later and formed a similarly structured cooperative with the same goals of securing financing and direct access to markets. The success of these cooperatives spawned a number of other copycat organizations.[29]

Twenty miles south of the city of Oaxaca, Centéotl, a local NGO dedicated to promoting sustainable economic development in Zimatlán and surrounding towns, has single-handedly sponsored the creation of dozens of independent grassroots organizations, most with fewer than thirty members. Its main funding comes from international foundations, which has increased dramatically since the late 1990s just as the stream of resources flowing from the state dwindled to a trickle. As a result, Centéotl has become an important alternative source of *apoyos* for hundreds of families in the area, triggering the defection of many from clientelist organizations. Despertar, which means "to awaken," was one of the first groups established by Centéotl. It began as a group of two hundred women who had been receiving *despensas*—a basket of such basic goods as oil, rice, flour, beans, and soap—from the PRI. But Centéotl was able to offer a similar basket of goods at a lower cost, a higher quality, and with more regularity than the PRI, eviscerating the membership of that group.

On the demand side, the poor I spoke with were "joiners," both because of their extreme need for assistance and because joining organizations to secure access to essential resources had become, after decades of state sponsorship of clientelist organizations, a core political repertoire. Although the benefits they might get from each individual organization were relatively small, on the order of fifty to one hundred dollars every few months, when combined they create a larger and more predictable income stream. Nonetheless, because their income levels are so low and the benefits coming from each organization so meager, the rural poor are extremely conscious of the costs and the benefits of membership in an organization and frequently change organizations if costs rise or benefits decline. Lourdes, a fifty-four-year-old widow living in La Ciénega, is a member of a peasant women's organization affiliated with the CNC and with a new group created by Centéotl in her town. As a widow, she relies on the remittances of her children living in the United States for most of her income, but these come at irregular intervals. The benefits she receives from organizations are a key supplement to her income. As a result, Lourdes is constantly comparing the benefits she receives from each organization. "The CNC group has given us some scholarships to take sewing classes, cooking classes," she said. "It is nice because they pay for us to take the classes [about $750 pesos]. In Centéotl they also want to give us classes on how to make children's clothes. That is nice, but it's not as beneficial because we won't get paid like we do in the PRI group."

When I asked what she liked about the women's group, Lourdes rattled off the costs and benefits as if reading from a balance sheet.

I like everything, because they have given us a lot of help. There's the scholarships, which I already told you about, later they also gave us fifteen hundred pesos to buy goats; then we got a credit of thirty kilograms of beans and garbanzos, then five hundred pesos to buy fertilizer. I've also received a credit of pigs twice.

[Do they ask for anything in exchange for this support?]

Well, yes. We simply have to accompany them to support the candidates and politicians at rallies. They also ask us to donate (*una cooperación*) so that the leaders can go to Oaxaca to apply for support. Sometimes they ask us for one or two pesos to pay for their bus fare. Just yesterday they asked for five pesos to establish a fund so that they wouldn't have to keep asking us for bus fare money. I've heard that in other groups they have to pay a lot more: fifty pesos for an event, or tortillas, eggs, soft drinks to entertain government representatives. But not with the Doña Katia. The other day a Congressman came to town and we contributed some money for his meal, but it wasn't much, only ten or fifteen pesos.[30]

Given the relatively small benefits people receive from PRI organizations, even small increases in costs or risks, or reductions in the benefits, are enough to discourage them from continued participation. Lourdes's situation is somewhat unique in that she has had good luck receiving benefits for little in exchange with the PRI group. Most everyone else I talked to complained about the declining frequency and quality of the benefits they receive from the CNC and government programs. Daniela, for example, also a widow from La Ciénenga who earns her income selling homemade cheese at the market, joined a PRI organization after her husband died. She had hoped to tap into government and party patronage. But she quickly came to resent what she perceived as unnecessary costs of membership, like the sanctions the leader imposes on members who fail to attend political rallies.

You see, I joined this group of peasant women to ask for *apoyos* from the government. At first we were free to do what we wanted and usually we would write up petitions and deliver them to our *diputada* (congressional representative). But when Señora Filomena of the CNC became the president, she wanted our organization to be officially registered to get any help. So we did all the paperwork to legalize the group. About a year ago we paid a notary five thousand pesos to process the paperwork. So now we have to pay annual taxes and the president goes to the government agencies to ask for *apoyos*. We also have to attend political rallies in Oaxaca, or events where the governor is speaking. It's really hard, it takes a lot of time, it's hot, and you are often gone all day. If we don't go, the leader fines us ten pesos, but going ends up being more expensive than paying the fine, because we have to buy food and something to drink. We end up spending thirty pesos, so I usually don't go.

When I spoke to Daniela, she had been a member of Centéotl for less than a year, so she was not yet willing to abandon the PRI organization in favor of Centéotl. But it was clear that if Centéotl proved to be a reliable source of benefits, she would stop participating with the CNC altogether. "The whole point of the organization is to get help from the government, to petition the ministries, to get *apoyos*," she recalled. "But there are fewer and fewer *apoyos* coming from the ministries, so I'm thinking of leaving the organization. They cheat us, they don't give us much help, or not very often. A lot of women have left already. The Centéotl group seems more serious, they all seem more responsible. I like to go to their workshops, to their meetings. I learn more and I don't have to pay anything. And just a couple of months ago, Centéotl lent me five thousand pesos to buy milk for my cheese business."

In Lidia's case, a mother of seven living in Zimatlán who had been a longtime member of PRI organizations, it was an increase in the risks of membership that persuaded her to leave the PRI organization and dedicate herself full-time to Despertar. "I used to belong to a group of peasant women through the CNC," she explained. "It was a good group because we could buy chickens to raise at good prices. We'd buy them cheap, raise them, and then sell them, and it was some extra money. But then one day I went to a protest rally in Oaxaca and someone from another party threw salt and chile in the eyes of one of our *compañeras*. Ever since then I stopped going. I come to Centéotl instead."

Although much has been written about the collective-action problems peasants face (Kurtz 2004, Popkin 1979, Scott 1979, and Bates 1981), the rural poor in Mexico may have a few advantages over their urban counterparts when it comes to forming and joining organizations.[31] Many of Mexico's urban poor are migrants from rural areas, creating an extremely heterogeneous, atomized group with few ties that bind them together. Work schedules and the location of poor *colonias* far away from places of employment (not to mention a lack of public transportation) means that many residents spend significant amounts of time away from home.[32] Although the urban poor come together quite willingly and frequently to cooperate on communal activities to improve living conditions in their neighborhoods, and though many participate in community assemblies to discuss key problems facing the neighborhood, feelings of collective identity tend to not be fully formed. There are simply too many factors—political affiliation, income and education levels, ethnic background, and length of residence, to name but a few—that divide rather than unite them.[33]

I found a great deal of individual-level atomization among squatters in Oaxaca. A common complaint among residents of Nezacubi was that people were too individualistic and unwilling to work for the common good. Rather than bringing them together, low incomes and precarious living conditions seemed to divide residents. Margarita, who returned to her home state after spending most of her adult years in Mexico City, was surprised by the attitudes she found in the neighborhood. "People are very individualistic and very jealous of what others have or get," she said. "They won't do any work unless they see everyone else contributing. In Mexico City it was different. People helped each other more. If we needed help with something, our neighbors would help out right away. I am not sure why it is different there, whether it is because there is more work [in Mexico City], or maybe because of better salaries which allows them to be more generous."

In addition to this atomization of individuals, I also found lower levels of organizational choice in Oaxaca's squatter neighborhoods than in surrounding rural towns where there were often several organizations to choose from and where people could switch organizations or hold overlapping memberships to hedge against declining government assistance. Much of this growth of independent NGO activity occurred in rural areas, which were seen as priority areas for funding agencies, leaving the urban poor with relatively few independent organizational options and fewer opportunities to supplement their income. Although Oaxaca neighborhoods may be unique, I did not see the proliferation of soup kitchens, women's centers, and similar grassroots organizations other scholars have observed in the urban areas in other Latin American countries like Chile and Peru (Dietz 1998, Oxhorn 1995, Schneider 1995, and Stokes 1995). Various church groups did exist in and around Nezacubi, but the diversity of sects—Adventist, Mormon, Jehovah's Witness, Pentecostal—tended to fragment rather than unite residents. And because many squatters work in informal sectors of the economy, they tend not to have access to traditional working-class organizations such as labor unions. This narrows their choice even more.[34] If resources dried up from one source, or an organization became too authoritarian, or the demands of membership became too onerous, the urban poor faced the unhappy choice of either continuing on despite the costs or dropping out and losing all access to future benefits.

Political Participation, Clientelism, and Exit

What impacts did these patterns of organizational memberships have on the political activity of the poor? The effect is far from straightforward and much depends on the characteristics and leadership of the organizations in which people are involved (Levine 1992). Rising prices, stagnant wages, and declining benefits from political organizations have made organizational membership an essential survival strategy for the poor, not just in Mexico but in other Latin American countries undergoing similar transitions to democracy and to market economies. A number of scholars have wondered whether this proliferation of popular organizations represents the beginning of a more democratic civil society that will strengthen democratic participation, representation, and accountability in the region. Optimists, drawing on the insights of Alexis de Tocqueville (1961) and Robert Putnam (1993), see in this growing pluralism an end to clientelism and the potential for creating an active, democratically inclined citizenry among the poor (Lipset 1981 [1960] and Pateman 1970). Beyond cultivating democratic attitudes and political engagement, membership in grassroots NGOs may give people opportunities to develop and hone civic skills that can serve as valuable resources for future political participation (Verba, Schlozman, and Brady 1995). There are good reasons to be pessimistic, however. Organizational fragmentation, lack of resources, and the continued strength of clientelist networks undermined many of the democratic gains that came from increasing organizational pluralism.

Organizations that succeed in maintaining their autonomy suffer from a lack of resources, vulnerability, and isolation that makes it difficult to mobilize members into political action. The positive externalities that organizational membership produces—new skills, more civic engagement, and more democratic attitudes—operate in the long term and are easily undermined by organizational mortality and authoritarian leadership styles (Fox 1994a and 1996, Holzner 2004, and Levine 1992). Most popular organizations do not survive for more than a few years, and those that do are frequently co-opted by local governments and political parties who offer the leaders resources and jobs in exchange for political support. Precisely because problems of autonomy and sustainability are chronic for these grassroots organizations, the process of fostering democratic attitudes and practices in members is easily sabotaged or aborted.

One of the illusions of civil society is that grassroots organizations are unified in opposition to the state and behind political projects that benefit the collective good. As Jonathan Shefner (2008) has reminded us, organized groups usually work independently and often at odds with each other to further their interests. Unity occurs rarely, usually in response to an overwhelming threat that affects most sectors of society. Some of these divisions are class-based, but organizational fragmentation is also a defining characteristic of popular organizations in Mexico. Most of the new organizations that emerged during the 1990s in Mexico were small, with very limited resources, and few if any links to broader movements or institutions. Relatively scarce resources from national and international funding agencies fosters competition among NGOs and other nascent peasant organizations. This hinders the formation of collective identity and the identification of common interests.[35] Fragmentation and atomization of popular organizations limits their capacity to aggregate the interests of the poor or to mobilize political action with any consistency.

Political independence may ironically lead to less political activity. People in Oaxaca who were members of organizations affiliated with political parties, especially clientelist organizations affiliated with the PRI and the PRD, were much more likely to be asked to participate in political activities than people involved in nonpolitical organizations such as weaving cooperatives or with Centéotl. In fact, members of these organizations tended to reduce their political activity, at least in the short term, precisely because they were able to exit from clientelist organizations. Without clientelist pressures, turnout among the poor tends to decline, especially in the absence of a party on the left that can galvanize the vote of low-income citizens. However, organizational fragmentation and weakness affect government-directed activities, such as petitioning and protesting, much more. To be effective, these activities require the support of important allies within government ministries and from local organizations that subsidize the cost of travel or whose leaders carry out the petitioning activity on behalf of local groups. With the decline of traditional organizations and the absence of new organizations that can be effective advocates, the poor with whom I spoke did not see themselves as having any channels through which to exercise their political voice.

This may seem strange since protests and marches appear to be a daily occurrence in most Mexican cities and receive much scholarly and media attention. However, poor people's predilection for disruptive acts tends to be overstated in the literature. The vast majority of the poor with whom I spoke saw protest as a risky, dangerous, and not very effective strategy, to be attempted only after all other options have been exhausted. But this preference for nonconfrontational tactics should not be interpreted as an attitude rooted in a political culture characterized by deference to authority, as some scholars have argued (Almond and Verba 1963 and Stokes 1995). Rather, it is rooted in a clear recognition of the risks, difficulties, and unlikelihood of success of protest activity, especially given the state's structural reforms that have raised the costs while decreasing the effectiveness of protesting (Jenkins 1983; McAdam 1982; McAdam, McCarthy, and Zald 1996; McCarthy and Zald 1977; and Tarrow 1998). To be successful, protest campaigns must target the highest levels of government over a sustained period of time. Of course, these are exactly the kinds of protests that are most visible and receive the greatest media coverage, but are practically impossible for increasingly unorganized and resource-poor actors to undertake. This helps explain why surveys report very little participation in protests and marches, and why the poor are much less likely to protest than the most affluent (see table 3.2).

Although many of Mexico's poor are voting less, are not attending political rallies, and disdain protests, declining efficacy and exit from the formal political arena does not mean that they have stopped looking for ways to improve their situation. Indeed, many are seeking solutions to their problems through private, nonpolitical strategies such as taking on an additional job, engaging in street vending, migration, or even petty crime.[36] Popular urban neighborhoods in Mexico are also alive with community activity that includes *juntas* and *asambleas* (meetings and assemblies), cooperation among neighbors to supply themselves with water and electricity, negotiations with local officials about pressing problems, and lively debates and talk about national and international politics and how it affects their lives (Gutmann 2002 and Rubin 1997).

This predilection for self-help and exit strategies is not unique to the poor living in Oaxaca.[37] Matthew Gutmann (2002), who studied low-income groups in Mexico City, noticed a similar impact of NAFTA and other free-market policies among low-income groups in Mexico City. According to him, the urban popular movements of the 1970s and 1980s that had sought broad structural and social change have been replaced with the "micromanagement of general social problems"—that is, activity designed to solve specific problems with little ideological compass or capacity of aggregation. In contrast, Shefner's *The Illusion of Civil Society* (2008) shows that under the right conditions, with substantial help from powerful organizational allies, grassroots organizations can successfully organize and mobilize the poor around larger campaigns for democratization and social justice. There too, however, once their allies withdrew funding, training, staffing, and organizing support, the organization was weakened, forced to focus more on fulfilling members' material needs, and vulnerable to clientelist incursions (ibid.).

On the whole, Mexico's growing organizational pluralism did not automatically translate into more voice and power for the poor. Organizations in civil society are small, underfunded, and fragmented; they are rarely able to launch effective grassroots efforts to oppose market reforms or advocate for the interests of popular groups. So although it is true that clientelist and corporatist organizations during the PRI's rule tended to demobilize popular groups by fragmenting them and forcing them to compete against each other for patronage, civil society in Mexico today is no less fragmented. Organizations face different but still strong pressures to compete against each other for resources and access (Kurtz 2004).

Students of Mexican politics anticipated that Mexico's shift from an ISI model of economic development to a neoliberal one would also erode the clientelist power of the PRI and free the poor to vote their true preferences. The reasoning is straightforward. The economic crises of the 1980s and 1990s forced the PRI governments to implement severe austerity measures and reduce funding for credits, subsidies, and antipoverty programs, damaging the party's revolutionary legitimacy among its core peasant and working-class constituencies. Declining legitimacy combined with increased electoral competition meant that the PRI would need an ever-increasing resource base to sustain its political machines. However, the same economic crises, austerity measures, and free-market policies meant that its ability to dole out patronage to loyal groups had shrunk. Efforts to maintain its electoral hegemony through clientelist practices would either bankrupt the state, the party, or both. Clientelist politics seemed impossible to sustain under neoliberalism.

The fact is that clientelism has not gone away in Mexico and may even be strengthening in many areas (Fox 1994a, Hellman 1994, and Holzner 2002). Decentralization has given governors new fiscal powers and autonomy from the federal government, shifting the apex of clientelist clusters downward from the president to governors (Hernández-Rodríguez 2003). In many cases (in Guerrero, Hidalgo, Oaxaca, Puebla, Tabasco, and Yucatán), governors used this power to build and maintain dominant electoral machines that allowed them to retain autocratic control over state politics, even as the PRI hemorrhaged votes in national elections. Politics in these autocratic enclaves is not very different from the clientelistic politics of years past, when party leaders used the state's resources to buy votes, co-opt the leadership of local organizations, punish competitors, and tamper with elections with relative impunity.[38]

Clientelist practices are not limited to autocratic PRI enclaves or to rural areas, however. The PRD, while usually operating and governing in more competitive contexts than the PRI, achieved much of its electoral success during the 1990s by luring away leaders of PRI clientelist networks, who in turn mobilized their clients to vote for the PRD using tried-and-true strategies of vote buying, promising access to government patronage, and in some cases electoral fraud (Bruhn 1997 and Hilgers 2005). The PAN, which has long worked to increase electoral transparency, governmental accountability, and transparency (Hernández-Rodríguez 2003, Cabrero Mendoza 1995 and 1996, Rodríguez 1998, Rodríguez and Ward 1995, and Shirk 2005), has also gotten into the act. Studies of clientelistic voting during the 2000 presidential elections show that the PAN was just as likely as the PRI to engage in election-day manipulation of voters (del Pozo and Aparicio 2001) and that vote buying and coercion (*compra y coacción*) were most common in urban areas where the PAN was competitive (Cornelius 2004).[39] In turn, joining clientelist organizations, petitioning local and regional patrons, and ritualistic attendance at rallies continue to be core strategies for the urban and rural poor who cling to old and new clientelist ties in an effort to secure government patronage that has become very scarce (Holzner 2004, Shefner 2001, and Tejera Gaona 2002).

Although neoliberalism certainly weakened the ability of corporatist organizations affiliated with the PRI to control members' political participation, the combination of free-market reforms, economic crises, and anemic job growth created strong incentives for both the poor and elites to choose political clientelism over other available political strategies. From the perspective of the poor and working classes, free-market reforms will reduce poor people's need for clientelist relationships only if reforms alleviate poverty and create alternative and autonomous sources of income, in the form of new high-paying jobs or access to new markets for agricultural products, for example (Lemarchand 1981). But people's need for subsidies, jobs, services, and income did not end with neoliberalism. On the contrary, with repeated economic crises, anemic growth rates, and austerity measures that cut subsidies and restricted the supply of government transfers, people's dependence on clientelist networks became more acute—if nothing else as a form of insurance against more severe deprivations. Although the hold of individual patrons over their clients may have weakened in the process, as these transfers became more scarce, they also became more valuable for everyone who benefited from them. In the absence of reliable alternative sources of income or credits, it made sense for the urban and rural poor to stick with clientelist arrangements even as the flow of benefits was reduced to a trickle (see also Shefner 2008).

Free-market reforms also created incentives for local elites and ambitious political entrepreneurs to rely more heavily on clientelist strategies to build their political base. Although local elites have always been fair-weather supporters of the PRI, during the period of economic expansion under ISI policies the abundance of resources flowing from the central state created a symbiotic relationship between the PRI and local caciques. As long as the party had a monopoly control over the state's political and economic resources, their loyalty appeared unshakeable because they had no incentive to defect from the party or openly show their displeasure. By doling out patronage and securing the allegiance of local bosses, who delivered the votes from their clientelist networks, the party was able to achieve electoral victories by supermajorities.[40] In turn, patrons enhanced their power and prestige by maintaining privileged access to government spoils.

Free-market reforms, austerity programs, and the retreat of the state from core activities broke apart this marriage of convenience. Whereas in the past the allegiance of caciques with the PRI made their position unassailable, the drying up of patronage from the central government eliminated their advantage over rival patrons, weakened their hold over their clients, and forced them to scramble to secure access to new resource streams. The flow of funding from international foundations, decentralization of fiscal resources away from the federal government, and opposition victories in many state and local elections created opportunities for new political entrepreneurs to establish organizations and entice the poor to defect from traditional organizations whose allegiance to the PRI no longer guaranteed them a monopoly over vital goods and services.

Fully aware that the drying up of patronage makes the poor more willing to shift allegiances, and fully aware that controlling the votes of large numbers of people is a quick and effective way to gain power and prestige within political parties, ambitious political entrepreneurs compete under this new political opportunity structure not by building state and national party organizations, which would take too long, but by building their clientelist networks and selling their services (votes) to the political party that offers them the greatest chance of winning an election. For many of these potential rival patrons their best chance of luring away clients has been to defect from the PRI and affiliate with an opposition party, usually the PRD, to win elections and gain access to valuable patronage. Thus Mexico's much celebrated electoral competitiveness is partly a consequence of neoliberal reforms that have allowed new patron-client pyramids to proliferate.

Mexico's massive institutional transformations have eroded much of the PRI's power over voters: its corporatist organizations are shells of their former selves, it has little or no access to the vast resources of the federal government with which to dole out patronage, and it faces the constant threat of defection from many of its most prominent leaders and organizations. And yet vote buying, ritualistic campaign support, and clientelist manipulation of citizens continues. What is different today is that the PRI has lost its monopoly control over clientelist networks, creating an extremely fluid situation in which local caciques frequently switch party allegiances to maintain access to government patronage. This stimulates a proliferation and in many cases a reinvigoration of clientelist clusters that no longer depends on a single party for their survival. Clientelist networks have not faded away in Mexico, just the PRI's ability to control and mobilize them.

Changing State-Society Relations

Political activity among the poor declined between 1990 and 2000 despite rapidly growing needs and grievances. Neoliberal policies, austerity measures, and economic crises contributed to this decline by diminishing the capacity of Mexico's poor, whether individually or collectively, to attempt political activities. Nevertheless, we know from the rational-choice and historical institutionalism literatures that needs, grievances, and resources do not provide a complete explanation of political behavior—or any other kind of human behavior for that matter. Rather, state institutions shape behavior most powerfully and directly by determining the benefits, costs, and expectations of success of these political activities; by constraining the range of political activities from which individuals can realistically choose; and, over time, by shaping the preferences citizens have for political activities. To ignore these effects of institutions is to completely misunderstand human behavior.

Neoliberalism is much more than a set of policy prescriptions designed to promote economic growth. It is a political project that seeks to remove the state from the economy. Specific policies—such as the elimination of trade tariffs, cuts in social-service expenditures, elimination of price subsidies, and industry privatization—are designed just as much to restructure the state and its relationship to citizens as to accomplish their ostensible goal of stimulating economic development. Popular groups' dependence on state and party patronage for their livelihood under ISI made state-directed political activities both desirable and necessary, since they were the surest way to gain access to the myriad goods distributed by the state (Eckstein 1977).[41] Most important, it created a set of citizens that was very attentive to shifts in the state policies and the institutional context, targeting different levels of government and adjusting their strategies according to which ones they think would be most successful with the least amount of risk and hardship.

The shift from an ISI to a free-market development model transformed the basic functions of the state—what it does and for whom—radically changing the relationship between the state and the poor in Mexico. Repeated austerity programs since the 1980s that gutted federal-spending programs and eliminated subsidies for basic foodstuffs, a decline in the spending and scope of rural development programs, and a general shrinking of state budgets made the state less relevant for the poor.[42] Other free-market reforms—such as the privatization of state-owned enterprises, the deregulation of the market for coffee and other cash crops without agricultural extension services, attempts to privatize *ejidos*, the signing of free-trade agreements, and the elimination of price supports—have privatized many of the relationships that were previously mediated by the state. So although grievances were high, the poor no longer saw many of their needs as subject to satisfaction through political activity.

Neoliberal reforms also raised the costs of political action by centralizing policymaking power at the executive level, in distant and inaccessible ministries, and by institutionalizing spending policies into ostensibly apolitical formulas and rules that eliminated the discretionary power of politicians to alter the allocation of resources. Under these conditions, petitions and protests—tried-and-true political strategies for Mexico's poor—were rendered ineffective. Moreover, the steady dismantling of Mexico's elaborate welfare system under neoliberalism did great damage to poor people's sense of political efficacy and engagement, leading many low-income Mexicans to the conclusion that politicians have turned their backs on Mexico's poor (Gutmann 2002). In short, Mexico's decisive shift to a free-market model of development increased the costs, decreased the benefits, and narrowed the opportunities the poor had for political action.

Social Spending and Poverty-Alleviation Programs

Central to this change in opportunities and incentives was the government's shift away from comprehensive welfare, poverty alleviation, and rural development programs to more limited programs that carefully target individuals on a need basis. Public policies, especially social-spending policies, create strong incentives for individuals and groups to become involved in politics not simply because beneficiaries develop a stake in maintaining and expanding these programs, but because public policies make the state an obvious target for mobilization efforts. Moreover, social-spending policies create opportunities for political action by multiplying the points through which citizens can access the state to make their opinions heard. In essence, public policies channel and focus activity into the political arena that might otherwise be directed toward private, nongovernmental actors or arenas. For these reasons state spending and poverty-alleviation policies are a fruitful place to examine how the state's actions have shaped the poor's political activity.

In Mexico the state's expansion into the lives of more and more Mexicans, which began in earnest with the presidency of Lázaro Cárdenas (1938–

1944) and grew quickly between 1950 and 1980, had precisely this effect of pulling people into politics. Rural development projects and large public projects in urban areas were core elements of the state's strategy to extend its presence as deeply as possible into the lives of the urban and rural poor. According to Merilee Grindle (1986), it was precisely because of state-building efforts during the 1950s and 1960s and because of comprehensive development programs like PIDER-COMPLAMAR, SAM (Sistema Alimentario Mexicano), and CONASUPO (Compañía Nacional de Subsistencias Populares) in the 1970s and 1980s that peasants had more and more incentives to target the state when seeking solutions to their material needs (see also Fox 1993). Ann Craig and Wayne Cornelius (1980, 378) noted the same effect beyond rural areas: "The agrarian reform program, agricultural credit, land titles for urban squatters, free or low-cost medical care . . . free lunches for school children, and low cost foodstuffs purchased through government retail outlets (the CONASUPO retail outlets) have . . . led many Mexicans to view the government as the most likely source of concrete benefits."

Like other groups in Mexico, such as unionized workers and government employees, the urban and rural poor had a large stake in government action that enhanced their motivation to participate in politics. It is likely, although hard to show because data is unavailable, that these policies had the largest mobilizing effect among low-income Mexicans, who depended on government programs the most.[43] It is no coincidence, for example, that the sharp increases in the mass mobilizations of both urban labor unions and rural peasant groups during the 1970s coincided with the rapid expansion of the Mexican state during the Echeverria and López Portillo administrations.[44]

The 1982 economic crisis triggered a slew of reforms that initiated a radical shrinking of the Mexican state and its relevance in the lives of the poor. Severe budget constraints forced the government to implement extensive austerity measures centered around limiting social spending wherever possible. Spending on health, education, social security, and poverty alleviation dropped in 1983 and remained below precrisis levels until 1993 (Mostajo 2000). In the short run this retreat of the state energized popular groups into forceful opposition to free-market reforms, culminating in 1988 with the presidential campaign of Cuahutémoc Cárdenas, who officially garnered more than 30 percent of the popular vote, due in large part to the support of urban and labor groups that defected from the PRI.[45] However, in subsequent years neoliberal reforms gutted the capacity of these organizations to mobilize opposition to the reforms.

The diminishing relevance of the state in the lives of the poor was temporarily halted by Mexico's new president, Carlos Salinas de Gortari. Although Salinas generally pursued policies designed to reduce the size of the state and consolidate free-market reforms, his ambitious poverty-alleviation program Programa Nacional de Solidaridad (or PRONASOL), also known as Solidarity, resumed the pattern of large-scale programs designed as much to alleviate poverty as to channel and control the political activity of popular groups (Cornelius, Craig, and Fox 1994). Solidarity was an ambitious, multidimensional program designed to repair Mexico's tattered social safety net, to fund urban and rural infrastructure projects—such as community electrification, road construction, and the building of schools—and to encourage productive projects to stimulate economic development among Mexico's poorest groups. This program has been heavily criticized for centralizing even more power in the hands of the president, for reviving clientelism and patronage politics, for focusing more on offsetting some of the costs of structural adjustment and the pursuit of neoliberal policies rather than combating the causes of poverty, and for using the funds to revitalize waning electoral support for the PRI.[46] However, there is little doubt that by its sheer size and scope, the program reactivated the relationship between the poor and the state in important and lasting ways (ibid.).

This expansion of the state into the lives of the poor was short-lived. A devastating economic crisis in 1995, severe budget constraints, and President Zedillo's commitment to deepening neoliberal reforms resulted in major cutbacks in social spending and antipoverty spending, both of which declined on a per capita basis and as a percentage of the gross domestic product between 1994 and 1997 (ECLAC 2006). Although social-spending levels have recovered somewhat, comparing social-spending levels with other Latin American countries reveals that even during boom times, the Zedillo administration gave a very low priority to social spending and poverty-alleviation programs. According to recent analysis by the UN's Economic Commission for Latin America and the Caribbean (ECLAC), Mexico ranks near the bottom on all indicators of the government's commitment to poverty alleviation. Between 1996 and 1999, for example, Mexico spent a smaller share of its gross domestic product on social services than twelve comparable countries in the region, including Argentina, Brazil, Colombia, and Venezuela. Mexico spent even less than Chile, which has been considered by many as a model for neoliberal reforms.[47]

Granted, a large portion of social spending in these countries is earmarked for health care, education, social security, and pensions—programs that are not explicitly designed to provide services and resources to the poor-

est sectors. Thus these programs may not reflect a government's true commitment to poverty alleviation. Nonetheless, if we break out the share of
social spending allocated to social assistance programs such as PROGRESA,
Oportunidades, and PROCAMPO, Mexico compares even less favorably.[48]
According to ECLAC, Mexico ranks second to last among large Latin American countries in the percentage of social spending it dedicates to poverty-alleviation or social assistance programs—half as much as Guatemala, a third
less than Chile, and one-fifth the level in Peru (ECLAC 2006, 145).

It is useful to compare the impact of the flagship poverty-alleviation programs of the Salinas and Zedillo administrations (PRONASOL and PRO-
GRESA, respectively) to see how public spending policies affected the
incentives and opportunities for the poor to engage in political activities during the 1990s. Recall that any analysis of incentives for behavior involves
more than simply weighing the costs and the benefits of an action; it should
pay attention to the overall expected utility of the act. The core insight behind the concept of an expected utility is that while the costs of an activity
are usually certain and immediate, the benefits are almost always uncertain
and deferred into the future. The concept of an expected utility takes this
uncertainty into account.[49] We should expect that political participation will
increase if the benefits increase, the costs decrease, or the likelihood of im-
pacting the government's decisions increases.

What effect did changes in poverty-alleviation strategies by the Mexican
government have on citizen political activity? Consider first the benefits provided by each program during their first four years of operation. By the sheer
size and scope of its programs and projects, Solidarity dwarfed PROGRESA
in the benefits it distributed (see figure 3.3). PRONASOL was a complex,
multidimensional social-spending program that targeted the rural poor, indigenous groups, and the urban poor. A large part of its expenditures, perhaps as much as 60 percent, was used for public works projects designed to
expand or improve infrastructure in poor urban neighborhoods and rural
communities.[50] A significant proportion of funding was channeled into productive and rural development projects in the form of credits to producers
and block grants to local governments; a still smaller amount was funneled
into direct transfers to poor families.

Although PRONASOL was certainly large—at its peak it distributed well
over $2 billion annually and accounted for 6 percent of the government's
programmable spending—its public presence was larger still. Information
about the number of beneficiaries is hard to come by, but the program was
national in scope, establishing Solidarity Committees and projects in 95 per-

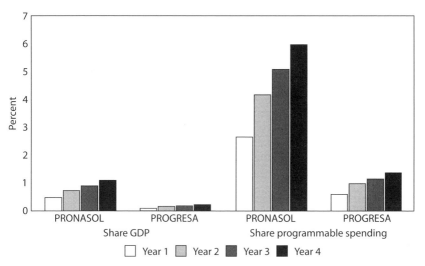

Figure 3.3. PRONASOL and PROGRESA Shares of GDP and Programmable Spending during First Four Years of Operation. *Source:* For PRONASOL, Lustig 1994; for PROGRESA, Levy 2006.

cent of Mexico's municipalities (Cornelius, Craig, and Fox 1994, 8). Furthermore, because such a large proportion of the funding was used to finance highly visible public works projects (such as schools, health posts, hospitals, sewage systems, electrification, and roads), even if people did not benefit directly from the spending, they likely knew about PRONASOL and viewed it favorably. The size, scope, and explosive growth of PRONASOL led some experts to declare that "it would be difficult to identify another government program in the postrevolutionary period whose penetration of Mexican society had been so rapid and extensive" (ibid., 8).

By contrast, PROGRESA's real and perceived footprint was minuscule, at least during its first years of operation. Whether measured as a share of GDP or as a share of the government's programmable spending, PRONASOL dwarfed PROGRESA during the first four years each program was in operation (figure 3.3). Although it too was designed to be a program with a national scope, PROGRESA was a highly focused, targeted income-transfer program that distributed money directly to very poor families to be used to cover food, education, and health care expenses. Unlike PRONASOL, however, none of its funds were earmarked for infrastructure projects. Even though participation in the program was conditional on recipients visiting local health clinics and enrolling their children in school, PROGRESA did

Table 3.3. Indicators of PROGRESA and Oportunidades Coverage, 1997–2005

	1997	1998	1999	2000	2001	2002	2003	2004	2005
Families covered (in thousands)	301	1,596	2,306	2,476	3,116	4,240	4,184	5,000	5,000
States	12	30	31	31	31	31	31	31	31
Municipalities	357	1,750	2,155	2,166	2,310	2,354	2,360	2,429	2,435
Localities	6,344	40,711	53,152	53,232	67,539	70,520	70,436	82,973	86,091
Total funding (millions of 2005 pesos)	876.4	5,5196	9,592	12,190	15,204	21,179	24,503	26,675	30,151

Source: Levy 2006.

not provide any funding for schools, hospitals, or health clinics. The vast majority of its funds, as much as 94 percent, were earmarked for cash transfers directly to poor families (Levy 2006, 32).[51] Thus much of the spending associated with PROGRESA was invisible except to recipients.

Gradualism was another defining characteristic of PROGRESA. Although the program grew rapidly after 1997 (table 3.3), it was designed to deliver benefits to the smallest and most marginalized rural localities first, then to the extreme poor living in less marginalized communities, and last to the urban poor.[52] As a result, though the number of families enrolled in PROGRESA reached 2.5 million by 2000 and the program had a presence in nearly 90 percent of municipalities, actual coverage was thinner than these numbers suggest. For instance, by 2000, PROGRESA had enrolled families in fewer than 2 percent of towns with more than twenty-five hundred inhabitants, which is where the majority of Mexicans live. On average, the program provided cash transfers to only about forty-six families per town (Levy 2006).

Even as spending for PROGRESA grew, actual coverage remained highly targeted, meaning that many of Mexico's poor that were not living in extremely marginal communities were excluded for several years from the program. For example, between 1998 and 2000 none of the residents of the three rural communities where I carried out interviews had begun receiving benefits from PROGRESA. Coverage in urban areas did not begin until 2002, well into the Fox administration, and spending in urban areas still accounts for only about 11 percent of PROGRESA spending.[53] The poor felt, quite understandably, that the government was not doing enough to alleviate the negative effects of economic crises or its free-market policies.

The frustration of one interviewee, Beatriz, was typical. Although her family of nine is undoubtedly extremely poor, living on an income of less than US$400 a month, she has seen almost no aid from the government. She lives with her husband and seven children in a two-room shack in the squatter neighborhood of Nezacubi. Her dwelling was among the poorest I saw in any of the towns in Oaxaca, whether urban or rural. A loyal PRIista, Beatriz has heard of many of the government's spending programs, but like many of Mexico's urban poor, she has not seen any benefits herself. "In the government no one cares about ordinary people," she said. "I hear that they plan to spend millions on a project somewhere down the valley, or that they will spend millions here and millions there, but we live so close to downtown Oaxaca and we still don't have water or sewage service? How is that possible? Why don't they spend their millions here?"

Beatriz's impression expressed to me in 2005 that the state was doing too little to help many of Mexico's poorest was grounded solidly in reality. Although the 1995 crisis had a devastating effect on wages, employment, and welfare, the government's reaction was to cut back on several highly symbolic food subsidy programs to balance its budget.[54] Moreover, because of budgetary constraints, the Zedillo administration phased in the cash transfers associated with PROGRESA only as other food subsidies were phased out (figure 3.4). However, subsidies were phased out more quickly than PROGRESA spending was phased in, which meant that the overall size of benefits distributed to the poor actually declined (Laurell 2003, 343). In fact, spending by PROGRESA did not begin until 1997, and coverage did not increase significantly until 1998, nearly three years *after* Zedillo took office and three years *after* one of Mexico's most devastating economic crises. [55] "In the interim," Carol Wise (2003, 183) has written, "there were no unemployment programs or effective safety nets in place to help offset the loss of more than a million formal sector jobs and a 12.5 percent drop in real wages in 1995 alone. As the drive against inflation pushed real interest rates to new heights, and social spending dropped by more than 12 percent in real terms under a tight fiscal policy, the Zedillo team floundered in offering basic relief measures."[56] We should not be surprised, then, to find that the poor felt like the government did not have its best interests in mind.

Even for those families participating in PROGRESA, the total benefits were small. Santiago Levy (2006) has estimated that all the cash and in-kind components of the program add up to an average transfer to US$35 per month per household, while households without children in school receive a substantially smaller transfer.[57] Given that poor families have on average

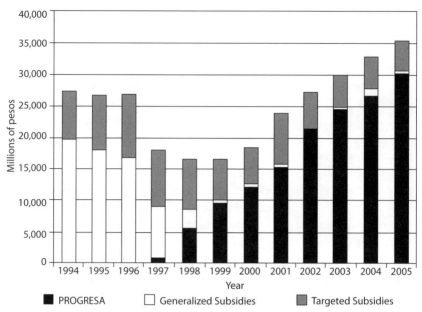

Figure 3.4. Contributions of PROGRESA/Oportunidades to Total Food Subsidy Budget, 1994–2005 (millions of 2005 pesos). *Source:* Levy 2006, Table 4-1.

4.8 members, this amounts to little more than, on average, US$7 per person per month (ibid., 23–25). I do not doubt that this supplementary income is very meaningful for poor families, especially for the rural poor, who cobble together cash from as many sources as they can. Small cash transfers have their biggest impact with the extremely poor, for whom this transfer might be enough to bring them away from the edge of economic insecurity. However, in most cases the transfer is too small to raise people above the poverty line and too small to be truly transformative.[58] The transfers may be enough of an incentive to encourage recipients to participate in politics to secure or expand the benefit, especially among families with several children. However, given the size of transfers, even small marginal increases in the cost of participation or declines in the likelihood of success of political action might be enough to outweigh the benefits of political action.

As with PRONASOL, appearances mattered. Although in reality PRO-GRESA and its successor, Oportunidades, grew rapidly after 1997 (expanding their coverage to nearly all of Mexico's municipalities by 2003), Zedillo and Fox's antipoverty efforts *appeared* smaller than they were and much smaller than efforts by previous administrations. There were several reasons for this. The initial transition from PRONASOL to PROGRESA actually produced an overall decline in antipoverty spending (figure 3.4). This created an impression among the poor that the state was doing too little to help them survive. This perception tended to persist even as the program doubled in size and expanded its coverage to nearly all of Mexico's municipalities. Objectively, actual government spending on antipoverty programs was higher overall than during the Salinas administration, but much of that spending was fragmented into dozens of separate programs that targeted distinct groups. PRONASOL, however, was designed to be a comprehensive umbrella program that encompassed all of the Salinas administration's poverty-alleviation efforts, giving it a much more prominent profile. Moreover, PRONASOL spending was dedicated to highly visible infrastructure projects, which reinforced the impression of an expansive government effort to combat poverty, even among people who did not benefit directly.

Perhaps most important, the Salinas administration went to great lengths to promote PRONASOL, designing its insignia as a blend of the Mexican flag (and the PRI logo) and displaying it prominently wherever projects were carried out. Salinas himself personally visited many of the communities that benefited from the program's funding, further reinforcing the impression that poverty alleviation was a priority for his administration.[59] Toward the end of his administration, Salinas institutionalized the agglomeration of programs under PRONASOL's umbrella in a new cabinet-level ministry, SEDESOL (the Ministry of Social Development), and hand-picked its head to be the PRI's presidential candidate in the 1994 elections.[60]

By contrast, PROGRESA was slow to gain momentum, its benefits were invisible to most even as its coverage grew, and it never received much fanfare from the Zedillo administration. One of the disadvantages of targeted cash transfer programs compared with more comprehensive programs like PRONASOL is that the benefits are only visible to recipients, which can create the impression that the state is doing little to combat poverty. Decisions to freeze new enrollments six months before the 2000 election, while politically laudable, further limited public awareness of the program. Finally, at the same time that Zedillo was underpromoting his poverty-alleviation strategy, news stories about the government's plan to spend $55 billion—about 10 percent of GDP—to bail out Mexican banks dominated the news cycle for much of his administration.[61] This controversial program known as FOBAPROA (Fondo Bancario Para la Protección del Ahorro) received much more publicity than PROGRESA, which sent a perverse signal to the poor about where the government's priorities lay. This made it hard to dispute the growing perception among the urban and rural poor who felt that the government cared more about the rich than the poor. From two interviews:

Well, for example, the sale of the Mexican telephone company, the privatization of PEMEX, who is that going to benefit? The rich! They have to take into account the needs of the whole country, and not just those of the few.
—MARGARITA, NEZACUBI

The problem is with the presidents; they don't do anything to help poor people. People don't have any money, but we have to pay for electricity, rent, taxes, and more. Where does all that money go? What do they do with all that money? They don't use it to help the poor but to pay the foreign debt.
—ARACELI, TEOTILÁN DEL VALLE

Given poor people's lack of financial resources, the increasing costs of targeting the state were more damaging to their political activism than declining benefits. PRONASOL could be considered a "bottom-up" program to the extent that it required beneficiaries to form local-level committees that participated directly in decisions about what kind of projects to undertake. Although there was large variability in the effectiveness of this kind of community participation, PRONASOL distributed large amounts of funds directly to state and local governments, which had considerable discretion about how the money should be used. By 1993 an estimated 120,000 Solidarity Committees had been formed. Although many were short-lived, as many as 40 percent of the committees established a real presence in their communities (Fox 1994b, 187). While not guaranteeing that communities would participate in funding decisions or that governments would actually listen to them, by bringing decisions and decision-makers closer to beneficiaries, PRONASOL did lower the costs of targeting the state with political activities. Actual experiences were mixed, but the evidence from field research shows PRONASOL was able to stimulate the autonomous participation of previously marginalized groups, giving them a more effective political voice than before (Graham 1994, 311).[62] From the perspective of the poor, PRONASOL created important new motivations and low-cost opportunities to become involved in politics.

PROGRESA (and now Oportunidades) was a top-down program. All of the relevant decisions about who benefits, how much money they get, where and when they collect their transfers are centrally made by the federal government. And because payments go directly to individuals and families, PROGRESA bypasses local governments and local organizations altogether. Furthermore, there is no community participation in the running of the program and no easy opportunities for beneficiaries to influence how the program is run or who is included among beneficiaries. Even the program's accountability mechanisms, through which beneficiaries can ask questions and file complaints, have strong top-down tendencies that discourage individuals from registering complaints, inhibit collective expressions of voice, and ultimately fail to adequately represent participants of the program. Given that all program decisions are made in Mexico City, and in the absence of interest groups to lobby on their behalf, the costs of targeting policymakers with political action is prohibitive for most potential and actual recipients. In addition, the selective allocation of social assistance to individuals rather than groups often divides communities between those receiving assistance and those left out of programs. This fragmentation of interests atomizes the rural and urban poor, placing them in competition with each other, thus raising the costs of collective action.[63]

Perhaps most damaging to political participation is that PROGRESA is much more technocratic than its predecessor. A central characteristic of the new era of government-sponsored poverty-alleviation programs like PROGRESA, its successor Oportunidades, and of agricultural subsidy programs like PROCAMPO, is that they target individuals on a strict need basis, using formulas or point systems for calculating the level of support individuals and households receive. This rationalization of public spending may be good economic policy because it insulates policymakers from political pressures and distributes funds where they are most needed, but by eliminating much of the discretionary power that parties, corporatist organizations, and politicians had in allocating benefits to their constituents, it makes political activity irrelevant if not irrational. There is simply no chance that political activity by individuals or groups will change who receives funding or how much they receive. Given the small amount of benefits coming from the government, and even slimmer chances of petitioning being successful, the expected utility of government-directed activity—contacting government officials, attending city council meetings, or protesting—approaches zero in this policy environment.[64] Under such circumstances, even very small increases in the costs of participation—due, for example, to weaker organizations, rising bus fares, or declining access to officials—or apparently insignificant declines in income are enough to dissuade the poor from political activity.

Another interviewee's experience illustrates how this logic works at the individual level. Although by 2000, Norma still was not receiving any cash payments from PROGRESA, as a member of an *ejido* community, she did receive transfers through PROCAMPO, which, like PROGRESA, provided direct cash payments to individual farmers based on predetermined and fixed criteria. Norma is a loyal PRIista who has voted for the PRI in every single election since she can remember, and she could be considered an activist: she is vice president of a women's group in La Ciénega, a member of Centeótl and of her *ejido* committee, she votes regularly, attends campaign rallies for all kinds of PRI candidates, and has a long history petitioning the CNC and the state for subsidies and credit. As this dialogue illustrates, she has noticed a change in the effectiveness of these strategies, however:

[How is it when you go to the CNC offices? How do they treat you?]

They treat us badly. Even when [the director] was there, we wouldn't get to see her; she would tell us to tell the secretary what we wanted.

[And did you get everything you asked for?]

No, they are sending very little. The only really big project they sent us was a package of seven goats, seven pigs, and fifteen hundred pesos. But it is not very much because there are thirty-two of us in the group.

[Did you get help from PROCAMPO?]

Yes, we did. We've been getting it for five years, but what do they give us? 130 pesos [approximately US$13.50] for each parcel! The money is just enough to pay for one pass with the plow, but what about paying for the tractor and fertilizer, and the ox, and the seeds, and feeding the ox so he will plow everything? It is not enough.

[Did you go to ask for help from PROCAMPO with the CNC group?]

No, because [the CNC] can't help with PROCAMPO. The governor said that whatever was on paper would stay as it was. It seems like they increased [the subsidy] because before they gave us 110 (pesos) and now they give us 137 pesos, but all that matters is the size of your plot.

Notice that Norma places particular emphasis on decreasing benefits, declining access, and an inability to use her position as a representative of the CNC to guarantee preferential treatment for her group—all consequences of the Zedillo (and Fox) administration's new approach to social spending, which distributes funds based on strict formulas that are insulated from political pressures. Programs like PROCAMPO and PROGRESA thus altered the links between the state and the poor in ways that reduced benefits, raised the costs, and reduced the likelihood that political participation would be effective. This created a vicious incentive structure that made political participation by the poor, at least political action that targets the federal government, less likely than before.

Although it is important to pay attention to the overall incentives public policies create for political participation, one of the most powerful ways that political institutions shape political behavior is by expanding or constraining the range of possible activities from which people can choose. To illustrate how the new era of spending programs narrowed the choice for political activism, let's compare the logic of political participation under PRONASOL and PROGRESA. Under PRONASOL local leaders and governments had to form organizations to receive benefits. This gave them strong incentives to recruit members and subsidize their political participation as they lobbied local and state governments for a share of PRONASOL funds. Citizens in turn saw a multiplication of opportunities through which they could become involved in the political process: they could join any number of organizations that tapped into PRONASOL funding; they could launch an organization themselves because the cost of targeting local and state governments was relatively low; and they could lobby local and state governments for a share of PRONASOL spending. The same group of citizens today has fewer choices than before. Local leaders have no incentive to form organizations to tap into PROGRESA funds because their efforts would not yield them any additional benefits. Individuals also have no reason to form organizations or to target local or state governments, since these (at least in theory) have no influence on who is included in the program or how much anyone receives. In theory, the poor could mobilize to target federal ministries or to lobby their representatives in Congress, but in practice the top-down, technocratic nature of PROGRESA rendered these strategies ineffective.

More generally, free-market reforms closed off opportunities for political participation in more subtle ways as well. By retreating from many core activities and encouraging the privatization of exchanges and relationships that previously were highly politicized—the provision of credits, inputs for farmers, land and labor disputes, job creation, and prices—people did not know where to turn for help or who to blame for their problems. For example, in the past the urban and rural poor benefited from low fixed prices for basic staples either because of government subsidies or because they could purchase goods at government-owned CONASUPO stores. If prices rose, they knew whom to blame (the government), whom to target with their political activity (CONASUPO stores, government and party officials), and what activities would be most effective (protests, marches, direct contacting). After subsidies were phased out and the CONASUPO program was dismantled in the 1990s, inflation became a private problem caused by market forces that were much less responsive to political solutions. Instead of targeting the government or elected representatives with their complaints, ordinary citizens now directed their anger and frustration at local merchants, distant multinational corporations, or at abstract "free markets."

These feelings of growing distance between the government and ordinary Mexicans has had a notable demobilizing effect. Their grievances are great—they mention poverty, inflation, low wages, privatization, and similar issues arising from macroeconomic reforms as the most important problems they face in their daily lives. However, for most, their geographic and psychological distance from the federal government places action against these policies beyond the realm of the conceivable. Even local activists who have a sophisticated understanding of politics in Mexico are keenly aware that there is little they can do to change macroeconomic policies. Liliana, for example, is active in community affairs in Zimatlán, but she feels much less empowered when thinking about changing the policies coming from the federal government. "There is nothing we can do about [the privatization of electricity or oil]," she said. "As long as we don't get any help from the government, everyone just has to look out for themselves and do the best they can to survive."

The fact is that most of the people I spoke with were paralyzed by the magnitude of undertaking action against these policies. Blanca, a sixty-year-old widow who lives in rural La Ciénega, has been active in local organizations. When I asked her what she thought the biggest problems facing Mexico were, she did not hesitate:

What I know is that the economic crisis affects Mexicans. Prices never stop going up, and that affects all of us because we have to continue buying things. We don't know what to do any more because the money we have is never enough to buy the things we need every day. All we know is that we can't do anything about it, because those policies come from very high up, from the governments in Mexico City, and we are too few, too weak to do anything.
[Are you happy with the government?]
No, but what does it matter? What can I do about it?

Institutions affect political participation directly by shaping the incentives and choices people have for undertaking political activities. They also shape behavior indirectly by affecting people's preference for politics—that is, their psychological orientations that would make them *want* to take part in political life (Burns, Schlozman, and Verba 2001, 99). These psychological orientations, also called political engagement, include how interested people are in politics, whether they feel like their participation matters, and

Table 3.4. Differences in Political Attitudes between High-
and Low-Income Groups, by Percentage

	Low income	High income	Difference
No interest in politics at all (2005)	36.8	21.5	15.3***
Followed 2006 electoral campaigns with interest (2006)	21.4	36.2	14.8***
Believed 2000 elections were clean (2000)	65.1	78.9	13.8***
Politics is not important to daily life (2005)	28.9	16.5	12.4***
The vote matters for what happens in Mexico (2006)	69.3	80.5	11.2**
Little or no trust in the judicial system	65.0	57.9	7.1**
Little or no trust in the federal government (2005)	56.0	50.6	5.4*
Little or no trust in Congress (2005)	75.1	70.8	4.3
Believed the 2006 elections were clean (2006)	35.5	39.0	3.5
Little or no trust in political parties (2005)	76.5	74.7	1.8

Sources: CSES 2000 and 2006; and World Values Survey 2005.
Notes:* $p < 0.1$ ** $p < 0.05$ *** $p < 0.01$

whether they trust governmental institutions. Recent survey evidence from Mexico confirms that the poor are less psychologically engaged than higher-income Mexicans. Table 3.4 reports the difference in a number of different measures of political engagement for low- and high-income individuals using both CSES and World Values Survey data. High-income individuals were more likely to respond favorably to almost all of the questions that measured political engagement. These class differences are important for an analysis of political participation because decades of research have confirmed the strong and positive relationship between political engagement and political activity.

We might conclude based on this evidence, as many others have, that the poor participate less in most kinds of political activities than the rich because they are less psychologically engaged with politics. Although this may be true in a narrow sense, that conclusion leaves a prior question unanswered: Why are the poor less engaged in politics than the rich? Whereas most theories of political participation attribute lower levels of engagement and efficacy among the poor to lower income and educational levels (Campbell 2003; Milbrath and Goel 1977; Verba, Nie, and Kim 1971 and 1978; and

Verba, Schlozman, and Brady 1995), E. E. Schattschneider (1960, 105) has suggested a better explanation for widespread nonparticipation in democracies: "Absenteeism reflects the suppression of options and alternatives that reflect the needs of nonparticipants. It is not necessarily true that people with the greatest needs participate in politics most actively—whoever decides what the game is about also decides who gets in the game."

That is an apt summary of a final pernicious consequence of the narrowing of opportunities for political action resulting from neoliberal reforms. The lack of choice can, in a relatively short period of time, lead people to feel more cynical, more apathetic, and less efficacious when it comes to politics. My interviews support the interpretation that poor people's preferences for politics are rooted in their experiences with the political process that has cultivated—and perhaps enhanced already existing—high levels of cynicism, apathy, and powerlessness. If restrictions to choice endure over time, and it has been more than twenty years since the government began slashing state budgets and retreating from what had been its dominant role in the economy, citizens may come to believe that all political activity is futile. They may therefore exit politics not as a strategic choice but because they prefer nonpolitical to political strategies. Although these habits of inaction and passivity may resemble a "culture of silence" or a "culture of poverty," it is important to recognize that they have their roots in enduring power relations manifested through institutional arrangements that tend to exclude the poor from government decision making (Gaventa 1980).

An important conclusion to this discussion is that although much of the demobilization and depoliticization of the poor occurs at the level of groups, by affecting their capacity to undertake collective action, the voice of the poor is silenced just as much by the cumulative effect of individual decisions to simply drop out of politics. Over time, this structurally induced "absenteeism" has the additional pernicious consequence of instilling among the poor a sense of powerlessness, inefficacy, and disengagement from politics that suppresses their political participation into the future.[65]

These findings are theoretically important because they support the book's main argument that the principal causes of political participation lie in the realm of politics—in the incentives and choices that political institutions provide for actors—not in the characteristics of individuals. Among the many political institutions that matter for political activity, the state has enormous power to draw people into politics or to shut them out. By carrying out its core tasks of making and implementing public policies, the state shapes the political choices and incentives actors face. It exerts enormous influence over the distribution of political resources and determines how much these resources matter for political participation.

I do not mean to argue that income, organizational resources, and psychological orientations toward politics do not matter. But the evidence shows that the state's actions are causally prior to the individual-level variables that have been shown to be important for political participation. Although the people I spoke with blame neoliberal policies directly for their disengagement from politics, it would be premature to conclude based only on evidence from my interviews, which were carried out exclusively with low-income Mexicans, that poor people's cynicism is not the result of their low socioeconomic resource endowments. Survey evidence from Mexico helps determine which of these two factors—personal background or political learning—is behind differences in the preferences the rich and poor have for politics.

CHAPTER 4

POLITICAL INSTITUTIONS, ENGAGEMENT, AND PARTICIPATION

Listening to people talk about their experiences with new economic policies implemented during the 1990s gives us insight into how institutional
changes linked to neoliberal reforms influenced their ability and desire to
participate in politics. New policies and different state-society relationships
suppressed the political activity of the poor by decreasing their capacity to
participate, by eliminating incentives for targeting the state and national
governments with political action, and by reducing their preference for political activity. Although interviews provide compelling evidence of the mechanisms linking institutional changes to changes in political activism, it is of
course possible that there is something unique about Oaxaca or about the
experiences of those interviewed. Is this institutional explanation of political
participation valid outside of the admittedly small number of cases used to
generate it? Does it hold true even after controlling for other possible explanations of political participation, such as income, education, and organizational involvement?

A series of rigorous statistical tests examines the various arguments.
Does political participation have its roots in political institutions, or is it best
explained by individual socioeconomic resources and political attitudes? Do

political institutions affect the political activity of the rich and poor differently? This is an important step for at least three reasons: (1) it will help determine whether the experiences of the poor in Oaxaca are unique or typical of people experiencing neoliberal reforms elsewhere in Mexico; (2) by including a variety of institutional factors into statistical models we will be able see which ones matter most for political participation, helping us refine our institutional theory of political participation; and (3) most importantly multivariate regression is a powerful means of testing the importance of institutional factors against other plausible explanations common in the literature, thus helping to rule out competing explanations of the decline in the political participation of the poor—namely that the poor participate less precisely because they are poor.

Key Hypotheses

Several key hypotheses are used to test the relationship between neoliberal reforms, socioeconomic status, and political activity. Together, they summarize many of the primary theoretical expectations that emerged from the institutional framework developed in chapter 2. These hypotheses serve as preliminary tests of that framework.

Income and education. Income, education, and other personal resources should still matter for political action. The key question is whether and how much they matter after controlling for the effect of institutional factors. If it is the case that institutional factors create obstacles for the poor to participate in politics, then

- Hypothesis 1: We should expect that the effect of income on participation will diminish after controlling for institutional factors.

Organizations. The literature predicts that organizations, especially labor unions and political organizations, will have a powerful impact on political activity. Nonpolitical organizations can also have a powerful mobilizing effect, particularly in new democracies as a more plural civil society creates opportunities for activism. However, neoliberal reforms weakened the mobilizing potential of many organizations in Mexico by reducing access to government officials, eliminating resources, fragmenting civil society, and encouraging many to focus on self-help activities rather than political action.

- Hypothesis 2a: Labor unions will have relatively small, if any, effects on political participation. To the extent that they do encourage political activism, their effect will be greatest among middle- and upper-income Mexicans who are more likely to be members.

- Hypothesis 2b: The effect of nonpolitical organizations on political participation will also be modest, especially among the poor.
- Hypothesis 2c: Clientelist political mobilization will remain important among the poor, so that people who are asked to participate in politics are offered gifts by political campaigns or who receive visits in their home by political organizers will be more likely to be active in politics.

Public policies, antipoverty programs, and access to government officials. Institutional factors that increase the benefits, decrease the costs, or increase the likelihood that activism will be successful should stimulate political activity.

- Hypothesis 3a: Government spending programs should have a strong effect on the political behavior of recipients who develop a stake in mobilizing to maintain access and increase the benefits. It may also make them feel "closer" to the government than people who receive no assistance. The effect should be greatest among low-income recipients for whom this assistance is more valuable.
- Hypothesis 3b: Government-assistance programs should impact government-directed activity more than electoral activity.
- Hypothesis 3c: The PRI and the PAN have been the parties that most consistently advocated and implemented neoliberal reforms, making the poor feel like neither party had their interests in mind. In contrast, the PRD's electoral platforms have emphasized economic nationalism, expansion of social-service spending, and rolling back free-market reforms. Although the PRD has not won the presidency, it has governed in several states (and in Mexico City) that have large budgets and the ability to promote their own economic development programs. Where the PRD governs at the state level (or in Mexico City), the poor should feel like they have more access to decision makers and that their political activity is more likely to impact the decisions of government officials. We should expect therefore that political activism among the poor will be greater on average where the PRD controls state-level governments.[1]

Psychological engagement and feelings of efficacy. If feelings of engagement and efficacy are rooted in childhood experiences and in levels of income and education, then measures of political engagement should be fairly stable over time. However, if they are instead rooted in people's direct and immediate experiences with politics, then we should see fluctuations in measures of engagement over time as government policies and actions have changed. Interviews with low-income Mexicans revealed growing feelings of distance from and disenchantment with the federal government after 1995 as a result of a devastating economic crisis, the implementation of NAFTA, deep cuts or elimination of subsidy and poverty-alleviation programs, and the slow introduction of a new more centralized and targeted poverty-alleviation program. Technocratic styles of policymaking that privilege economic over political factors, along with economic policies that seem to favor large corporate and foreign interests, made citizens feel like they could do nothing to influence the decisions of federal governments. This created feelings of distance to the federal government and reduced people's psychological engagement with politics.

- Hypothesis 4a: We should expect to see average levels of political attitudes fluctuate, probably with some lag, in the aftermath of important institutional changes. In particular, we should expect to see a sharp decline in levels of political engagement among the poor (and perhaps the middle class, who also suffered during this period) after 1995.
- Hypothesis 4b: The institutional factors will have an effect on levels of political efficacy even after controlling for the effects of income and education.

Disparate effects. If I am right, neoliberal reforms harmed the political activity of the poor the most because they relied most heavily on government spending, because they have fewer resources with which to overcome the rising costs of political action, and because their feelings of efficacy suffered the most as a result of the retreat of the state from traditional roles. It is standard in statistical studies of political participation to include all income groups in the same regression equation. That is a valid strategy if we assume that the social and political processes that influence people's level of political activism are the same for all income classes. However, one of the main arguments of this book is that public policies and political institutions—and the opportunities and obstacles they create for political activity—impact the poor differently than higher-income individuals. The logic of this argument requires analyzing separate regression equations for the poor and for the middle class and the rich to test whether changes in features of the political environment have the same effect on the political activity of the poor as they do on higher-income groups.[2]

- Hypothesis 5a: Institutional factors will not have uniform effects on political attitudes and political behavior across income groups.
- Hypothesis 5b: Similarly, we should not expect the same institutional factors to have uniform effects across political activities. In particular,

because neoliberal reforms involved a radical restructuring of the state, we should expect them to influence state- or government-directed activities more than electoral ones.

Political Engagement and Political Institutions

A good first step in tracing the influence of institutions on political participation is to explore the degree to which people's preference for politics are rooted in their direct experiences with political institutions and with the political process. Political engagement is the set of political attitudes or psychological orientations toward politics that makes someone *want* to take part in the political life of their communities (Burns, Schlozman, and Verba 2001, 99). This set of opinions and orientations include what people think and feel about political parties; what they think about local, state, and national governments; whether they believe political leaders actually listen to ordinary citizens; whether they harbor strong policy preferences; and whether they care about or are interested in politics. Taken together, we can think of these orientations as people's taste or preference for politics. As such, we should expect that people with a greater taste for politics will participate more often in a wider variety of activities.

Decades of research on political participation have confirmed the strong and positive relationship between political attitudes and political activity. Later I explore how these orientations influence political participation, but there is a prior question: Where do these orientations come from? Most of the literature conceptualizes political attitudes as attributes of individuals—as beliefs, opinions, and psychological orientations—developed by individuals over relatively long periods of time through early socialization experiences in school or within their families, or with experiences in such adult institutions as church, the workplace, civic organizations, or in the neighborhood context.[3] Other studies, noting that the poor are on average much less engaged with politics than more affluent groups, have attributed differences in political attitudes to their level of education or level of income, both of which give individuals the capacity and motivation to become politically active.[4] As diverse as these explanations are, they share two characteristics: (1) they assume that political predispositions are attributes of individuals and so once acquired, they are relatively stable over time; and (2) they ignore the impact that the political environment might have on someone's preference for politics.[5]

What if preferences for politics were not just the product of a lifetime of socialization experiences, but also shaped by people's direct and recent political experiences? If this were the case, rather than thinking about political engagement solely as an attribute of individuals, we could think of it as a measure of how the political system works. From this perspective lower levels of political engagement and political efficacy among the poor would be evidence not that they are uninterested in politics or apathetic, but that they have had different experiences—likely more negative experiences—with political institutions and with the political process than the rich. If we can establish that political attitudes have some of their origins in political institutions, and in turn that these attitudes affect political participation, we will have a much better understanding of the mechanisms through which political institutions affect political participation.[6] So the first step is to determine to what extent people's psychological orientations toward politics—their taste for political activity—are rooted in their political experiences. The basic expectation is that the way political institutions and the political process work opens and closes opportunities for political activity. As opportunities close for some groups and individuals, their levels of efficacy and engagement should drop. Conversely, as opportunities broaden, people become more politically engaged. The period between 1990 and 2000 was turbulent for Mexico, characterized by enormous institutional changes. If attitudes are related to political opportunities, we should see significant fluctuation in Mexicans' orientations toward politics.

The decade can be roughly divided in two. Mexico's boom years were 1990 through 1994, characterized by robust economic growth, declining inflation, and a massive social-service program (PRONASOL) that sought to ameliorate some of the worst impacts of neoliberal reforms. The year 1994 was a turning point. Most neoliberal reforms had been implemented by then, including the historic North American Trade Agreement (NAFTA) between the United States, Canada, and Mexico, which guaranteed that free-trade policies would be pursued long into the future. Mexicans seemed to validate the government's neoliberal turn by turning out in great numbers and electing the PRI's candidate Ernesto Zedillo in elections that were mostly free (although they were not fair). Despite these strengths, major cracks in the system became evident that year. The Zapatista guerrilla army launched its uprising in Chiapas on the same day that NAFTA went into effect; the PRI's initial presidential candidate, Luis Donaldo Colosio, was assassinated at a campaign rally in Tijuana in March; and by December the bottom had fallen out of the Mexican economy, producing a deep economic crisis that devastated the incomes of millions of low- and middle-income Mexicans. Although the government moved quickly to stabilize the economy and return to growth, its strategies required deep cuts in social-service spending, eliminating subsidy programs and delaying the implementation of a new poverty-alleviation program. When PROGRESA was finally introduced, the income of working-class Mexicans had declined by about a third (Pastor and Wise 2003).

There was, of course, a silver lining associated with these turbulent events: the 1997 congressional elections saw the PRI lose its majority in the Chamber of Deputies for the first time, while the 2000 presidential elections finally saw an opposition party win. Mexico's transition to democracy could be dated to 1997, because the elections were unambiguously free and fair and its results made the system of checks and balances between the legislative and the executive branches a practical reality for the first time since the Mexican constitution was ratified in 1917. In turn, Vicente Fox's victory in 2000 marked a definitive end to nearly two centuries of authoritarianism in Mexico, ushering in a new era of democratic governance.

This was a decade of historic highs and lows that impacted ordinary Mexicans deeply. I carried out the bulk of my fieldwork between 1998 and 2000, when people were still recovering from the consequences of these institutional changes and economic crises, when they were dealing with the realization that neoliberal policies were not the panacea to poverty as the government had claimed. They were looking forward with some guarded optimism toward the 2000 elections. Despite the prospect of democratization, the poor I spoke with felt less able to afford the increasing costs of political action, and they were increasingly pessimistic about their ability to influence the decisions and actions of their governments. More and more often, they were choosing to drop out of politics. Were these experiences typical? If so, we should expect feelings of political engagement to have improved during the early part of the decade, then to have suffered a sharp decline after 1995. If feelings of political engagement did not change much during this tumultuous decade, we would have powerful evidence against an institutional explanation of political attitudes and political participation.

Cross-sectional evidence, the kind that is most often used when studying political attitudes and political participation, is of little use. Table 3.4 reported differences in the political engagement of the poor as compared with the rich at a fixed point in time. The low levels of engagement reported by poor Mexicans could be explained either by institutional or individual factors, so the information cannot help us distinguish which explanation is right. Panel data is the most appropriate for exploring causal relationships between the political process and political attitudes and beliefs. There is no such data available for the entire decade, but the 2000 Mexico Panel study collected three waves of interviews in the months preceding and one wave immediately after the historic 2000 presidential election—all with the same respondents. This valuable data can help identify what impact, if any, the democratic transition had on political attitudes.

Published studies show that political opinions and beliefs, even deeply held ones, are not stable in Mexico. James McCann and Chappell Lawson (2003) have found that Mexicans' ideological dispositions and preferences on some policy issues fluctuated during the six-month presidential campaign; overall they were more volatile than in consolidated democracies. Interestingly, the educational background of Mexicans did not have much impact on the stability of most political beliefs—that is, the political beliefs of highly educated Mexicans were just as unstable as the beliefs of less-educated citizens (ibid.). Roderic Ai Camp (2004) also found that the democratization of the political process had powerful and immediate effects on people's assessment of Mexico's political system. Whereas before the election only 40 percent of respondents believed Mexico to have been a democracy, the number jumped to 63 percent immediately after Fox's victory. Because the two surveys interviewed the same people, Camp (ibid., 39–40) concluded that "for the first time in Mexico's political history, we have empirical evidence of a cause-and-effect relationship between the political system's performance (in this case, a presidential election) and political values. . . . This finding . . . demonstrated definitively that structures and behavior determine political attitudes."[7]

Longitudinal data collected by the World Values Survey in 1990, 1995, and 2000 (three critical periods) are an excellent source of information about Mexicans' political attitudes. This provides some of the leverage to distinguish between individual and institutional explanations of political attitudes. The surveys asked two questions that tap into people's preference for politics: (1) "How interested would you say you are in politics?" and (2) "How important would you say politics is in your life?" Responses are measured on a four-point scale, ranging from "very interested" or "very important" to "not at all interested" or "not at all important." Of course, these are general questions about people's orientations toward politics, so we cannot be certain what exactly they measure. Conceptually, questions that ask about people's interest in politics are intended to tap into their psychological engagement with politics. Hundreds of studies have found this to be an important predictor of all kinds of political activity. Questions that ask about the importance of politics in people's daily lives are less common, but they may

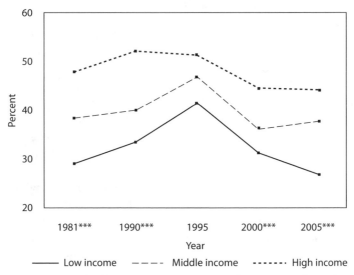

Figure 4.1a. Percentage of Mexicans Very or Somewhat Interested in Politics. ***
indicates that the differences are significant across income groups. Only the political interest question was asked in the 1981 wave, included here for comparison.
Source: World Values Survey, 1981–2005.

be a more direct measure of the impact of reforms of the state and neoliberal
policies.

Under Mexico's state-led development model (in place until the 1980s),
the state played an enormous role in the lives of both the urban and the rural poor through highly visible social-spending programs, investments in
infrastructure, and public enterprises that provided jobs and purchased and
sold foodstuff at subsidized prices. Neoliberal reforms affected the lives of
the poor by cutting back on state spending and dismantling state institutions that had been so important in their everyday lives. As a consequence,
politics—and in turn political activity—became much less relevant for the
poor. Questions about the importance of politics in people's lives can be interpreted as a measure of the relevance of the state's actions on people's daily
lives. Together these two measures allow us to see if the feelings of growing political disengagement experienced by the poor in Oaxaca were more
widely shared.

Figures 4.1a and 4.1b show how levels of interest in and the importance
of politics fluctuated in Mexico for low-, medium-, and high-income Mexicans. The first general pattern to notice is that political attitudes fluctuated

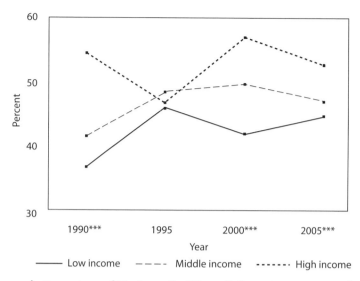

Figure 4.1b. Percentage of Mexicans for Whom Politics Was Very or Rather Important. *** indicates that the differences are significant across income groups. *Source:* World Values Survey, 1981–2005.

significantly during the decade, suggesting that these measures of political engagement do tap into people's experiences with the political process, in addition to long-held opinions. The second pattern is that low-income Mexicans were less politically engaged than the affluent in most years, although the gap is not stable over time. It was quite wide in 1981, 1990, and 2000, but the gap narrowed significantly in 1995. This narrowing calls into question a common explanation for the engagement gap that exists today: that the poor in Mexico have always been more cynical and apathetic than the affluent. The poor certainly report being less engaged most times, but as recently as 1995 the gap was small or nonexistent.

Finally, although the evidence in these figures is not definitive proof of a causal relationship between reforms of the state and people's preference for politics, it is encouraging to note that levels of political engagement follow important political and institutional changes in the expected direction. Interest in politics increased for all income groups between 1981 and 1990 (see figure 4.1a), which could be the result of the interest generated by Cuahutémoc Cárdenas's nearly successful opposition movement that challenged the PRI in the 1988 presidential elections. Both measures of political engagement continued to increase for the poor and middle class in the first half of the decade, a period of economic growth and political optimism (and the period during which PRONASOL operated). However, levels of interest in politics plummeted for all income groups between 1995 and 2000, evidence of widespread disillusionment with government policies and reactions to the various crises it faced. Measures of the importance of politics in people's lives (see figure 4.1b) also tell a compelling story. For the poor the importance of politics in their lives increased between 1990 and 1995, quite possibly due to the size and visibility of PRONASOL. However, after the economic crisis of 1994 and 1995 the government was forced to eliminate most subsidy programs on essential goods; it put antipoverty spending on hold and did not have the resources to launch a new social-spending program until later in the decade. When the Zedillo administration did roll out its antipoverty program, it was small, highly centralized, and impermeable to political pressures coming from below. As a consequence, the poor Mexicans I spoke with, and likely others across the country, felt that politics offered few if any opportunities to satisfy their needs. This was not the case for more affluent citizens, who on average felt like politics was more important in their daily lives in 2000 than in 1995. Another meaningful finding is that levels of engagement do not follow the same pattern for different income groups. Whereas the importance of politics in the lives of the poor declined in 2000 and increased in 2005, it did the opposite for middle- and high-income respondents. Levels of interest also followed markedly different patterns in 2005, as the engagement gap widened dramatically between the poor and the more affluent. This is evidence that political opportunities quite often have divergent effects on people from different income groups.

The evidence presented provides good reason to believe that political attitudes are quite responsive to changes in the political opportunity structure citizens face. But we have to consider the possibility that it was one of these other institutional changes, or some combination of them instead of neoliberal reforms, that caused poor Mexicans to become less engaged with politics (the impact of democratization on political attitudes and political participation is detailed in chapters 5 and 6). There are reasons to be confident that public policies associated with free-market reforms are at least partially responsible for this growing detachment from politics. First, we would expect democratization and decentralization, which open rather than close opportunities for political action and influence, to have positive effects on citizen attitudes, particularly if citizens perceive the new rules of the political game to be fair and to be functioning well (Moehler 2008, Catterberg and Moreno 2005, and Weitz-Shapiro 2008).[8] Second, my interviews provide valuable information that helps us interpret the story told by aggregate survey data. The people I spoke with (almost unanimously opposed to neoliberal reforms) were disappointed with levels of government antipoverty spending. The new technocratic policies made them feel like there was nothing they could do politically to change the situation. In contrast, they were on the whole happy with their local governments and targeted them more frequently with political action (Holzner 2004). Their feelings toward democratic reforms were more mixed but tended to be positive if they thought the leftist PRD had a chance of winning elections. They were more disenchanted if their choice was limited to either the PRI or the PAN, both of which advocated deepening neoliberal reforms.

The data presented thus far provides quite a bit of evidence that political orientations are in fact related to people's recent and direct experiences with political institutions. This helps to support the argument that the massive institutional reforms associated with Mexico's neoliberal turn dampened poor people's enthusiasm for politics. We should expect this growing engagement gap to produce greater inequality in the political activity between the rich and the poor in Mexico. Before testing whether this is so, we need to establish more clearly a causal link between changes in the political environment and changes in political attitudes. The next step in the analysis, therefore, is to test whether political efficacy, which has consistently been shown to be a strong predictor of political activity, is in fact caused by institutional factors. If we can link political participation to political efficacy, and political efficacy in turn back to its institutional origins, we will have established a much stronger case for the institutional roots of citizen political activity.

Causes of Political Efficacy

Political efficacy is one of the most studied political attitudes and lies at the heart of many explanations of citizen political involvement (Verba, Schlozman, and Brady 1995, 346). Although it has been measured in many different ways, the core concept taps into feelings people have that governments are responsive to their needs and that their political activity can have some influence over the decisions of government officials. My measure is an additive scale (ranging from 0 to 16) of four measures of external efficacy used by the Comparative Studies of Electoral Systems (CSES) surveys.[9]

Among the many free-market policy reforms implemented by the Mexican governments during the 1990s, perhaps none created a greater gulf between the poor and national governments than cutbacks in *apoyos* (subsidies and direct government assistance). The 2003 Mexico wave of the CSES

Table 4.1. Political Efficacy by Income and Federal Government Assistance

	Received government assistance		Means Test
	Yes	No	
Low income	9.06	8.35	***
Medium income	8.37	8.30	
High income	7.05	8.06	
Means test	**		

Source: CSES-CIDE 2003.
Notes: * p < 0.1   ** p < 0.05   *** p < 0.01

surveys collected information about people's levels of efficacy and whether they received any kind of government assistance through a state or federal spending program such as Oportunidades or PROCAMPO. Accordingly, this gives us a sense about whether these feelings of disempowerment are common among the poor in Mexico and whether public policies can influence levels of efficacy among citizens.[10] Table 4.1 presents the result of a means test of the relationship between government assistance and political efficacy for people in different income categories. The results are entirely consistent with the arguments made in chapter 3. Receiving government assistance increases feelings of efficacy only among the poor, and among those who receive government assistance, the poor are the most efficacious of all. To the extent that feelings of efficacy encourage political participation, this is strong evidence that government-spending programs that target the poor could help decrease the participation gap that exists between the rich and the poor in Mexico.

Although this bivariate analysis is consistent with the argument about the relationship between institutional factors and political attitudes, to be more certain that a causal relationship actually exists, we need to control for additional variables such as age, education, gender, and socioeconomic context that might also influence people's political orientations. Table 4.2 presents the result of an OLS (ordinary least squares) regression analysis that estimates the effect of a variety of individual and institutional variables on political efficacy.[11] Because my argument is that efficacy really measures people's perception of how well the political system works, the key explanatory variables include a number of measures of institutional performance and access. The analysis in chapter 3 suggests that union membership (UNION), receiving government assistance (GOVASST), and perceptions of how well the economy is doing (NATECON) affect how efficacious people

Table 4.2. Testing the Relative Importance of Individual and Institutional Factors for Efficacy (OLS)

Variable	Full sample (1)	Sample with only low-income respondents (2)	Sample with only medium- and high-income respondents (3)
INDIVIDUAL FACTORS			
Income	−0.08 (0.081)	0.31 (0.27)	−0.07 (0.13)
Education	**−0.02 (0.05)**	**−0.13 (0.07)***	**0.09 (0.08)**
Male	−0.01 (0.18)	0.18 (0.25)	−0.26 (0.28)
Age	0.002 (0.007)	0.00 (0.009)	0.001 (0.01)
Member of a labor union (UNION)	−0.07 (0.29)	−0.18 (0.46)	−0.10 (0.38)
State GINI score above national average (GINIAVG)	−0.23 (0.22)	−0.28 (0.26)	−0.15 (0.41)
INSTITUTIONAL FACTORS			
Receive government cash payments or subsidies (GOVASST)	**0.47 (0.23)****	**0.51 (0.28)***	**0.27 (0.43)**
National economic situation improved during past year (NATECON)	0.27 (0.08)***	0.30 (0.11)***	0.24 (0.12)**
PRD in power at the state level (PRDGOV)	**0.09 (0.26)**	**0.63 (0.36)***	**−0.40 (0.39)**
PAN in power at the state level (PANGOV)	−0.19 (0.23)	−0.42 (0.32)	−0.10 (0.35)
Past elections were not clean (FRAUD)	−0.30 (0.06)***	−0.35 (0.08)***	−0.25 (0.09)***
Elections do a good job in ensuring politicians will represent voters (ELECREP)	0.78 (0.1)***	0.91 (0.14)***	0.60 (0.16)***
Corruption is widespread (CORRUPT)	−0.63 (0.15)***	−0.40 (0.19)**	−0.96 (0.26)***
Political and human rights are well protected (HUMRTS)	**0.40 (0.11)*****	**0.46 (0.14)*****	**0.26 (0.16)**

Source: CSES-CIDE 2003.
Notes: Standard errors reported in parentheses.
Rows in boldface indicate results are different across income groups.
* p < 0.1   ** p < 0.05   *** p < 0.01.

feel.[12] Unions declined in strength and influence under neoliberalism, so I would expect, contrary to conventional wisdom, that their contribution to efficacy will be minimal and perhaps nonexistent for the poor who are unlikely to be members. Government assistance should boost levels of efficacy among recipients, while those who feel like the economy is performing well under neoliberalism have more reason to feel efficacious than people who think the economy is deteriorating.

Another potentially important variable is whether the PRI, the PAN, or the PRD governs at the state level. Since 1988, the PRI and the PAN have been allied in implementing ever deeper free-market reforms and have come to be perceived as parties that favor the interests of businesses and international companies over those of workers or ordinary citizens. The PRD, however, has been among the most consistent critics of neoliberal policies. We would expect therefore that the poor living in states where the PRD governs would feel more efficacious than those living in states where another party is in power. I test this effect with dummy variables to indicate whether the PRD or the PAN is in power at the state level. Because only three parties have won governorships in Mexico, the PRI is the comparison category.

A full model of political efficacy should test whether factors associated with democratization and the rule of law also matter, so the model in table 4.2 includes measures of people's perceptions of fraud (FRAUD), whether corruption is widespread (CORRUPT), whether the state successfully protects political and human rights (HUMRTS), and whether the electoral process produces representative outcomes (ELECREP).[13] Although Mexico has made great strides toward consolidating its democracy, the actual spread of democratic practices and protection of basic civil and political rights is still very uneven in Mexico. So where fraud is more prevalent, elections produce less representative outcomes, or where the rule of law is not adequately enforced, we should expect political efficacy to suffer. Finally, the model includes five control variables: income, education level, gender, age, whether someone lives in a state with above-average levels of socioeconomic inequality (GINIAVG).[14]

Because I am interested in testing whether political variables have disparate effects on low- versus medium- and high-income Mexicans, the table reports the estimated effects of the independent variables using the full survey sample (column 1), and the estimated effects on just low-income and medium- to high-income respondents (columns 2 and 3). The results are surprising, since neither income nor education affect levels of efficacy once we control for institutional factors.[15] Instead, the data provide strong confirmation that the state's actions have powerful effects on people's levels of political efficacy. People who receive assistance through spending programs or who perceived the economy as performing well thought the political system was more open and representative. The results also confirm that institutional factors need not have uniform effects across income groups. Some factors, like receiving government assistance and whether a leftist party is in power locally, matter a great deal for the political attitudes of the poor, but not at all for the affluent. Thus, whereas declining government assistance damages the efficacy of low-income Mexicans, it does not create a feeling of cynicism or apathy among middle- and high-income citizens. Also, where a party that opposes neoliberal reforms governs at the state level, the poor feel like they have more access and influence with government officials compared with states where the PRI governs. In contrast, this kind of political alternation in power does not appear to be a significant political opportunity for the affluent.

Institutional variables associated with features of the democratic political process are also very influential. Perceptions that fraud and corruption are widespread harm feelings of efficacy for all Mexicans, while thinking that elections do a good job in producing representative outcomes enhance it. In contrast, the poor appear more vulnerable to breakdowns in the rule of law, since only their feelings of efficacy suffer among people who perceive that the state does not do a good job protecting political and human rights. These are important findings because they establish the institutional roots of political efficacy and lend credence to the argument that measures of efficacy do measure institutional performance rather than individual political competence. Surely socialization experiences in the home and at school instill in people a core set of political beliefs and attitudes that might be quite stable over time. This may explain, for example, why for most periods the poor in Mexico show lower levels of psychological engagement with politics than do more affluent Mexicans. However, the analysis makes clear that we cannot think of individuals as efficacious or inefficacious, engaged or detached in any absolute sense. Rather, people's political attitudes and beliefs are also rooted in concrete experiences with issues, with political institutions, and with the political process. Thus they should vary from group to group and person to person according to individual and group experiences. We can think of political orientations as measuring people's preferences or tastes for politics, but like all preferences they are developed and formed within a specific institutional context (March and Olsen 1984 and Wildavsky 1987).

Interpreted in this way, questions that probe people's feelings of political efficacy, trust in institutions, and political engagement that are ubiquitous in studies of political participation can be interpreted as indicators of how political institutions and the political process actually work rather than measures of individual political culture or dispositions (Dennis 1991). This conceptualization of political orientations has the advantage of avoiding problems of reverse causation with political participation, since institutional factors such as government responsiveness are temporally prior to and unlikely to be influenced by the political activity of any given individual. Furthermore, because many surveys already collect information about political efficacy, trust in institutions, and interest in politics, we have ready-made proxy measures of how the political process and how political institutions work in a particular context.[16] These variables make it possible to use existing survey data to test some of the effects of institutions on political participation even in the absence of more direct measures of political opportunities. The key is to interpret measures of political attitudes not as characteristics inherent in individuals, but as evidence of the way institutions actually function.[17]

Explaining Political Participation by Individual and Institutional Factors

It is now time to test the argument that the institutional changes—reduction in state spending, a shift to more targeted poverty-alleviation programs, the growth and simultaneous fragmentation and weakening of labor unions and organizations in civil society—are partly responsible for the stratification by income of political participation in Mexico. After testing, we can have greater confidence that the class differences in political activism are not the fault of the poor. Rather, these differences are the result of the new rules of the political game that closed off opportunities for the poor to become involved in politics, while affecting higher-income groups much less.

We can explore the impact of government policies on the political activity of people from different income groups by analyzing some bivariate relationships between political participation and institutional factors that tap into these new state-society relations. Because each of the three major parties in Mexico have different philosophies and strategies of governing, one such factor is whether the PRI controls the executive branch of state governments. At one time almost all politics in Mexico was national, with state and local governments subordinated to the federal government, and to the executive branch in particular (Fagen and Tuohy 1972 and Rodríguez 1997). But recent research has documented the increasing importance of politics at the state level in the lives of citizens (Beer 2003, Cabrero Mendoza 1998, Díaz-Cayeros 2004, Hernández-Rodríguez 2003, and Rodríguez 1997).[18]

After the PAN gained control of the presidency in 2000, state governors quickly moved to assert their autonomy from the executive branch and sought to use their newfound power and independence to build up local bases of power. Patronage from the federal government had been declining under the Zedillo administration and dropped even further under Fox. However, many governors, particularly PRI governors, used the significant resources now under their control to continue buying votes, to undermine PAN and PRD candidates, and to reinforce their new position at the top of clientelist pyramids (Hernández-Rodríguez 2003 and Magaloni 2006). Following the logic of vote buying under autocracies, PRI governors attempting to establish hegemonic control over state politics targeted the poor with patronage much more often than middle- and upper-income individuals who are less likely to sell their vote.[19] Consequently, the poor living in states with PRI governors were more likely to be mobilized into politics and could expect to receive more government patronage than low-income individuals living in states governed by the PAN or the PRD. Of course, if they keep their part of the clientelist bargain, we should also see higher participation rates by low-income people living in states governed by the PRI.

Table 4.3a compares the mean number of political acts by individuals with different income levels living in states governed by the PRI or by other parties.[20] It shows that the poor participated in more activities when they lived in states with PRI governors. The effect was reversed for medium- and high-income individuals, who are much less susceptible to clientelist mobilization. Notice also that although political participation is very stratified by income where the PRI does not govern, the negative effects of income and education are mitigated where the PRI controls the executive branch. This is indirect evidence of the power that clientelist mobilization strategies still have in Mexico, particularly among the poor for whom the reactivation of clientelist networks gives them more channels of access to political leaders and so feel like their political activity will be rewarded—quite literally (Holzner 2004). Higher-income groups, in contrast, do not benefit much from clientelism and so come to resent these authoritarian practices that give them little access to decision makers at the state and local levels.

The increase in political participation from 1.1 acts to 1.27 acts among the poor who live in states with PRI governors may seem trivial politically, but when we aggregate the impact across a large population the effect mounts quickly.[21] If we assume there are approximately fifty million Mexicans of voting age, of which approximately half live in poverty and half live in states governed by the PRI, then this increase of 0.17 acts per translates into an in-

Table 4.3a. Impact of Having the PRI in Power at the State Level on Political Participation, by Income

	PRI in power at the state level		Means test
	Yes	No	
Low	1.27	1.10	**
Medium	1.19	1.47	***
High	1.30	1.78	**
Means test		***	

Source: CSES-CIDE 2003.
Notes: * p < 0.1   ** p < 0.05   *** p < 0.01

Table 4.3b. Impact of Government Assistance on Political Participation, by Income

	Received government assistance		Means test
	Yes	No	
Low	1.49	1.12	***
Medium	1.50	1.25	*
High	1.79	1.43	
Means test		***	

Source: CSES-CIDE 2003.
Notes: * p < 0.1   ** p < 0.05   *** p < 0.01

crease of more than two million distinct political acts each year. This means that the poor living in states controlled by the PRI potentially have considerably more voice, more representation, and more clout than their counterparts elsewhere in Mexico.

Receiving assistance through established government programs should also boost the poor's political activity and help equalize levels of participation across income groups because it gives recipients a tangible stake in policy decisions.[22] Although the effect might occur among all income groups, the impact of government assistance on political participation should be greatest among the poor, for whom government benefits have a much higher marginal utility. The results in table 4.3b are consistent with these expectations. Not only does government assistance boost the political activity of the poor the most, it is also a great political equalizer because it eliminates systematic differences in the volume of political activity between the rich and the poor. This result is not new or surprising, but it does suggest that whereas ISI policies tended to level the political playing field, encouraging the poor to become active in politics, cutbacks in state spending associated with neoliberal reforms tend to reinforce the political inequalities that arise from Mexico's very high levels of income inequality.

It seems that the actions of states and governments can have powerful effects on citizens' political activity, either by encouraging or discouraging their participation. Public policies—how money is spent and who benefits—seems to be an especially crucial factor that can help boost the motivation and ability of low-income people to participate in politics, or alternatively to discourage them from ever trying to influence the political process. The next step is to test an institutional model of political participation that also controls for individual socioeconomic and demographic characteristics, such as education, age, and gender. The main theoretical goal is to determine whether the institutional factors we have identified thus far as important still have an effect on political behavior after controlling for these competing explanations.

Tables 4.4, 4.5, and 4.6 report the results of statistical analyses that test many of the hypotheses outlined at the beginning of the chapter.[23] The first two columns of table 4.4 show for purposes of comparison the coefficients obtained from estimating a narrow socioeconomic status model of political participation and a model that includes measures of organizational effects. The second model approximates the standard model of political participation that is common in the literature, and so can be thought of as a baseline for comparing the institutional model in column 3. The standard model tests the effect of union membership on political activism as well as membership in political and nonpolitical organizations.[24] These two variables count the number of organizations in which respondents were active, with values ranging from 0 to 5 for each variable. The third model adds measures of political opportunities including perceptions of the openness and representatives of the political system (efficacy), whether the respondent received financial assistance from the federal government, whether the PAN or the PRD is in power at the state level, and the number of times (ranging from 0 to 3) someone was recruited by political campaigns to participate in politics. In most democratic systems political recruitment is a core part of electoral campaigns and a key mechanism through which individuals are mobilized into politics. This is true in Mexico as well, with the additional wrinkle that much of this recruitment happens within clientelist networks, so the variable also measures undemocratic forms of political mobilization.[25]

The institutional model in column 3 works quite well as an explanation for political participation. As expected, those who perceive the political system to be open and representative, who received some kind of government assistance, and who are recruited by political campaigns (often using clientelist mobilization strategies) are more likely to be active in politics. Although many recent studies have documented the importance of nonpolitical organizations for political participation (most notably Burns, Schlozman, and Verba 2001; and Verba, Schlozman, and Brady 1995), the results confirm that in Mexico they may be too small, fragmented, and short-lived to have much impact. Political organizations, such as *ejido* groups or hu-

Table 4.4. Political Participation Models (OLS)

Variables	SES model (1)	SES + organizations (standard model) (2)	Standard model + political opportunities (3)	Low-income respondents only (4)	Middle- and high-income respondents only (5)
INDIVIDUAL LEVEL					
Education	0.03 (0.02)**	0.018 (0.02)**	0.04 (0.02)**	0.03 (0.022)	0.04 (0.024)
Income	0.03 (0.02)	0.04 (0.02)**	0.03 (0.02)	-0.02 (0.08)	0.04 (0.04)
Male	0.17 (0.06)***	0.06 (0.06)	0.03 (0.06)	0.07 (0.07)	-0.01 (0.09)
Age	0.008 (0.002)***	0.007 (0.002)***	0.01 (0.002)***	0.008 (0.003)***	0.01 (0.003)***
Union member	—	0.22 (0.09)**	0.26 (0.09)***	**0.11 (0.15)**	**0.34 (0.12)***
Political organization count	—	0.36 (0.05)***	0.39 (0.05)***	0.34 (0.06)***	0.48 (0.09)***
Nonpolitical organization count	—	0.08 (0.04)***	0.05 (0.04)	0.065 (0.05)	0.003 (0.06)
POLITICAL OPPORTUNITIES					
Efficacy	—	—	0.04 (0.008)***	0.04 (0.01)***	0.04 (0.01)***
Receive government transfers	—	—	0.19 (0.07)***	**0.20 (0.09)**	**0.13 (0.13)**
Political recruitment	—	—	0.28 (0.03)***	0.23 (0.04)***	0.33 (0.05)***
PRD in power at state level	—	—	0.14 (0.08)*	**-0.07 (0.11)**	**0.41 (0.12)***
PAN in power at state level	—	—	0.05 (0.07)	0.00 (0.10)	0.15 (0.10)
Constant	0.70 (0.12)***	0.55 (0.12)***	-0.26 (0.16)	-0.004 (0.25)	-0.46 (0.28)
	$R^2 = 0.017$	$R^2 = 0.075$	$R^2 = 0.156$	$R^2 = 0.131$	$R^2 = 0.201$
	$N = 1,836$	$N = 1,753$	$N = 1,551$	$N = 860$	$N = 673$

Source: CSES-CIDE 2003.
Notes: Results that vary across income groups are highlighted in boldface.
* $p < 0.1$ ** $p < 0.05$ *** $p < 0.01$

man rights organizations, have a much stronger effect on all income groups. Finally, whether the PRI controlled the governorship mattered for political participation. To test this effect, the models in table 4.4 include dummy variables for states where the PAN and the PRD are in power, so that the coefficient of these variables can be interpreted as the effect of having the PAN or the PRD in power at the state level on political participation relative to states where the PRI is in power at the state level. The coefficients for these variables show, somewhat counterintuitively, that where the PRD governs, the political activity of the affluent is bolstered.

Overall, individual-level variables do not affect political participation as much as the standard theories would lead us to expect. Although age and education both have positive impacts on political participation, when looking at the whole sample, neither income nor gender mattered. The results also show how leaving institutions out of models of political participation can produce misleading results. The results in column 2 confirm the importance of income, education, and membership in nonpolitical organizations as predictors of who participates and how much. This is where most analyses of political participation stop. However, once we add measures of political opportunities to the model, income and membership in nonpolitical organizations cease to be significant predictors of political activity.

What are political opportunities for some may be political constraints for others, so we should not expect institutional factors to have the same effect on low- and high-income groups. For this reason I estimate separate regression models for low- and middle- to high-income individuals (see columns 4 and 5, respectively) to explore which institutional factors have disparate effects across income groups. As expected, the analysis shows that there are important income differences in the way participatory factors shape political activity (highlighted with boldface). Multiple regression confirms the earlier result that government assistance only boosts the political activity of the poor. The effect of union membership proved to be strong and positive when looking at the entire sample. Although this is a common result in studies of political participation, given how much neoliberal reforms weakened unions in Mexico, I did not expect them to have a powerful effect on citizen activism.[26] However, when we look at the results in columns 4 and 5, we see that unions only mobilized middle- and high-income Mexicans into politics and had absolutely no impact on the political activity of the poor. This makes sense because workers lucky enough to belong to the more established unions tend have much higher incomes than average workers *and* receive more pressure to participate in political activities. Most low-income workers are not unionized, so it is not surprising that union membership has no effect on their political activity.

Thus far the analysis has focused on explaining the overall volume of political activity. It is unlikely that the same features of the political system will affect all modes of political action equally, since different activities have different resource requirements and are more or less sensitive to different features of the political environment.[27] For example, voting is quite a unique act. Compared with other political activities such as contacting a government official or protesting, it is a very low-cost activity that requires relatively few skills or resources. It also conveys very little information about an actor's preferences. From the perspective of the individual voter, voting has a very low likelihood of making any impact on policymakers (Verba, Schlozman, and Brady 1995, 23–24).[28] In large part, because of these characteristics, explanations of voting behavior found in the literature are fundamentally different than explanations for other acts. For example, voting is very sensitive to some institutional configurations that do not affect other political acts at all, such as voter registration laws, the number of parties competing, and how close elections are (Aldrich 1993, Powell Jr. 1986, Rosenstone and Wolfinger 1978, and Rusk and Stucker 1991). In short, we should not expect to find a single institutional explanation that fits all modes of political participation. Reality is messier than that.

Table 4.5 summarizes the results of a logistic regression analysis of the factors that influence the likelihood of undertaking four political acts: voting, volunteering for a political campaign, contacting a government representative, and participating in a protest or march. The interpretation of coefficients that result from logistic regression is less straightforward than OLS coefficients, so I have replaced coefficients and standard errors with (+) and (−) symbols to indicate the direction of the impact of each variable where that impact is significant. Blank cells indicate variables that are not statistically significant explanations of the participatory act. Among individual factors, level of education mattered for government-directed acts but not for electoral ones. Age, however, mattered for all acts except protests and marches. This means that older Mexicans who were socialized under authoritarianism are more likely to vote, volunteer for political campaigns, and contact government officials than younger Mexicans. Despite common depictions of Mexico as having a male-centered culture, men and women are just as likely to be politically active. Most studies of political participation in Mexico have focused on voting behavior, but a quick glance at the table reveals that the same factors that explain voting behavior cannot be gener-

Table 4.5. Political Participation Models for Electoral and Government-directed Activities (Logit)

Variables	Electoral activities		Government-directed activities	
	Voting	Campaign activities	Contacting	Protesting
INDIVIDUAL LEVEL				
Education			+	+
Income	+++		+++	
Male		++		
Age	+++		++	
Union member				++
Political organization count	+	+++		+++
Nonpolitical organization count			++	
POLITICAL OPPORTUNITIES				
Efficacy	+++	+++	++	
Receive government transfers			++	
Political recruitment	+++	+++	+++	+++
PRD in power at state level	+++			
PAN in power at state level				
	$LL = 1738.92$	$LL = 1144.38$	$LL = 975.84$	$LL = 816.71$
	$X^2 = 108.28$	$X^2 = 60.81$	$X^2 = 108.1$	$X^2 = 69.38$
	X^2 prob. $p \leq 0.000$	X^2 prob. $p \leq 0.000$	X^2 prob. $p \leq 0.000$	X^2 prob. $p \leq 0.000$
	$N = 1,579$	$N = 1,574$	$N = 1,574$	$N = 1,574$

Source: CSES-CIDE 2003.
Notes: The dependent variables are dichotomous variables indicating whether an individual undertook one of the political acts.
+ Positive effect at 0.1 level   ++ Positive effect significant at 0.05 level   +++ Positive effect significant at 0.01 level
LL = log likelihood

alized to other political acts. For example, it is well established that income is an important predictor of voter turnout in Mexico, but once we control for political factors, income does not influence campaign or protest activity at all. Income is an important predictor of political contacting, perhaps because it has become relatively costly to do so. Similarly, although evidence shows that receiving government transfers influences voters' *choice* among parties, favoring whichever party happens to be in power (Camp 2006; and Díaz-Cayeros, Estevez, and Magaloni forthcoming), it does not make it more likely that people will vote. It does affect contacting activity, because receiving transfers gives citizens clear incentives to target government officials with political action.

Table 4.5 also shows the dissimilar influence organizations have on different modes of political participation. Unions mobilize members to protest but are much less influential than other kinds of political organizations when it comes to mobilizing members to vote or participate in campaign activities. This is further evidence of unions' weakened capacity to mobilize workers into politics. Curiously, although nonpolitical organizations had no effect on overall levels of political activity, once we disaggregated political acts we can see that organizations in civil society do support contacting activity. However, membership in political organizations encourages participation in all kinds of political acts *except* contacting. Finally, political action of any kind is most likely when people are asked to participate by political elites.

Table 4.6 depicts differences across income groups for voting and contacting government officials. Table 4.4 showed that receiving government transfers was one of the important predictors of overall political activism. However, once we disaggregate the analysis by income level and by political activities, we see that government-spending programs enhance the political participation only of the poor and only for government contacting. Feelings of political efficacy matter for all activities and for all income groups. One somewhat unexpected finding is the positive effect on voting for all income groups when the PAN (as opposed to the PRI) is in power at the state level. Given the PAN's pro-business stance, I would have expected the poor to feel more alienated from politics when the PAN controlled the executive branches at both the federal and state levels. Perhaps this result suggests the power that democratization has for voting behavior, since early on in Mexico's democratic transition PAN victories signaled to voters that Mexico was indeed a democracy and that their vote would truly count (Camp 2004 and Lawson and Klesner 2004). PRD victories at the state level did not have

Table 4.6. Political Participation Models for Voting and Contacting, by Income (Logit)

Variables	Voting		Contacting government officials	
	Low income	High income	Low income	High income
INDIVIDUAL LEVEL				
Education				
Income	+++	+++	–	+
Male		+++		
Age	+++	+++		
Union member				
Political organization count		+++		
Nonpolitical organization count				++
POLITICAL OPPORTUNITIES				
Efficacy	+++	+++	++	++
Receive government transfers			++	
Political recruitment	+++		+++	+++
PRD in power at state level				++
PAN in power at state level	++	++		
	$LL = 1014.56$	$LL = 694.94$	$LL = 454.80$	$LL = 486.62$
	$X^2 = 41.90$	$X^2 = 79.47$	$X^2 = 27.33$	$X^2 = 77.44$
	X^2 prob. $p \le 0.000$	X^2 prob. $p \le 0.000$	X^2 prob. $p \le 0.007$	X^2 prob. $p \le 0.000$
	$N = 885$	$N = 676$	$N = 882$	$N = 674$

Source: CSES-CIDE 2003.

Notes: The dependent variables are dichotomous variables indicating whether an individual undertook one of the political acts.
+ Positive effect at 0.1 level   ++ Positive effect significant at 0.05 level   +++ Positive effect significant at 0.01 level
– Negative effect at 0.1 level LL = log likelihood

this effect, and only increased political contacting among the most affluent. This result might be skewed by the influence of Mexico City, where the PRD dominates and which has a greater proportion of medium- and high-income residents. Because most federal ministries and the offices of the legislative branch are located in the capital, in some ways national politics are local politics for residents, who face lower costs to contacting than Mexicans living in the provinces (Holzner 2007a and 2007b).

It turns out that membership in political organizations, which showed up as a significant predictor of voting behavior in the full sample, only mobilized middle- and high-income Mexicans. Similarly, although it was encouraging to see that nonpolitical organizations mobilized Mexicans to contact government officials, their positive effect is limited to the affluent, who already have more resources with which to participate. This is a problematic result for theories of civil society that see it as directly supporting democracy and democratic outcomes, especially in its role of instilling democratic values, mobilizing interests, and holding the state accountable. In Mexico it appears that civil society is not only divided and stratified, as Jonathan Shefner (2008) has reminded us, but also contributes to political inequality, skewing the voices heard by the state and to whom it is ultimately accountable.[29] In contrast, and somewhat ironically, clientelist political recruitment is one of the only factors that holds some promise for reducing the participation gap between the rich and the poor. Whether clientelist voting gives the poor a real voice or encourages more autonomous participation in the future is debatable, but we would be hard-pressed to argue that more voting is worse than less, even if it is clientelistic voting. This is especially true today because the secrecy of the ballot is guaranteed in Mexico, giving the poor opportunities to shirk on their side of the clientelist bargain: they are now free to accept payment from their political boss but then vote for whomever they wish (Magaloni 2006).[30]

The analysis in this chapter produced three important theoretical findings: (1) that the opening of political opportunities and positive institutional performances have robust and significant positive effects on political activism, even after controlling for socioeconomic factors, age, gender, and organizational involvement; (2) that institutions influence behavior in part through their effect on political attitudes; (3) and that institutional factors do not have uniform effects across income groups. These findings go a long way toward establishing the institutional origins of political inequality and suggest a need to reinterpret the standard socioeconomic status and resource theories of political participation. Specifically, excluding measures of political opportunities from regression models can bias the results by making the influence of socioeconomic and organizational measures appear greater than they truly are. Analyses that lump low- and high-income groups together risk missing important pieces of the story—namely that the process through which institutions shape political activity is not uniform across income groups. Therefore something like a "general theory of political participation" is probably out of our reach. The specific factors that enable and constrain activity will differ across political contexts and will affect different groups of people—the rich and poor, men and women, the young and old—differently. This should not be discouraging; it is as it should be. What we *can* generalize about is the mechanisms through which institutions matter, something we actually already understand quite a bit about.

The results also have important practical implications. Perhaps the most important lesson is that governments have powerful tools at their disposal to decrease the participatory gap between the rich and the poor, particularly in societies that struggle with large income inequalities. In particular, if properly structured, antipoverty programs can motivate the poor to become more engaged and active in politics, thus producing positive social, economic, and political outcomes at the same time. Over the longer term, if programs like Oportunidades can increase their reach and the amount of support they provide, they may create new kinds of political citizens among the poor who are socialized into democratic participation and eschew clientelist mobilization, much like the Social Security program in the United States helped created a highly active elderly population. A more troubling implication of the analysis is that civil society may not be a vehicle for promoting political equality and governmental accountability for all citizens in Mexico. On the contrary, Mexico's class, gender, ethnic, regional, and status hierarchies also divide its civil society, which then function as yet another mechanism for the perpetuation of power asymmetries in Mexico despite the best intentions of organizations themselves (Fox 2007 and Shefner 2008).

□ □ □ □ **CHAPTER 5** □ □ □ □

UNEVEN AND INCOMPLETE
DEMOCRATIZATION IN MEXICO

In order to understand how people behave, we have
to understand where they live.
—CLAUDINE GAY, 2001

While neoliberal reforms had powerful effects on the political attitudes and
activity of the poor, depressing their political involvement to levels much
lower than that of other groups, the shift away from an ISI development
model was only half of the massive institutional changes experienced by
Mexican citizens during the decade. The transition from a one-party authoritarian regime to a multiparty competitive democracy also occurred between
1990 and 2000, rewriting the rules of the political game and potentially
creating incentives and opportunities for participation that balanced out the
negative effect of economic reforms.

Although this democratic transformation has been long in the making, beginning by some accounts as early as 1977, most of the democratic
gains were made between 1990 and 2000. There were three key institutional transformations in Mexico's political process: the establishment of
free and fair elections with strong safeguards against systematic fraud; the
emergence of dynamic electoral competition between the PRI, the PAN, and
the PRD at the local, state, and national levels; and intragovernmental competition—that is, the competition that arises between political parties when
they control different branches or levels of government. This gives them all
opportunities to govern, wield enormous fiscal resources, and check each

other's behavior and power. Together these changes created a radically new strategic context for political mobilization and participation. Analyzing these major changes to Mexico's political process helps identify what effect these new opportunities and constraints had on citizen political activism.

The political science literature gives us reason to think the swift transition from autocracy to democracy created political openings and opportunities for participation for all. Research in Mexico and elsewhere has shown that political participation increases when elections are perceived to be free and fair, when elections are more competitive, where opposition parties win elections, and where the risk of state repression declines (Aldrich 1993, Barnes and Kaase 1979, Clarke and Acock 1989, Cook 1990, Davis 1983, Eldersveld and Ahmed 1978, Jenkins 1983, Klesner and Lawson 2000, Lawson and Klesner 2004, Macedo et al. 2005, McCann and Lawson 2003, Powell Jr. 1986, Rodríguez 1998, Tamayo and Valdés Zurita 1991, Tanaka 1995, and Tarrow 1998). However, the picture that emerges in Mexico is complex and inconsistent.

Contrary to the expectations of much of the scholarly literature, turnout has declined despite the elimination of fraud in national elections, intense electoral contests, and aggressive campaigning by all parties. Indeed, turnout reached an all-time low for congressional elections in 2003, and although it bounced back in the hotly contested 2006 presidential elections, it was still 5.5 percent below the turnout registered in 2000 and nearly 20 percent lower than in 1994. During the 2009 congressional elections a well-organized campaign prodded Mexicans to abstain or to soil their ballots, evidence of growing disenchantment with political parties and electoral politics (see also Camp 2006).[1] Survey evidence also shows that political participation was still stratified by income in 2006 (see figure 1.3), suggesting that the political process in Mexico continues to create obstacles for low-income citizens. Perhaps most important, the spread of political competition and of democratic political practices has been uneven in Mexico, creating a complex mix of pluralist enclaves coexisting with authoritarian strongholds and semidemocratic provincial regimes (Beer 2003; and Fox 1994a and 1996).

The mix of democratic openings and enduring authoritarianism creates a complex behavioral landscape in which democratic, autonomous, and elite challenging political behavior coexists with authoritarian and clientelistic practices that reproduce and reinforce the power of authoritarian leaders. It turns out that where someone lives in Mexico matters much more for their political attitudes and political behavior than whether they are rich or poor, educated or illiterate, young or old (see Klesner 2007 and Lawson 2006).

Still, Mexico's poor are much more likely to experience the authoritarian dark side of the political system, meaning that their choices and opportunities for participation are different, and probably much narrower, than the choices and opportunities available to more affluent actors.

Opposition Victories, Political Competition, and Reduction in Fraud

One of the defining characteristics of Mexico's political system between the 1930s and 1980s was the lack of meaningful political competition in elections at any level. The PRI regularly won local elections with 100 percent of the vote, it never lost a presidential or gubernatorial election, and won every single senate seat before 1988.[2] The PAN, a pro-business party established in the 1920s in northern Mexico, has been the most consistent challenger to the PRI. But until it won the 2000 elections, the PAN rarely received more than 20 percent of the vote in presidential elections (Shirk 2005). Numerous other parties, particularly on the left of the political spectrum, have come and gone since the 1920s, some even won municipal elections, but none of them ever posed a serious challenge to the PRI's electoral hegemony. Many of these small parties—such as the PPS (Partido Popular Socialista) and the PARM (Partido Auténtico de la Revolución Mexicana) during the 1960s and 1970s and later the PT (Partido del Trabajo) and the PVEM (Partido Verde Ecologista Mexicano) in the 1990s—made up a loyal opposition that exercised little autonomy from the PRI (Levy and Székely 1987).

Most explanations of the PRI's electoral dominance emphasize the party's corporatist structure that allowed it to control the political activity of labor, peasants, and state employees. The PRI also used electoral fraud to pad its own votes and dissuade potential dissidents from defecting to opposition parties. Also, there was the PRI's occasional but decisive use of violence to repress groups that challenged the state or sought to democratize the political system (Greene 2007, Langston 2002, and Magaloni 2006). However, these strategies alone could not have preserved the legitimacy and stability of Mexico's one-party authoritarian regime for so long. The *legal* foundations for Mexico's electoral authoritarianism and the PRI's ability to monopolize state offices were set in place with the electoral law passed in 1946 were also important (Levy and Székely 1987).[3] Key features of this electoral system included (1) a single member simple plurality (SMSP) electoral system to elect representatives to the Chamber of Deputies; (2) the self-certification of elections through which newly elected members of congress confirmed the election results that put them into power; (3) elections were organized and the votes counted by the Ministry of the Interior; (4) provisions that made it difficult for new political parties to emerge; and (5) an absence of real campaign finance laws, which allowed the PRI to use its almost unlimited access to state resources to outspend opposition parties by a huge margin.[4] Each of these five features would have to change before elections in Mexico could become free, fair, and competitive.

The most important initiative for the long-term prospects of democracy in Mexico was the creation of the Federal Electoral Institute (Instituto Federal Electoral, IFE) in 1990, a decentralized entity in charge of organizing federal-level elections. Although at first the IFE remained under the control of the Ministry of the Interior and had little independent power to organize and monitor elections, over time its power and autonomy were bolstered in ways that produced free and fair elections by 1997, making possible the PAN's landmark victory in the 2000 presidential elections (Crespo 2004 and Gómez Tagle 2004). Today the IFE is the institutional keystone of Mexican democracy and remains one of the few political institutions trusted by most Mexicans.

During its first few years in operation, the IFE implemented a series of reforms to minimize the likelihood of fraud in elections. One of the PRI's most common strategies to ensure electoral victories by large margins was to add votes to its own tally rather than taking them away from opposition parties (Cornelius 1996, 60).[5] This was accomplished by inflating the voter registries in certain districts to allow brigades of PRI supporters to vote in multiple polling places, or simply by stuffing ballot boxes before the polls opened. To prevent this kind of fraud, the IFE was given control over the voter registry and voter identification cards, and both became subject to external audits by each party. New voter identification cards were issued that included the person's name, address, photograph, signature, and fingerprint to safeguard against counterfeiting. Polling booth officials were no longer to be party members but ordinary citizens chosen independently of their party affiliations. To prevent the stuffing of ballot boxes before the polls opened, the IFE began using transparent ballot boxes and numbered ballots. To prevent people from voting multiple times, each voter had his or her fingers marked with indelible ink after casting a ballot (Cornelius 1996 and Domínguez and Poiré 1999). Since then, there have been additional improvements—in particular, guarantees for the secrecy of the ballot and efforts to educate citizens about what kinds of activities qualify as electoral crimes.

Further reforms in 1994 overhauled the IFE, giving citizen councilors more power and eliminating electoral self-certification by granting the IFE and the recently created Federal Electoral Tribunal (Tribuno Federal Electoral, TFE) the power to certify the election of federal deputies and sena-tors.[6] Although during the 1994 presidential election the PRI could (and did) outspend all other parties by a large margin, and even though it received a disproportionate share of the media coverage, the victory of the PRI's presidential candidate, Ernesto Zedillo, is generally regarded as legitimate (Crespo 2004 and Gómez Tagle 2004).[7] The final bastions of the PRI's elec-toral authoritarianism crumbled with electoral reforms proposed in 1996 and passed by congress in 1997 that finally eliminated all government con-trol over elections by placing them fully in the hands of a strengthened Fed-eral Electoral Institute. The 1997 law also changed the way campaigns were financed to level the playing field between the PRI and the opposition. The new law set upper limits for campaign spending, limited private sources of financing to 10 percent of total campaign expenditures, established new oversight mechanisms for campaign spending, greatly increased public fi-nancing for campaigns, and expanded access to radio and television for all parties (Domínguez 1999 and Gómez Tagle 2004). Because it was still the largest party in the country, the PRI received a larger share of this public funding and media coverage than the PAN or the PRD. However, under the new proportional-financing formulas both the PAN and the PRD saw huge increases in public financing, giving them the resources with which to mount effective electoral challenges to the PRI (Bruhn 1999).

As important as these reforms were for establishing truly free and fair national elections in Mexico, other reforms were necessary to increase their competitiveness. The first serious efforts to increase the competitiveness of elections in Mexico can be traced to the 1977 reforms of the electoral system that modified the winner-take-all system by creating one hundred propor-tional representation seats in the Chamber of Deputies, increasing the to-tal number of seats from three hundred to four hundred.[8] The law had an immediate effect on political competition. Three new parties formed and competed in the 1979 midterm elections.[9] By 1985 nine parties had partici-pated in national elections—five more than before the reforms. President de la Madrid's administration (1982–1988) enlarged the lower house once again in 1986, creating an additional one hundred proportional representa-tive seats in the Chamber of Deputies, bringing the total number of seats to five hundred, its current number (Crespo 2004, 69–70). Political competi-tion was further enhanced in 1996 with reforms that introduced a complex system of proportional and minority representation in the way senators were elected, dramatically increasing minority party representation in that cham-ber (Díaz-Cayeros 2005 and Gómez Tagle 2004, 94–95).

Decentralization in Mexico was another institutional innovation that enhanced political competition and created new incentives for citizens to become involved in politics. Although Mexico's constitution outlined a federal system similar to the one that exists in the United States, in practice almost all power was concentrated in the federal government, with most of that in the hands of the president. According to Richard Fagen and William Tuohy (1972, 20–21), in Mexico "each successive level of government is weaker, more dependent, and more impoverished than the level above. Since the municipality is at the bottom of the federal-state-local chain, it is in reality . . . the least autonomous unit of government in the republic. An *ayuntamiento* or municipal government is normally constituted at the pleasure of state authorities, is in the control of very few funds, and is limited juridically and politically to caretaker and administrative functions."[10] Given this rigid power hierarchy, the political energies of political parties and of ordinary citizens were often focused on state and national politics, hindering the development of alternatives to the PRI at the municipal level.

Serious efforts to decentralize power began under the de la Madrid administration with reforms that granted municipal government the capacity to raise revenues on their own through property taxes and from the provision of public services (Rodríguez 1997, 73–76). President Ernesto Zedillo (1994–2000) made decentralization a priority in his administration and designed a program called New Federalism to further strengthen the financial and administrative capacity of municipal and state governments (ibid., 83–88). As a result, the situation for state and local governments has changed dramatically. For the first time municipal governments, particularly those located in larger urban centers, had the means and the technical capacity to carry out infrastructure projects, fund police forces, and carry out activities of great relevance to residents, making them increasingly important arenas for political participation (Cabrero Mendoza 1998 and Ward 1998). Nevertheless, analysts generally agree that the push to decentralize power away from the federal level benefited state governments much more than municipalities (Cabrero Mendoza 1998, Díaz-Cayeros 2004, and Rodríguez 1997).

These institutional changes had positive consequences for political competition, electoral choice, and ultimately democratization. Opposition candidates began competing and winning local elections in both the north and the south of the country in the 1980s, when the PRI's hold over national politics was still firm. During the 1990s both the PAN and the PRD focused on building regional party organizations where they had some electoral strength—in the north and the center for the PAN and in the south and in

Mexico City for the PRD, building their portfolio of electoral victories as they prepared to take on the PRI at the national level (Klesner 2005; see also Shirk 2005 on the PAN and Bruhn 1997 on the PRD). The devolution of fiscal powers to state and local government was immensely important in these efforts. On the one hand, it gave opposition parties enormous resources with which to build party organizations and enhance their electoral prospects locally and nationally.[11] On the other hand, it gave them the resources with which to demonstrate to skeptical voters that they could govern effectively and therefore be viable alternatives to the PRI at the national level (Magaloni 1999). Indeed, the PRI lost control of many state and municipal governments well before it lost control of the presidency in 2000. As recently as 1988, the PRI controlled 100 percent of all governorships, 90 percent of all municipal governments, and more than 90 percent of all elected positions. By the time Fox became the first opposition party president in seven decades, the PAN and the PRD already governed in nearly half of Mexico's states and municipalities, in most of its large cities, and in many regional capitals.

Intragovernmental political competition also increased rapidly in congressional elections during the decade. Early electoral reforms in 1977 and 1986, coupled with growing voter disenchantment with the PRI, sparked an increase in the number of winner-take-all districts that were competitive, but as late as 1991 the PRI still did not face a significant electoral challenge in more than 60 percent of the congressional races. Electoral competitiveness increased dramatically in the 1994 elections when the IFE organized a presidential election, monitored campaign spending, and tallied the votes as an independent agency for the first time. Although the PRI once again captured the presidency and won a majority in congress, the vast majority of congressional elections were competitive that year (Klesner 2005). By 1997 fewer than 10 percent of districts could be characterized as PRI-dominant. More important, the PRI lost control of the Chamber of Deputies for the first time, marking the beginning of an era in which Congress could and would exert its constitutional prerogative to check presidential power.

These aggregate numbers understate the symbolic importance of many opposition victories during the 1990s. Each time the PAN or the PRD won a gubernatorial election, it added a chink in the PRI's armor while convincing Mexican voters that opposition party candidates could govern effectively, making them more viable candidates for future contests. Opposition parties, the PAN in particular, also governed in many provincial capitals in the industrial north as well as in poor states like Oaxaca and Chiapas, while the PRD made its biggest splash by winning control over Mexico City's government in 1997 and 2000, giving both parties more visibility and clout than the sheer number of victories might suggest. One statistic is particularly telling: by the end of the decade opposition parties governed in cities and states that made up more than half the country's population.

As important as the emergence of electoral competition was for Mexico's democratic transition, the rise of intragovernmental competition, measured by the number of elected government posts controlled by opposition parties, may play a larger role in shaping political participation. This kind of political competition receives less attention, but it is relevant for the case of Mexico, where one party has had a monopoly on political power.[12] Although electoral competition sends signals to citizens that their vote matters in established democracies, in dominant one-party systems citizens have little reason to think that a vote for the opposition will actually yield a victory until the dominant party loses elections with some consistency. In addition, without also demonstrating that they could govern effectively, opposition parties in Mexico found it difficult to convince citizens that they were a credible alternative to the PRI (Magaloni 1999). Thus, early on in Mexico's democratic transition, intragovernmental competition may have been a more important motivator of political participation than political contestation alone.

Another difference is that electoral competition is likely to have its greatest impact on electoral modes of political participation, such as voting and volunteering for campaigns, while intragovernmental competition should impact government-directed modes of participation such as petitioning and protests as well. In addition, while the act of voting may increase people's sense of political efficacy, research has shown that voting may be less important for efficacy than seeing one's preferred party win an election (Clarke and Acock 1989). Therefore electoral victories by the PAN and the PRD should boost supporters' feelings of efficacy and also their political participation more generally (Camp 2006).

Democratic and Autocratic Subnational Games

The transition from a dominant one-party system to a competitive multiparty democracy is without a doubt one of the most significant transformations of Mexico's political environment. However, there are several important caveats to this otherwise optimistic story. First, at least until 2003, both the PRD and the PAN were still regional parties that found it difficult to win elections outside of their strongholds (Klesner 2005 and Shirk 2005). So although Mexico had a three-party system at the national level, it is more accurate to describe Mexico's party system at the time as parallel two-party systems, with PRI-PAN competition in the north and center and PRI-PRD competition primarily in the center and south. Few states had a true thee-party system (Oaxaca may have been one of them, for a time), and fewer still saw competition between the PRD and the PAN.[13]

Second, the left did not live up to the promise it showed by almost defeating the PRI in the 1988 presidential elections. In 1991, 1994, 1997, and 2000, the PRD was competitive in only a relatively small number of federal districts, managing to win only 8, 16, 25, and 19 percent of the vote in each of these elections, respectively. As for Cuahutémoc Cárdenas, after officially receiving 33 percent of the vote in 1988, he never again won more than 20 percent of the vote in a national election. The strong showing of the PRD in the 2006 presidential election, when it came within 250,000 votes of winning, turned out to be short-lived as well, as its support dropped by nearly two-thirds in the next national elections.[14] Part of the weakness is also due to the PRD's internal divisions, disorganization, lack of programmatic platforms, and inability to build a strong nationwide party organization with enough loyal cadres to nominate candidates from within the party structure (Bruhn 1997 and Wuhs 2008). To be competitive in state and local elections, it often had to rely on defectors from the PRI and the PAN who had questionable loyalties to the party (Bruhn 1999). Throughout the 1990s, and even into the next decade, there were large swaths of the country in which the left was not a factor in elections at any level. This weakness of the left in Mexico continues to be a constraint on the political involvement of the poor, who may not see opportunities for activism when only the pro-business PAN is competitive and able to win elections.

Most concerning is the survival and sometimes the strengthening of subnational autocracies in many states and hundreds of municipalities across Mexico. Although studies have argued that political competition at the provincial level has been an important catalyst for democratic changes at the national level (see Beer 2003), the subnational political arena is also where authoritarian leaders are making rather successful last stands. The strongest resistance to democratization typically comes from state governors who use the power of their position to perpetuate local autocracies even as national politics become more competitive and open. Although opposition parties compete for power in such settings, the dominant party typically wins a large majority of legislative seats (in addition to its control over the executive), which enables it to exercise unchecked influence over political institutions and processes. As a result, electoral fraud and misconduct, along with other abuses of power and challenges to the rule of law, go largely unchecked at the local level (Magaloni 2006, 32–36).

Indeed, fraud is still a common occurrence in many state and local elections across Mexico. Although the bolstered IFE has been able to guarantee free and fair elections at the federal level after 1997, state and local elections are still under the responsibility of state electoral authorities (called State Electoral Institutes, or Institutos Electorales Estatales, IEEs). The quality, professionalism, and independence of these bodies from state authorities are very uneven.[15] Many of the IEEs are still susceptible to manipulation from powerful governors and frequently enable electoral mischief (Gómez Tagle 1997). As a result, vote buying, stolen ballot boxes, coerced or mobilized voting by local bosses, and even computer crashes when the PRI is losing are still part of Mexico's electoral landscape.

Public opinion surveys that ask respondents whether they thought elections were conducted cleanly and fairly are a good way to measure the pervasiveness of authoritarian practices across Mexico. The 2006 CSES-CIDE survey (Comparativo de los Sistemas Electorales–Centro de Investigación y Docencia Económicas) asked people to evaluate the 2006 presidential elections on a five-point scale according to whether they were clean, somewhat clean, neither clean nor fraudulent, somewhat fraudulent, or totally marred by fraud. Overall perceptions of fraud were quite high (32 percent) and nearly twice as high as in 2000. However, perceptions of fraud varied significantly across states (figure 5.1), ranging from a low of 4 percent in Nuevo León to a high of 61 percent in Mexico City. Perceptions of fraud were highest in poor southern states, particularly in states where the PRD won the largest share of the vote. In Chiapas, Guerrero, Mexico City, Mexico state, Oaxaca, Tabasco, and Tlaxcala—all states carried by the PRD—more people doubted the cleanliness of elections than thought they had been free and fair.[16]

Electoral irregularities appear to be much more common in poor states, towns, and neighborhoods (del Pozo and Aparicio 2001), which means that the poor experience the authoritarian side of Mexico's political system more consistently than higher-income citizens.[17] Indeed, according to CSES survey results, the poor consistently perceive elections as more fraudulent than the more affluent. Figure 5.2 compares the perceptions of electoral fraud across income groups between 1997 and 2006, precisely the period *after* elections were supposed to have become free and fair in Mexico. In 1997, 2000, and 2003 perceptions of fraud were highest among low-income respondents, although perceptions of fraud spiked for the most affluent in 2006.[18] This per-

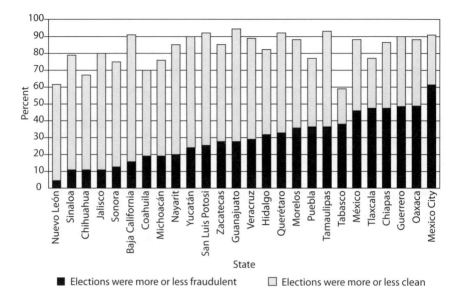

Figure 5.1. Perceptions of Fraud by State, 2006. The survey measured perceptions of fraud on a five-point scale. The figure shows the percentage of respondents who thought the elections were more or less fraudulent (that is, those who
thought they were very or somewhat fraudulent) and the percentage who thought
they were more or less clean (that is, those who thought they were clean or somewhat clean). The numbers do not add up to 100 percent because they do not include a neutral category: neither clean nor fraudulent. *Source:* CSES-CIDE 2006.

ception gap across income groups may help account for lower turnout rates
by the poor since perceptions of fairness of elections is among the most powerful predictors of turnout in Mexico (Domínguez and McCann 1996, Lawson and Klesner 2004, and Levin and Alvarez 2009).

It would be naïve to dismiss these subnational autocracies and authoritarian practices as anachronistic remnants of Mexico's authoritarian past,
destined to wither away as democratic rules, norms, and practices take root
and strengthen elsewhere. The coexistence of democratic and authoritarian party systems is not a uniquely Mexican phenomenon. Edward Gibson
(2005) has reminded us that subnational authoritarianism is a fact of life in
most democracies in the developing and postcommunist world. The empirical literature on clientelism is also full of examples of political machines that
thrived in rich democracies, including the powerful party machines in the
United States and Italy that survived well into the twentieth century (Banfield and Wilson 1965, Chubb 1981, Erie 1988, Key 1956, Scott 1969, and

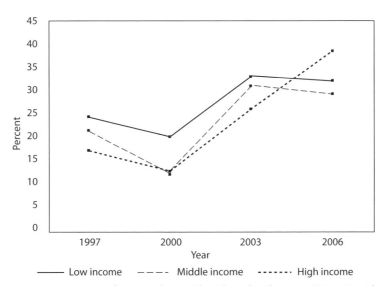

Figure 5.2. Percentage of Respondents Who Thought Elections Were Not Clean, 1997–2006. Low income: 0–3 times the minimum wage; middle income: 3–7 times the minimum wage; high income: more than 7 times the minimum wage. *Source:* CSES 1997–2006.

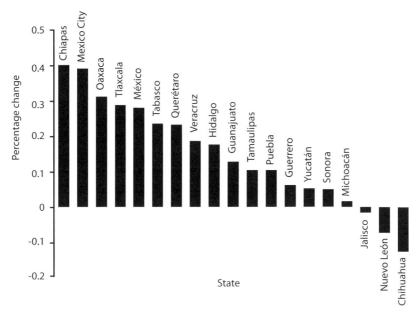

Figure 5.3. Change in Perception of Fraud between the 2000 and 2006 Mexican Presidential Elections, by State. *Source:* CSES-CIDE 2000 and 2006.

Wolfinger 1972). There is no reason to think Mexico will be an exception to these patterns. On the contrary, Wayne Cornelius (1999, 11) sees local and state-level governments as "the principal source of inertia and resistance to democratization, rather than the prime breeding ground for democratic advances." After declining between 1997 and 2000, as we would expect given the strengthening of the IFE, perceptions of fraud increased sharply for all income groups in the most recent elections (see figure 5.2), a most troubling sign for the consolidation of democracy in Mexico. Furthermore, figure 5.3 shows that perceptions of fraud increased in all but three states included in the 2000 and 2006 CSES surveys, in some cases by as much as 40 percent, suggesting that authoritarian practices are gaining an upper hand over democratic ones in most Mexican states.

Democratization and the Emergence of Competitive Clientelism

How do we explain this stubborn resilience of authoritarian practices, particularly in state and local politics? We can trace part of the answer to the enduring strength of clientelist politics in Mexico, which continues to structure the political competition between parties and condition the political behavior of ordinary citizens. Political parties in Mexico do compete with each other on the basis of programmatic appeals, sophisticated campaigns to mobilize partisans and appeal to undecided voters, and by demonstrating they can govern effectively. But this is only half the story. A great deal of electoral competition in Mexico still follows the logic of competitive clientelism, in which national political parties compete by establishing a network of links to existing patron-client clusters at the local level and incorporating them into their structure. Under this dynamic parties grow not by appealing to independent voters but by recruiting unattached leaders of clientelist networks or by luring them away from rival parties. Candidates in elections are often the leaders of these clientelist clusters, who have demonstrated the capacity to mobilize large numbers of supporters using whatever means necessary (Scott 1972). As these patrons win elections and gain in power, the political process becomes increasingly marred by fraud, vote buying, voter intimidation, co-optation of opposition leaders, *dedazos*, and the monopolization of political institutions to ensure that elites can carry out these strategies with impunity.[19] In short, politics proceeds much as it did during the glory days of the PRI.

Today, both kinds of electoral competition coexist and intermingle in Mexico without clear-cut boundaries, influencing electoral dynamics and voter behavior locally and nationally. Despite losing its hegemonic position, the PRI has continued to cultivate and rely on state and local-level political machines to win elections at all levels.[20] Clientelist practices have also spread beyond autocratic PRI enclaves and rural areas, influencing electoral dynamics across Mexico and in national elections. The PRD achieved much of its electoral success during the 1990s by luring away disaffected leaders of PRI factions, who in turn mobilized their clients to vote for the PRD using tried-and-true strategies of vote buying, promising access to government patronage, and in some cases electoral fraud (Bruhn 1997 and Hilgers 2005). The PAN, which has always been critical of clientelist mobilization strategies, has also gotten into the act recently, driven by the imperative to win elections.[21] Studies of clientelistic voting during the 2000 presidential elections show that the PAN was just as likely as the PRI to engage in election-day manipulation of voters (del Pozo and Aparicio 2001 and del Mercado 2007) and that vote buying and coercion (*compra y coacción*) were most common in urban areas where the PAN was competitive (Cornelius 2004).

The staying power of clientelism, despite greater organizational pluralism, increased political competition, clean elections, and drying up of state patronage is puzzling and largely unanticipated by recent scholarly work on Mexico's process of democratization. The optimistic expectation was that greater political competition and electoral transparency, particularly at the local level, would strengthen the hand of clients and make it harder for patrons to coerce and cajole them into political activities. But these expectations have proved too optimistic. So what explains the resilience of clientelism in Mexico? The answer to the puzzle contains a great deal of irony. The same reforms that enabled a democratic multiparty system to emerge at the national level—decentralization, campaign finance reforms, and neoliberal reforms that delinked many voters from the PRI—also produced provincial party systems where the logic of competitive clientelism drove parties' efforts to compete and win elections.

Austerity programs and free-market economic reforms altered the role of the state in the economy, decreasing the amount of patronage available to the president and to the PRI's corporatist organizations. This loosened the links between national PRI organizations and local elites, making them and their rank-and-file supporters available for mobilization by opposition parties *and* by alternative clientelist networks. In response to these changes in the electorate, all major parties repositioned themselves as catchall parties to attract independent voters (Klesner 2005 and Wuhs 2008). All of them, though the PAN less than the PRD and the PRI, also sought out links to local and regional leaders of clientelist networks who had the power to mobilize large numbers of supporters for whichever party secured his or her allegiance. Because the economic reforms have failed to create jobs in sufficient numbers with sufficient wages to pull millions of Mexicans out of poverty, Mexico's poor remain vulnerable to clientelist manipulation and may actually choose to support authoritarian elites instead of democratic alternatives.

Decentralization policies and the PRI's loss of control over the federal government also did not end clientelism; they simply shifted its apex further down the chain, so that now governors—and in the case of Mexico City, the mayor—are the absolute leaders of extensive clientelistic networks. Decentralization significantly strengthened state governments relative to both local and federal governments, giving governors the financial and political autonomy to pursue their own self-interested ends not beholden to any one or any group higher up in the party structure. Sometimes they govern democratically, but many have no intention of doing so. Instead, a number of autocratic governors have used their financial and political resources to assert control over regional political machines, to isolate and displace rivals from power, and to limit electoral competition through both legal and illegal means (Gibson 2005, Hernández-Rodríguez 2003, and Magaloni 2006). Many also used their capacity to mobilize large numbers of supporters to enhance their standing at the national level by delivering votes to other candidates from their party in federal elections and by demanding representation of allies in important government posts (Gibson 2005).

In this institutional context increased political competition and electoral victories by opposition parties have helped patron-client dynamics to survive and even thrive. Though losing control over the presidency might once have been considered devastating to state and local PRI political machines when power was more centralized, by the time Vicente Fox became president in 2000, governors had carved out a great deal of autonomy from the federal government and rebuilt their local-level political machines. Indeed, there is evidence that the election of Fox and his decision to not intervene in state-level political conflicts (Eisenstadt 2004) only served to strengthen the position of authoritarian governors, who no longer faced challenges from PRI rivals within the central government (Gibson 2005). The imperative of political parties to win electoral contests has also driven many of them, sometimes willfully and sometimes by accident, to engage in practices that strengthened patron-client networks.[22]

One common response to increasing electoral competition was to recruit local leaders who commanded the loyalty (or at least were able to control the political participation) of large numbers of people.[23] Although this linking to local networks does not necessarily reproduce clientelist practices, given how pervasive and entrenched clientelist networks and practices were in Mexico, that outcome was almost inevitable. The PRD built its early portfolio of electoral victories by running candidates who had defected from the PRI, bringing with them the support of their local clientelist network (Bruhn 1997).[24] This happened most commonly when one PRI faction was shut out from power, as occurred in the gubernatorial elections in Zacatecas in 1998 and in Baja California, Tlaxcala, and Nayarit in 1999 or in scores of local elections across the country.[25] Since then, small parties like Convergencia and Nueva Alianza have achieved regional and national prominence very quickly by mobilizing the supporters of dissident PRI factions.[26] The PAN resisted this strategy the longest, relying instead on candidates with proven loyalty to the PAN or businessmen who did not have much prior political experience. However, the PAN has also come to rely more and more on these kinds of links, especially since its disappointing showing in the 2003 midterm elections (Wuhs 2008).

Electoral competition also created strong incentives for local clientelist leaders to switch party allegiances to preserve their access to government resources, without which they could not maintain control over members' political activity. This was especially true for PRI dissidents whose faction found itself out of favor with dominant state or national party groups. Ironically, the more opposition parties compete for the allegiance of these leaders, the more leverage they have within the party structure to exert their influence and demand more prominent posts for themselves and their allies. In a relatively short period of time, clientelist factions came to dominate party competition in hundreds of local and state elections, forcing all parties and candidates to play by the rules of the clientelist game or risk being shut out of power altogether.

The crucial point is that this strengthening and proliferation of authoritarian and clientelist practices in Mexico happened because of increased electoral competition, not in spite of it.[27] As a result, much of what passes as multiparty competition today is really competition between rival clientelist leaders who adopt the party label that gives them the best chance of winning elections and who mobilize supporters by promising more access to government patronage. These local-level practices inevitably influence national elections as well, as parties come to rely on local power brokers to deliver the votes of their supporters and encourage them to attend campaign rallies and events. If successful, local patrons can gain enough leverage within the party to demand that they or that their allies be nominated as candidates for national-level posts. This allows the clientelist practices to contaminate what had hitherto been relatively democratic national-level political processes.

The consequences for the future of democratization in Mexico are not promising. Early research has found abundant evidence that decentralization and political competition in state and local elections created positive feedback loops to the national level in ways that strengthened democratic institutions and practices at all levels (Beer 2003). This may have been true for a time, and may still be true in certain parts of Mexico—Guanajuato, Nuevo León, and Querétaro, for example. However, when political competition is based on competition between rival clientelist clusters—as it is in Guerrero, Mexico City, Oaxaca, and elsewhere—the institutional consequences tend to be nearly the opposite of what Caroline Beer has observed: stronger executives, less separation of powers and professional legislatures, less accountability, less rule of law, and less representation; in short, less democracy (Gibson 2005, Hernandez-Rodríguez 2003, Hiskey and Bowler 2005, and Holzner 2009). The reality is that widespread democratic party competition coexists with perhaps equally widespread clientelist competition in Mexico. Both coexist, not as parallel systems that do not interact—democratic politics in the north and at the national level immune from authoritarian practices in the south and in Mexico City—but as interlocking webs of mutual influence and interaction, where it is sometimes difficult to distinguish one from the other.

A basic lesson that emerges from the preceding analysis is that where someone lives in Mexico matters for how they experience the political process and for how they behave politically. Thus we might find that two people with identical backgrounds, educational and income levels, and political beliefs participate very differently in the political life of their communities if they find themselves in different places, say Monterrey or Oaxaca. Mexico's 2006 presidential election confirmed how important regional differences have become. This election was the closest and most contested in recent memory. In the end the PAN's candidate, Felipe Calderón, edged out the PRD's Andrés Manuel López Obrador by the narrowest of margins: 35.9 percent to 35.3 percent. Despite the polarizing class rhetoric of the campaign, region not socioeconomic class was the dominant cleavage in the election (Klesner 2007 and Lawson 2006). Each candidate won sixteen states, Calderón mostly in the center and the north, López Obrador in Mexico City and the south. However, within each state the candidates won what were essentially landslide victories: the average margin of victory for the PAN in the sixteen states it won was 23 percent, while the PRD's average margin of victory was 17 percent. Where someone lived in Mexico also affected people's basic political beliefs and opinions about the political process. For example, whereas 93 percent of Calderón supporters considered the elections to have been clean, 81 percent of López Obrador supporters considered them dirty; supporters of the PAN are also much more likely than supporters of the PRD to believe that Mexico is now a democracy (Camp 2006).

A core question is how Mexico's overlapping democratic and authoritarian political contexts affect the political activity of ordinary people in Mexico. Chapter 6 tackles this question using the same combination of in-depth interviews and representative survey data used in chapters 3 and 4. Because where people live in Mexico matters for how they behave, the next section describes Oaxaca's complex local politics to provide some context for the interview evidence presented in chapter 6. Some readers may object that politics in Oaxaca is not representative of politics in the rest of Mexico. Fair enough. By the same token, politics in Mexico City or Guanajuato are also not representative of the rest of Mexico. Place matters in Mexico, so any analysis of how the political system works and what effect it has on citizen attitudes and behavior needs to be sensitive to the importance of place. Nonetheless, because authoritarian state-level politics coexist with relatively democratic and pluralistic enclaves in Oaxaca, politics in the state does reflect broader political dynamics found across Mexico, giving us a window into how these two systems interact and what effect they have on the opinions and behaviors of ordinary Mexicans.

Political Change and Continuity in Oaxaca

What did the political context in Oaxaca look like during this period? Though a strong democratic and antiestablishment streak runs through Oaxaca's political history, on the whole state-level politics are among the most authoritarian in Mexico and epitomize how subnational autocratic leaders can survive (and thrive) despite national-level democratization.[28] The opposition never won control over the state government, losing every election for governor held since the 1930s, and never came close to winning a majority of seats in the state's legislature. The PRI faced its stiffest challenge in the 2004 gubernatorial elections, but it still managed to retain control of the governor's seat in elections marred by allegations of fraud. It won 60 percent (twenty of forty-two) of the seats in the state legislature—the maximum number possible given the state's system of proportional representation (Gibson 2005 and Holzner 2002).

As a result, the PRI in Oaxaca governs much as it always has, with none of the institutional benefits that electoral competition is supposed to bring: the state still has an authoritarian executive who faces few or no checks from the state legislature, and the PRI still recruits unpopular candidates to run in elections. The state government is notorious for its lack of responsiveness and accountability; it uses its supermajorities to unilaterally control state-level institutions and perpetrate electoral misconduct and engages in aggressive vote-buying campaigns through its clientelist networks. From the perspective of individual citizens, particularly opposition supporters, the political situation appears little changed, which is generating a great deal of frustration, disillusionment, and disengagement from politics despite democratic gains at the national level.[29]

It is also important to recognize that local politics in Oaxaca is unique in several ways. With 570 municipalities, Oaxaca has by far the largest number of municipalities of any of Mexico's thirty-one states.[30] This means that municipalities tend to be small in size, in the number of villages or *agencias* that exist within municipal boundaries as well as in the number of inhabitants. This creates a context in which local governance is highly fragmented but potentially also more representative and accountable because the population tends to be more homogeneous and local leaders have close ties to the community. On the flip side, because of their small size, remote location, and poverty, most of Oaxaca's rural towns have few means to raise funds themselves and depend almost completely on financing from the state and federal governments.

Another unique feature of Oaxaca's political landscape is the large number of municipalities ruled by *usos y costumbres*, or customary law.[31] Oaxaca is one of the most ethnically diverse states in Mexico, and many small towns have preserved their traditional cargo system inherited from precolonial times (see Stephen 1991 for details). The physical and cultural remoteness of municipalities from the influence of the federal government means that many have maintained a great deal of autonomy from the central state. Many municipalities were able to preserve local political institutions and insulate themselves from excessive control by the PRI and the expanding state. Although the PRI had nominally dominated elections in rural municipalities in Oaxaca, capturing 100 percent of the vote in the vast majority of local elections, a closer analysis reveals that this control was superficial. In most cases rural communities elected their leadership according to traditional practices (usually in open assemblies) several weeks before the official election date. Then, on the date of the elections, these local leaders were presented as the winning PRI candidates with no competition from other parties. As a practical matter, there has been little organized presence of any political party, including the PRI, in the majority of rural municipalities in the state of Oaxaca (Díaz Montes 1994).[32]

The uneven presence of the PRI and the national bureaucracy is true of larger towns as well. Writing about Juchitán, a city located in the southern part of the Isthmus of Tehuantepec, Jeffrey Rubin (1996) has emphasized the capacity of political elites in the region to exercise a significant degree of local autonomy, based in part on Zapotec language and ritual practices: "The PRI barely existed in the isthmus between 1930 and 1960, with power exercised primarily by a local *cacique*, often in opposition to incursions by the central state rather than as a mediator for state-centered development and political control" (ibid., 104). Through much of the 1980s and 1990s the town was governed by the COCEI, a coalition of students, workers, and peasants that has "proved to be one of the most militant and enduring popular movements in Mexico" (ibid., 105). The case of Juchitán and other municipalities in Oaxaca challenges the dominant narrative of the origins of Mexico's transition to democracy that emphasized the electoral opposition by PAN militants in the industrialized states of northern Mexico. Democratic movements in rural communities in the states of Guerrero, Oaxaca, and Veracruz have contested the hegemony of the PRI since the revolution, in some cases winning local elections years before the PAN did so in the north.

As with the rest of Mexico, political competition in Oaxaca began at the municipal level, then trickled up to higher levels of government. The PRD has had the most success among opposition parties, winning 29 municipal elections in 1998 and 36 in 2001 (of 152), but the party is plagued by factional infighting and has had trouble developing a strong organizational base outside of the Isthmus region, where the COCEI filled the party ranks with experienced organizers. Although the PAN won 2 successive elections in the state capital and controls several other urban areas in the state, it has a thin organizational presence elsewhere. In the 1998 municipal elections, for example, it failed to win a single vote in 101 of the 152 elections and received less than 15 percent of the vote in 117 of the 152 municipalities (77 percent). In 2001, the PAN failed to run candidates in 34 percent of municipal elections, while the PRD did not run candidates in 17 of 152 local elections. The PAN did slightly better in 2001 but suffered a severe setback when it lost control of the capital city's government for the first time in six years.

Given the weakness of opposition parties, the amount of choice citizens have is unevenly distributed across Oaxaca's municipalities. Residents of the capital city and other urban areas in the state have quite a bit of choice, while the majority of people living in rural areas have almost none. And because municipalities, especially rural ones, depend on resources disbursed by the state and federal governments, which at the time of my interviews were still dominated by the PRI, the actual scope of choice available to the poor in Oaxaca was narrower still. The four municipalities in Oaxaca where I carried out my interviews represent much of the diversity of local political opportunity structures that exist across Mexico. La Ciénega epitomizes local politics, where the PRI still dominates by mobilizing patron-client links to exclude other parties from power. Two of the municipalities have competitive local party systems, the city of Oaxaca with PAN-PRI competition that is typical of regional capitals and Zimatlán with PRD-PRI competition, more typical of rural towns. Although it is relatively poor and rural, Teotitlán del Valle enjoys politics as open and competitive as anywhere else in Mexico, with all three major parties finding significant support. This diversity of contexts makes these towns good places to explore the impact of Mexico's uneven spread of democratic politics on the political attitudes and behaviors of ordinary Mexicans. Thumbnail sketches of politics in each of these towns helps to contextualize the interview evidence in chapter 6.

La Ciénega

La Ciénega is a typical case in which the mechanisms of political control deployed by the Mexican state and by the PRI created and sustained PRI hegemony over local politics. La Ciénega is a rural town of about three thousand residents located approximately fifty kilometers (30 miles) south of the city of Oaxaca. During the 1970s residents of the town who worked on a local hacienda organized a series of successful protests and land occupations to force the government to expropriate the privately held land and redistribute it in the form of an *ejido*. Because La Ciénega is an *ejido* community, the affairs of residents and local organizations are woven together with various state institutions and PRI party organizations into a network of hierarchical relationships through which the state exercises political control over the town. *Ejidatarios* do not own their own land, so they depend almost completely on the state for most resources, including credits, fertilizer, seeds, and often even the sale of their crops. In addition, access to public goods and services requires that *ejidatarios* belong to the Confederación Nacional Campesina (the CNC), the national peasant confederation that is one of the PRI's three mass-based corporatist organizations.[33]

Thus all members of La Ciénega's *ejido* community, and of most other local organizations for that matter, are members of the PRI and participate regularly in political events organized by the party. This monopolistic dependence on the state and the ruling party for resources meant that peasants, regardless of their political preferences, really had no choice but to join the PRI, vote for its candidates, and participate in political events organized by the party. To do otherwise would mean jeopardizing their only access to the resources they need to survive. As the president of the *comisariado ejidal* told me: "Here we all belong to the PRI, and we have to, otherwise [the government] won't give us anything."[34] There was absolutely no party competition in local elections in La Ciénega before 1995, with the PRI winning 100 percent of the vote in nearly every election. The PRD began to compete in local elections in 1995, but even as late as 1998, when I was carrying out my research in the town, the PRI remained the dominant local party, capturing 65 percent of the vote in municipal elections. Although the PRD won the next elections by a razor-thin margin (six votes), the PRI once again regained control over the town in 2004. Residents also supported the PRI at almost all state- and national-level elections.[35] Despite the radical changes that weakened the PRI elsewhere in Mexico, politics in La Ciénega seemed to proceed as usual.

Zimatlán

Politics in Zimatlán provides a comparative counterpoint to La Ciénega. On the surface the local political context in Zimatlán differed little from the situation in La Ciénega and hundreds of other rural municipalities across Oaxaca. There are several *ejido* groups in Zimatlán located primarily in the periphery of the municipality, but because Zimatlán is much larger and also a commercial center for the region, they weigh less heavily on the affairs of the municipal government than the comparable groups in La Ciénega. The PRI maintained a stranglehold on local politics until 1992, controlling and co-opting opposition groups with great success. But cracks began to appear in the PRI's local hegemony shortly after 1988 when, encouraged by Cardenas's strong showing in the presidential election, local political activists affiliated themselves with the PRD and ran a candidate to oppose the PRI in the 1989 municipal elections. They won a surprising 23 percent of the vote in 1989 and just over 40 percent in 1992. The next mayoral elections in 1995 were extremely competitive, with the PRD finally succeeding in dethroning the PRI after a leader of a local PRI faction defected to the PRD, bringing with him a slew of supporters.[36] The PRI recaptured control of the municipal government in 1998, but lost it again in 2001 to Convergencia, a relative newcomer to electoral politics.

Although at first glance Zimatlán appears to have a competitive multiparty system, what the electoral results do not show is that most of this electoral competition follows the logic of competitive clientelism, in which marginalized patrons defected from the PRI (and later the PRD) when their prospects for advancing their political careers within the party narrowed. When the PRD emerged as a viable party vehicle after 1989, it offered leaders of these smaller factions the means of winning power outside of the dominant party. Although the newly minted PRD leaders were able to capture the support of independent voters who were upset with PRI rule, particularly after the 1994 peso crisis, the large gains the PRD made between 1989 and 1995 were not the result of ideological appeals but of clientelist bandwagoning—that is, of local leaders defecting to a rival party and mobilizing their clientelist base through a combination of vote buying and coercion. In turn, the PRD welcomed these defectors and the votes they could deliver because its local organizational presence was relatively weak. Similarly, the PRI's victory in 1998 was facilitated when a PRI dissident left the PRD to return to the PRI. In turn, the meteoric rise of Convergencia in the 2001 mayoral elections was also the result of an elite split, not of grassroots organizing by newcomers to politics.

Oaxaca

Politics in the city of Oaxaca epitomize the democratization of local political contexts that so many analysts have celebrated. Because it is the capital city and the largest urban center in the state, greater incentives for opposition parties to participate in local elections have always existed there. In addition to the symbolic value of winning control of the most important city in the state, city council seats have been distributed according to proportional representation since 1980, six years before anywhere else in the state (Díaz Montes 1994, 94–95). This lowered the threshold that opposition parties faced for winning some representation in the city's government. Still, with the exception of the 1983 elections, when the PRI failed to win a majority of the local vote, there was a wide gap between the electoral support enjoyed by the PRI and opposition parties on the right and left. In fact, until 1992 the PRI could be considered a hegemonic party in the city since it defeated the second-place party by fifty percentage points or more in most elections.

The city is also unique in the state because the PAN has been the most competitive opposition party.[37] Elsewhere in the state the PRD is the strongest opposition party, but in the capital it suffers from internal divisions and is not a factor in local elections. It managed to win only 10 percent of the vote in 1998 and just over 6 percent in the 2001 mayoral elections. This does not mean that the party does not enjoy local support. In fact, in 1998 the PRD's gubernatorial candidate, Hector Sánchez, won a plurality of votes in the capital (35 percent), defeating both the PRI's candidate, José Murat (31 percent), who won the overall election, and the PAN's candidate, Pablo Arnaud (30 percent), a very popular local politician and former mayor of the city. The political situation was made even more fluid with the emergence, seemingly from nowhere, of a fourth party—the Convergence Party (Partido Convergencia, known as Convergencia)—which won the mayoral election in 2001. Thanks to key defections from the PRI, access to key PRI networks, and some very powerful political patrons, Convergencia quickly replaced the PAN as the city's largest party.[38]

This political volatility and alternation in power at the local level created new opportunities for residents of the city to become involved in politics and voice their demands. Whether residents of Nezacubi saw the PAN's victory as an opening in the local political opportunity structure depended on how closely tied they were to clientelist networks in the area. Most squatters in Nezacubi welcomed PAN administrations because it gave them an alternative to the clientelistic neighborhood association controlled by PRI leaders that had failed to deliver any substantial improvements to their living situation over the past decade. PRI supporters, however, saw the PAN's victory as a closing of access and were forced to experiment with new forms of political action because traditional clientelistic relationships became less effective. Many were recruited to participate in disruptive protests against the local PAN government in an effort to hinder its ability to govern; others increased their contacts with state-level PRI organizations in an effort to win the ear of the governor; and still others dropped out of politics altogether, waiting until the PRI returned to power in the city.

Teotitlán del Valle

Teotitlán del Valle is a town of artisan weavers, where Zapotec cultural traditions and practices still organize the town's political, social, and religious life. Visitors see evidence of its Zapotec roots in the tapestries hanging outside of artisans' shops, in the ancient hieroglyphics carved into stones in the walls of the Catholic church, and in the conversations overheard among residents in the city streets.[39] What is less obvious is that Teotitlán del Valle's local political structure is based on customary law inherited from pre-Hispanic times. All of the officials who occupy the most important political posts in the village, including the mayor (*alcalde*) and council members (*síndico* and *regidores*), are elected in village assemblies where political parties are prohibited from running candidates. This indigenous political structure, combined with the town's reliance on commerce rather than patronage for its economic survival, insulated residents from many of the political pressures faced by nearby agricultural communities, allowing the town more political autonomy than most other rural towns in Oaxaca.[40]

Although the cargo system structures municipal-level politics, residents of Teotitlán del Valle and of other towns governed by customary law participate normally in state and national politics. For these elections Teotitlán del Valle has developed one of the few three-party competitive systems in the state. Support for the PRI was high before parties were excluded from local affairs, but after 1995 support for the PAN and the PRD increased quickly, suggesting an independent streak among local residents despite the town's rural location and low incomes. Residents voted for the PRD in slightly larger numbers than for the PRI in the 1997 congressional elections, but the PRD received twice the votes of the PRI in the 1998 state elections. The PAN then became very popular, improving its standing locally on the coattails of Fox's victory in the 2000 presidential elections. The PRI's vote stabilized at around 21 percent, but it is no longer competitive locally.

The elimination of fraud in elections, the emergence of viable opposition parties that challenge the PRI in elections for all levels of government, and intragovernmental party competition created a new strategic context that changed the incentives and opportunities ordinary citizens have for undertaking political action. However, Mexican citizens do not face a monolithic political opportunity structure. Instead, the uneven spread of political competition and democratic political practices across the country created a complex mix of pluralist enclaves that coexist with authoritarian strongholds and semidemocratic subnational regimes (Beer 2003 and Fox 1994a and 1996). These local variations are immensely important for political participation, because it is at this level where people have their most frequent and meaningful experiences with the political process, form their ideas about how the political system works, and learn to how to participate (Hiskey and Bowler 2005).

Optimists consider the spread of political competition across cities and states as beneficial for the consolidation of democratic practices in Mexico. After all, both citizens and government officials must learn democratic politics, and state and municipal governments where the opposition competes and wins elections make a good school for democracy (Fox 1994a and Beer 2003). By the same logic, however, the survival of authoritarianism at the state and local levels means that undemocratic practices are also constantly reproduced and reinforced. Thus Mexico's mottled, uneven, and incomplete transition to democracy simultaneously encourages democratic practices and allows authoritarian ones to thrive.

CHAPTER 6

DEMOCRATIZATION, POLITICAL COMPETITION, AND POLITICAL PARTICIPATION

Most accounts of Mexico's democratic transition emphasize its gradualism, suggesting perhaps that ordinary Mexicans had sufficient time to adapt their behavior to the emerging institutional context. However, the evolution of political competition in Mexico (in Oaxaca in particular) reveals that the transition to democracy was full of inconsistencies and paradoxes. For example, although the transition began in local and state elections and eventually spread to the national level, today democratic practices are much more solidly established at the federal level. Local elections in many states and municipalities are still marred by fraud, clientelism, and lack of choice among parties. Democratic openings are distributed unevenly across states and municipalities in Mexico. So while some citizens live in local contexts with high levels of electoral competition and the alternation of parties in power, many Mexicans still live in cities and states where autocratic leaders control local-level participation and political competition. For these citizens democratic reforms and even President Vicente Fox's victory in 2000 did not open up new opportunities for political activism. Rather, Mexico's political system looked much as it had in previous decades.

These varied and often contradictory local, state, and national institutional environments offer Mexico's citizens starkly different incentives and opportunities for political action. Mexicans are struggling to read these mixed signals and to adjust their political behavior to these new and often contradictory opportunity structures. As a result, neat generalizations about how politics works or about how people respond to political stimuli may not be possible. In situations like these, in-depth interviews and detailed analysis of local political contexts are useful research strategies for disentangling the interlocking and often inconsistent political opportunities ordinary Mexicans face when contemplating political action. At the time of my interviews (1998–2000), Oaxaca was controlled by an autocratic clique and political participation was often mobilized through local and regional political machines. Thus the interviews cannot give us much insight into how politics works in states governed more democratically. Nonetheless, three of the towns where I carried out interviews had competitive local party systems, providing a window into how overlapping authoritarian and democratic political systems interact and what effect they have on the opinions and behaviors of ordinary Mexicans. Special attention must be paid to the ways in which the evolving political opportunity structure influenced the costs and benefits of political action, how it expanded or constrained choice for action, and how it affected the poor's levels of political engagement. I then analyze national-level survey data to see if these patterns are typical of politics throughout the rest of Mexico.

Electoral Reforms, Political Competition, and Political Participation

Reforms that guarantee the secrecy of the ballot are necessary to eliminate fraud and to build confidence among citizens so they are free to vote for whomever they please. In the past, especially in rural communities but also in popular urban neighborhoods, there were never any independent election observers present at polling booths, making it almost impossible to guarantee the ballot's secrecy. Such practices as husbands casting the ballots for the entire family or *ejido* leaders voting for the entire organization at once were common. This served not only to ensure PRI victories locally but also to show party higher-ups that the organization, village, or neighborhood was loyal to the PRI and deserving of *apoyos*, or governmental support. It was usually local caciques and organizational leaders, not necessarily representatives of the state or the PRI, that supervised how rank-and-file members voted. One interviewee in Teotitlán del Valle, Hector, remembers this kind of public voting, when he voted for the first time: "Yes, when I began voting, I voted for the official party (the PRI). Well, I voted for the official party because I did not know for whom to vote. I would ask my parents how to vote:

What do you do when you get to the polling station, what do you say when you get there? They told me, 'Son, just go there and tell them you want to vote for the majority.' I didn't know any better, so two or three times I went to vote and told the poll worker, 'I'd like to vote for the majority,' and he would cast my ballot for me."

The relative secrecy of the ballot is also important for the power balance between patrons and clients. There is a commitment problem facing political parties using clientelist strategies to mobilize voters (Stokes 2005). The basic clientelist contract in which political leaders exchange material resources for votes would quickly break down without the ability to observe how clients actually vote. If political leaders cannot monitor what party people vote for, the poor are in principle free to accept goods and services and then vote for whomever they please. Clientelistic voting works best, at least from the perspective of political parties, when people's votes can be observed. The greater the secrecy of the ballot, the greater the freedom citizens have to vote their preferences without fear of sanctions from a local boss or members of the group to which they belong. This is especially important among the poor, who are vulnerable to clientelistic manipulation. Liliana, from Zimatlán, expressed what is by now a common lesson in independent voting learned by many of Mexico's poor. "Look, it is not right for the parties to distribute pigs, or building material, or food baskets right before an election," she said, "but if they are handing things out, I'll take it. But when it comes to the moment of voting, only I will know who I vote for, because what they are giving out is not a handout—it comes from my money too, from the taxes I pay."

Independent voting became possible after the government implemented a series of electoral reforms aimed at protecting the secrecy of the vote, beginning with the 1994 presidential elections. These measures included new voter identification cards with pictures, requiring all polling booths to have electoral observers from opposition parties present, and allowing citizen groups, such as Alianza Cívica, to staff polling places with independent observers. The IFE even designed new voting booths for the country's 112,500 polling stations to ensure the secrecy of the ballot for the 2000 elections. These reforms have tipped the power balance between political parties and the poor in favor of the latter. However, clientelistic voting remains common in part because many doubted the effectiveness of the IFE's reforms. Even though it is objectively impossible for political parties or the government to know how individuals vote during elections, grassroots organizations still employ multiple strategies to create the *perception* among poor citizens that party leaders and the government can credibly monitor how individuals vote (Holzner 2004). Before the 1998 local elections, the local PRI group in Zimatlán distributed farm animals to most anyone who gave the leaders a photocopy of their electoral identification card and signed a petition declaring that they were members of the PRI. The intention was to make people think that the PRI had their personal information and could use it to find out whether they had actually voted for the PRI. These are not isolated instances but common strategies used by clientelist leaders from both the PRI and the PRD across Mexico.

Given their general mistrust of the state and of politicians, the poor do not need much convincing. Approximately two-thirds of the people I interviewed, in both rural and urban settings, believed there were ways for the PRI and the state to find out how people vote in elections. In some ways they are right. Ironically, the increased transparency of election results, which are now publicly available for every single polling place in Mexico, gives political analysts *and* political parties an extremely detailed picture of where support for each party comes from.[1] So even though an individual's vote is secret, how a neighborhood, village, or *ejido* community has voted is more public than ever, transferring power back to political parties and leaders. This information is used by clientelist leaders to monitor how territorially based groups have voted during local and national elections and punish communities that failed to deliver the vote.[2]

Citizens also mistrust the intentions of authorities, because they know all too well what party and state officials are capable of to win elections.[3] Indeed, electoral manipulation and sleight of hand are not relics of Mexico's distant past. Although the IFE is highly professionalized and organizes world-class elections, state and local elections are the responsibility of state-level electoral institutes (IEEs), which are often less professional and less impartial than the IFE. Typically, where state-level politics are truly competitive and no political clique has monopoly control over key institutions like the state legislature, IEEs organize free and fair elections locally. However, when states are under the control of autocratic governors, as is the case in Oaxaca, IEEs often enable all sorts of electoral shenanigans, becoming another tool used by governors to solidify their control over state politics. Oaxaca is one of the states where fraud in elections continues to be a problem. While observing local- and national-level elections in 1998, 2000, 2003, and 2004, I heard about and witnessed hundreds of acts of fraud, vote buying, intimidation, and clientelist mobilization of voters. The 2004 gubernatorial elections were a particularly egregious example, perhaps because the ruling clique had to respond to its most significant electoral challenge to date. Oaxaqueños who experienced this dark side of the political system directly quickly lost faith that democratization had taken root in Mexico and either dropped out of politics or clung to clientelist networks, aware that that they were still the most important game in (their) town. Others who did not witness fraud but heard the allegations of electoral misconduct in the news also lost confidence in the integrity of elections and turned out less in the future.

In the aftermath of the 2004 elections, many of the most active residents of Nezacubi became deeply disillusioned with the progress of democracy in their state. They had high hopes that the unified challenge by PAN, PRD, and Convergencia parties against the PRI's candidate would finally wrest control over the state government from the PRI and bring real change to local politics. The PRI's victory, combined with the allegations of widespread fraud, were a punch in the stomach. Many, if not most, dropped out of politics for a while, and the once vibrant neighborhood association became inactive. When the PRI recaptured control over the city's government a few months later, in part because of very low turnout, the long-dormant PRI faction in Nezacubi regained strength and took control of the neighborhood association. The new leadership focused on reestablishing links to local PRI groups and resumed the personal, clientelistic politics residents had eschewed during the past few years. Residents willing to engage in clientelist politics generally became more active, while those who valued their political independence dropped out of politics altogether.[4]

Overall the impact of fraud on participation may be mixed. Cleaner elections tend to increase turnout because voters have greater confidence that their vote will actually matter. However, elections need to be clean at all levels for this positive effect to occur. The persistence of dirty politics locally may skew people's perceptions about politics nationally so that they may *perceive* federal elections to be fraudulent when in fact they are not. This undermines the positive impact that free and fair elections at the national level might have on turnout. Where IEEs are compromised so that local leaders can buy votes, coerce and cajole people to the polls, and even tamper with the results, opportunities open up for clientelist leaders and local political machines to mobilize supporters through all kinds of authoritarian tactics. This may increase turnout in a specific election, particularly among the poor, who are most vulnerable to these tactics.[5]

According to conventional wisdom in political science, greater political competition in local and national elections should stimulate electoral participation for three reasons: (1) because it makes the election more relevant to citizens, (2) because political leaders have more incentives to mobilize voters on election day, and (3) because people are exposed to more political stimuli (Aldrich 1993, Caldeira and Patterson 1982, Jackman 1987, Patterson and Caldeira 1983, and Rosenstone and Hansen 1993). Evidence from Mexico suggests that this is indeed happening, with opposition parties and the PRI undertaking vigorous efforts to recruit and mobilize voters (Domínguez and Lawson 2004, Domínguez and Poiré 1999, Klesner and Lawson 2000, and Ziccardi 1998). This kind of electoral mobilization was evident in both urban and rural towns in Oaxaca, and much of it came from the PRI itself, which faced stiff competition from the PAN at the national level and from the PRD in statewide elections.

It is no coincidence that the PRI established numerous grassroots groups just before the 1994 presidential elections in rural towns like La Ciénega and Zimatlán, where the party's dominant position was at risk. Many of the people in rural towns with whom I spoke had voted and attended campaign events for the first time only a few years before, usually after joining one of these local organizations had mobilized them at election time. Much of this political activity was clearly designed to support PRI candidates and boost the standing of local leaders with party higher-ups. Nevertheless, the experiences were valuable for the people with whom I spoke, particularly women, who felt they gained in experience, savvy, and self-confidence. In some cases this kind of mobilized political participation transformed into more autonomous behavior. Daniela from La Ciénega exemplifies how political participation that begins as clientelistic can become more democratic. "I was afraid to vote before," she said. "I did not know what it was about. Then, after joining the [Confederación Nacional Campesina, or CNC] group, I learned how to vote: the green one is the PRI, the blue one PAN, and so on. Now we go to campaign rallies and yell 'Que Viva el PRI!' And so I began to vote, and I liked it, and then I went because *I* wanted to." This kind of transformation was sparked by the imperative of political parties to mobilize new voters in response to local-level elections that had become more competitive. Thus political competition, even if it occurs between rival clientelist networks, is often an important opening in the local political environment, creating fresh incentives and opportunities that can draw previously inactive citizens into the political arena.

However, true political competition was far from the norm during most of the 1990s in Oaxaca. There was some ambivalence among the people I spoke with about whether the political system was truly opening up. My impression was that the effect of political competition on people's political attitudes and behavior depended on their political preferences and on the local political opportunity structure. If someone's preferred party had a chance of winning elections locally, their interest in politics and political activity increased; if parties other than their own were competitive, people might not be drawn into politics even if elections were very close. A comparison of how PRD supporters in La Ciénega (a PRI stronghold) and Zimatlán (where the PRD was competitive) reacted to increasing political competition shows how local contexts combine with political preferences to produce different kinds of political behavior. Daniela in La Ciénega voted for the PRI candidate in the 1998 municipal elections, mostly because she was encouraged to do so by the leader of her organization. But in a small act of defiance, and probably to experiment with the power of her suffrage, she decided to vote for the PRD in the most recent elections for governor. With relatively little party competition at the municipal or state level, she recognized that her act was somewhat futile and said she is thinking of dropping out of politics altogether.

[Do you think your vote matters?]
    Well, they say that things can change if we all vote, for example, voting for the PRD. But I don't think things will ever change.
    [So what are you going to do now?]
    I don't know. I guess I won't vote for anyone. See what happens. Or maybe I'll go again. I don't know.

Since then, Daniela has wondered about the value of her vote, because so little has changed with state-level politics. Most of the time she voted out of a sense of civic duty, but with the PRI dominating state and local politics, democracy has not brought about much positive change, as far as she was concerned.

    Zimatlán has a similar history to La Ciénega, but a victory by the PRD in the 1995 municipal elections broke the PRI's stranglehold on power. This made voting more meaningful for residents, especially those who had tired of PRI rule. The competitiveness of the PRD locally gave the rural poor a real *choice* at election time, for the first time in memory. Like Daniela, Fortina had become disillusioned with local and national PRI governments, so she decided to vote for the PRD in Zimatlán's municipal elections in 1995. But unlike Daniela, who still faced a hegemonic PRI locally, the PRD's victory in Zimatlán drew Fortina further into politics.

The first time I voted for the PRD I did it to see if there would be a change in the way they ran the town, without much corruption, to see if they worked better. But seeing that they worked in the same way, the whole town was disillusioned. Everyone was disillusioned, because no one votes now.

[In the most recent elections did you vote for the PRI?]

I voted for the PRI because I thought maybe they had changed, that they wouldn't act badly and were going to try to do better, and it seems like they are.

Even though Fortina switched her vote back to the PRI in 1998, her support for the PRI has a different meaning than it did in the past. In the past Fortina's support for the PRI had been mobilized through community organizations in which she had participated, hoping to get her share of benefits through clientelistic channels. Now her support for the PRI is more autonomous and designed to punish the incumbents. Just as important, although in the past Fortina's voting behavior had been constrained by the lack of choice—she could either vote for the PRI or abstain—elections now provide her and others in Zimatlán with a real choice among parties.

Political competition in Zimatlán has also had a positive effect on many residents' feelings of efficacy. Liliana, in her early thirties, had never participated in politics, not even in PRI groups. She had just finished telling me how disenchanted she was with state and national politics, and how little people like her could not do anything to curb corruption among politicians. I asked if she thought there was anything the people (*el pueblo*) could do to defend themselves from corruption and lack of accountability. "Well, only through the vote," she responded. "I think that is the way to accomplish something, by voting for other people. Because if some politician is corrupt and we keep voting for him, when are things going to change? Never. Only by voting for a different party can we really change things. We have to try." Liliana voted for the first time in her life in the 1998 municipal elections; she chose the PRD "to see some change, to see if they really keep their promises." Competitive elections in Zimatlán inspired more political interest and more activism in Liliana. During the campaigns she attended political rallies held by both the PRI and the PRD, not as part of a group in support of the candidates but as a private citizen trying to make up her mind. "I like to listen to what each party has to say," she told me. "It is important to hear what one says, then what the other says, what alternatives they propose, what they plan to do to help the people, what promises they make."

Why did Liliana suddenly decide to become active, and why did she decide to do so by voting? Certainly she had been upset about corruption before 1998. She had considered participating in marches or protests, but she thought those were largely ineffective and too difficult to organize. The

PRD's electoral victory in the 1995 municipal elections expanded Liliana's choice and made it more likely that her vote would not just count: it would matter.[6] In short, her behavior and attitudes changed not because of skills she had gained in organizations, nor because she had acquired more resources (such as income or education); rather, the PRD victory created novel openings in the local political opportunity structure.

Of the four towns I studied, the capital city of Oaxaca has the longest history of political competition, with the PAN winning two successive municipal elections in 1995 and 1998. Convergencia's victory in the mayoral election in 2001 made it three consecutive terms in which the PRI had failed to win a local election in Oaxaca city. This electoral competition stimulated a great deal of electoral activism among squatters in Nezacubi, who became more interested in politics, felt more efficacious, voted more regularly, and in many cases also volunteered for the first time for election campaigns. As in Zimatlán, electoral competition boosted the activism among those who opposed the PRI the most, but it had the opposite effect on PRIistas. Pilar's case is typical of people who had tired of PRI rule. She is twenty-eight years old and has been interested in politics ever since her first vote at age nineteen. Pilar says she has disliked the PRI as long as she can remember: she disliked its clientelist mobilization strategies, she disliked the corruption by party leaders, and she disliked their neoliberal policies. As long as the PRI was certain to win elections, Pilar wondered whether it was even worthwhile voting: "You know what my husband would say to me? Why vote if the PRI always wins? It doesn't matter who you vote for, they always win. I'd tell him to vote because you never know, maybe your vote could decide an election. I'd vote and hope, hope with all my heart that they would lose, but he was right, they always won, and often by cheating, by stealing ballot boxes or filling them with votes."

After the PAN's first electoral victory in Oaxaca in 1995, Pilar's views and behavior changed dramatically. She became involved in the neighborhood association almost immediately after the PAN won its first local election. Despite raising three sons and taking care of her ailing mother-in-law, Pilar was gradually drawn into other modes of political activity. When I met her in 1998, she was attending weekly meetings of the neighborhood association (from 9 to 11 p.m. on Saturday nights!) and attending the associations weekly *tequios* (at 7 a.m. on Sunday mornings!).[7] She made monthly visits to city hall and to government agencies to petition for water and sewage services for her neighborhood. She volunteered in Pablo Arnaud's gubernatorial campaign in 1998, in part because she was recruited by local PAN activists but mainly because Arnaud was Oaxaca's first opposition party mayor. He had worked hard to bring services to the previously marginalized squatter settlements. "More than anything I liked him," Pilar explained, "because he would come to the marginalized neighborhoods to give us his support, to make sure that we got the services we needed. The PRI really tried to put up roadblocks so that he wouldn't be able to accomplish much, but even if progress was slow, I saw that he was trying, that he was always working, that he would not give in to the pressure of the PRI."

In contrast, many loyal PRIistas were skeptical that an increase in party competition would improve their personal situation. Beatriz, who lives in urban Nezacubi and has always voted for the PRI, just felt confused and overwhelmed by political competition. I asked her whether she thought elections were effective at forcing the government to take citizens' preferences into account. "Who knows," Beatriz said. "It's hard to tell because there are now four, five, even six candidates in every election—all of whom promise things, criticize each other, claim they are the good ones and all the others are crooks. Our leaders also pick sides, telling us that we should vote for this one, or for that one, or that this one promised us more. . . . I just feel confused. It's harder than ever to tell whom one should vote for."

Other PRIistas were frustrated by Nezacubi's support of the PAN instead of the PRI, feeling like it reduced their chances at receiving patronage from the governor. Ernesto, was one of the original leaders of the neighborhood association and was otherwise very active politically, but he refused to take part in any of the community's affairs after the PAN won the mayoral elections in 1995. To the extent that he remained involved in politics, Ernesto did so through his PRI networks, focusing on state-level politics. "This neighborhood committee has always opposed the PRI," he said. "I have always told them that it is useless to swim against the current. The governor is from the PRI but the mayor is not. And while the mayor is the local authority, he doesn't have the economic or political power to change things. I try to tell them that the federal and the state government has children and it has stepchildren. The children belong to the PRI, the stepchildren belong to other parties. Stepchildren receive something from the parent occasionally, and only if there is anything left over or to shut them up. But children get everything on a silver platter." This skepticism toward increased party competition is often rooted in people's experiences with clientelist politics that characterized their political participation in earlier decades. Rather than creating opportunities, opposition victories threaten PRIistas' access to government patronage. For opposition supporters, the opposite is true. Because they typically have been shut out of clientelist benefits in the past, local-level PRI losses open access to government officials, often for the very first time.

The positive impact of increasing political competition based on the political participation of the poor has also been limited; the party system has yet to provide many of them with a viable alternative to the clientelistic exchanges that organized politics in the past or with a credible alternative to the PRI in local elections. The PRI was (and probably still is) the only party that has the organizational capacity to field candidates and mobilize voters in all of Mexico's municipalities. The PRD and the PAN are credible contenders in national elections and in local elections in Mexico City, but in states like Oaxaca they simply could not field electable candidates in most municipal elections. Where local party systems excluded one or both major opposition parties, partisans still felt like the choices democratic politics offered them were too limited.

From the perspective of the poor, a two-party competitive system in which the PAN and the PRI vie for power often holds little appeal. At the national level both parties support free-market economic reforms, a reduced role of the state in the economy, and eliminating traditional government subsidies. Although the PRD's platforms may have moderated over the years, it still favors a renegotiation of NAFTA and opposes a deepening of neoliberal economic reforms. It also advocates for more spending for poverty-alleviation programs and a greater emphasis on distributive policies. These policies appeal to the poor. "Neither the PRI nor PAN care about Mexicans," Natalia from Nezacubi told me. "If the dollar goes up or the peso falls, it is better for them. They don't know what it means to be poor. The PRD cares more about the poor." Many would like to vote for the PRD locally but do not because it is too disorganized and faction-ridden to run competitively in elections.

Even those who vote for the PAN locally and approve of the way it governs see it as a second-best option. Edmundo from Nezacubi echoed the sentiments of many in the *colonia*: "The PRD is my party. You have no idea how much I want them to win the presidency, and I would love it if they could get themselves organized here in Oaxaca. But they are a mess. On the other hand, the PAN has governed well. I have to give them credit for that. So here in Oaxaca I vote for the PAN because there is no other option, but whenever I can, I support the PRD." Despite the PAN's electoral success in the capital, many of the poor still do not feel like elections offer them much choice because the PRD is often not competitive. In fact, people had serious misgivings about the prospect of the PAN coming to power at the national level. Many expressed a combination of fear, disgust, and animosity toward the party:

I've always voted for the PRD. Up until now because they've had the most direct work for the people. But now, who knows? At the local level it's a disaster. The PAN isn't an option because they think they're the masters, and the day they take power, it's going to be frightening. They are arrogant and are going to want to grab everything for themselves.

—CARMEN, OAXACA

I don't know the PAN very well, but as a party I'd be afraid if a person from the PAN became president. What can you expect from people with money, from people who have always been well off, who have never had to suffer hunger? And in some way, even in the PRI there are people who have suffered . . . who know what it means to work for a tortilla. But not in PAN, the majority are rich.

—TIBERIO, NEZACUBI

Statistical evidence from the 2003 CSES Mexico survey confirms that political competition between the PAN and the PRI is not enough to stimulate activism among the poor. Table 6.1 compares the mean number of political acts by income groups for people living in states where the PAN is competitive in gubernatorial elections and where it is not.[8] The PAN competition at the state level decreases the political activity of all income groups, except the most affluent, with the largest decrease occurring among the poor. Where the PAN is competitive, political participation is heavily stratified by income, but where it is not, the poor are actually the most politically active. Thus in Mexico it appears that political competition by itself is not enough to pull people into politics; where the PRD is not competitive, it may actually discourage participation.

Although political competition is certainly vibrant in Mexico, this evi-

Table 6.1. Impact of Political Competition on Political Participation, PAN 2003, by Income

	PAN competitive at the state level		
	Yes	No	Means test
Low income	1.12	1.68	***
Medium income	1.28	1.61	
High income	1.46	1.47	
Means test	***		

Source: CSES-CIDE 2003.
Notes: Table shows the mean number of political activities in which people engage using the same scale as in chapter 4.
* p < 0.1   ** p < 0.05   *** p < 0.01

dence hints at the troubling fact that Mexico's parallel two-party system of-ten does not represent well the poor's political preferences. Survey evidence confirms that Mexicans are deeply disillusioned with political parties. Most consider themselves independents, have little or no trust in parties, and base their voting decisions more on the personal qualities of candidates than on party platforms (Klesner 2005 and Camp 2006). Many of the interviewees were already looking beyond party labels and making voting decisions based on individual candidates. Tomás's comments are typical: "I think the person matters most, because that is who is taking on the authority. The person has to solve the problems, not the party. Once a candidate is elected, once he oc-cupies his post, then the party becomes secondary." Tiberio's views are more radical. He migrated to Oaxaca in 1996 from Mexico City, where he had ex-perience with a squatters' movement and participated in numerous protests. He liked the PRD and its leader Cuahutémoc Cárdenas, but in Oaxaca he had found few outlets for his political energies. This lack of choice led him to a disturbing conclusion about his political options. I asked if there was any hope of changing the system. "No. Well, not through elections," Tiberio said. "I'm in favor of an uprising. People that are part of the system are never going to want to leave power, and the fact that the PAN is winning, for ex-ample—it's not going change anything."

The presidential candidacy of Andrés Manuel López Obrador for the PRD in 2006, the first candidate from the left to have a credible chance of winning the presidency, provided something of a test of the importance of voter choice for turnout. While cynicism and feelings of inefficacy have been growing among the poor since 1994, because presidential elections offered them the unpalatable choice between PRI and PAN candidates who differed little on their economic policy platforms, López Obrador's candidacy ener-gized many who had felt disaffected with party politics in Mexico. He was the charismatic candidate people like Tomás had been looking for, and his campaign slogan—"For the Good of Everyone, the Poor First"—resonated with people like Carmen, Edmundo, and Tiberio who had felt shut out of politics. His populist policy proposals and anti-neoliberal rhetoric were im-portant for low-income Mexicans, and his status as the frontrunner during much of the campaign gave the poor real incentives to pay attention to the campaign and turn out to vote.[9]

In the end López Obrador lost a hotly contested election, which devas-tated millions of his supporters. Because levels of cynicism and distrust with politics are high in Mexico, supporters of López Obrador were quick to believe his allegations that Calderón's victory was the result of electoral fraud orchestrated by national and international business interests to keep the PRD from taking power (Estrada and Poiré 2007). López Obrador's aggressive protests of the electoral results and scathing criticism of Mexico's electoral institutions divided the PRD and nourished poor people's skepticism in the ability of democratic politics to represent their interests. By the midterm elections in 2009, electoral support for the PRD was halved, with many former PRD supporters switching their vote to the PRI or simply choosing not to vote at all. Oaxaca followed this national trend. After voting for the PRD by a margin of 46 percent to 32 percent in 2006, in 2009 Oaxaqueños once again voted for the PRI by an overwhelming margin: 44 percent to 16 percent.

Decentralization and Intragovernmental Competition

Decentralization policies, coupled with the growing number of opposition party victories in municipal and provincial elections, did more to muddle the political opportunity structure Mexicans faced than any other of the major institutional reforms implemented since 1990. On the one hand, decentralization strengthened municipal governments, made local politics more relevant than ever for ordinary Mexicans, and created new incentives and opportunities for citizens to become involved in politics. The fact that municipalities can now collect taxes and carry out public works projects *with their own funds* means that political parties have greater incentives to contest local elections, and citizens have more reasons to target local government officials with political activity. On the other hand, as political parties contest local elections more vigorously, quite often winning them, citizens' political energies are directed more toward local government offices and so increase overall levels of participation, especially among people tired of PRI rule. Electoral competition locally can also produce more accountable and responsive administrations that over time socialize residents and elites into more democratic kinds of political practices (Beer 2003). These openings of the political space may be particularly important for the poor, who often cannot bear the costs of participation when this means traveling to distant state capitals or meeting with unreceptive government officials.

However, whether decentralization and intragovernmental competition actually opens opportunities for participation depends on whether citizens have, or *perceive* themselves to have, access to state and local governments. Access encourages participation because it increases the expected utility of political action and expands the choice of possible activities available to ordinary citizens. Access depends on the support base the political party in power relies on, as well as on individuals' party preference. Where political competition occurred between well-organized parties that compete based on programmatic appeals to voters, access may increase for all, because candidates and parties have incentives to attract as many supporters as possible. This is most often the case when the PAN, and sometimes the PRD, has challenged the PRI at both the state and local level, such as in Nuevo León, Quéretaro, Aguascalientes, Guanajuato, and Baja California. In those states the PAN governments set a higher standard for "good government," which forced the PRI to select better candidates, minimize corruption, and deliver tangible results to an increasingly independent and demanding electorate. However, in states where autocratic governors continued to dominate local politics, or where political competition followed the logic of competitive clientelism, access for both elites and ordinary citizens requires membership in a clientelist network. If someone's group lost an election, they were routinely denied access to power and government resources until the next election, while those not affiliated with any clientelist cluster were excluded indefinitely. In states like Oaxaca, where a powerful political machine dominated state-level politics but relatively autonomous and democratic local political systems emerged and survived, citizens faced a very different political opportunity structure depending on where they lived and which party they supported in elections.

New Opportunities and Constraints in Oaxaca

Decentralization coupled with opposition party victories in municipal elections opened up multiple new opportunities for participation for residents of the city of Oaxaca. During the 1990s opposition governments in Mexico developed innovative governing styles and strategies to promote local economic development and establish links between citizens and municipal governments that emphasized greater popular participation in local affairs (Beer 2003; Cabrero Mendoza 1995, 1996, and 1998; Rodríguez 1998; and Rodríguez and Ward 1995). This was the case in the city of Oaxaca, where the PAN administration reached out to citizens to encourage their participation in municipal affairs. One such initiative, launched in 1996, was the establishment of neighborhood committees called COMVIVES (Comités de Vida Vecinal, or Committees of Neighborhood Life). These had the goal of increasing involvement of residents in the management and problem-solving activities of their neighborhoods, giving neighborhoods direct access to the city government to voice their complaints, petition for public works, and coordinate and oversee public works projects carried out by the city. In addition to encouraging the participation of residents in the affairs of their community, the PAN administration also hoped that COMVIVES would compete directly with PRI neighborhood associations, weaken the power of local bosses over squatters, impair the PRI's mobilizing capacity, and promote new forms of citizen participation.

These innovations in the links between the state and citizens can have powerful effects on people's sense of efficacy and on their willingness to become more politically active. For example, Oscar, who lived in Nezacubi, had long been disillusioned with corrupt local and state PRI administrations and had given up on most kinds of political activity. After the PAN administration set up a COMVIVE in Nezacubi, however, he was elected by his neighbors to manage the *colonia's* land-titling program, which required Oscar to make frequent visits to city hall. His perception of government has changed as a result of the PAN's more open governing style. "I used to think people in the city government were a bunch of despots," he told me. "I would walk into the offices like a dog with my tail between my legs. Now I see the government as more tangible, like I have more access than before. You know, it feels like a veil has been lifted. In the past I used to think that the government was something distant, something that was up there somewhere. Now I feel like we can actually go up there where they are, address them, ask for their help."

Overall, decentralization and opposition party victories together have created fresh opportunities and incentives for involvement in both electoral activities and government-directed activities, such as contacting and protesting. Participation in Nezacubi's COMVIVE drew residents into a slew of political activities many had never even contemplated before. They might begin by attending a weekly community assembly (or *tequio*), where they would hear about the city's land-titling program. Interested in acquiring legal title to their plot, residents then might attend a couple of city council meetings, where the titling program would be discussed and where they would enroll. In the meantime the residents would see the city government paving roads in the neighborhood, improving trash pickup, and building a basketball court nearby. Impressed with the interest the city was showing in the plight of squatters, residents might accept an invitation to attend a campaign rally for the next PAN mayoral candidate. They might then make the extra effort to turn out and vote for him. As long as the residents perceived the city government to be fair, well-run, and concerned with their welfare, opposition party victories created a virtuous circle of more political engagement and governmental accountability in the city.

This dynamic also encourages people to redirect their political activity *toward* local and state government offices and *away* from federal bureaucracies that are relatively distant and perceived to be inaccessible. Roderic Ai Camp (2006), among others, has argued that local elections matter more to Mexican voters than federal elections. In 2003 turnout averaged 38 percent when only congressional districts were contested, but jumped to 49 percent when local deputies or city councils were up for election, and to 54 percent if the governorship was contested (ibid.).

The positive effects of decentralization on political participation may be most pronounced among the poor, who can least afford the expense of contacting state and federal officials. The 2003 Mexico wave of the CSES survey asked respondents whether they had petitioned or contacted a government official during the past twelve months, and to what level of government they had directed their petitioning. Table 6.2 shows that the poor target local and state governments almost exclusively with their political demands, contacting federal government officials only 16 percent of the time. The relationship is largely reversed for respondents from the higher-income categories, who petition the federal government nearly three times as often as the poor, suggesting that they can best afford the expense of petitioning at this level and depend least on organizations to subsidize the cost. Thus decentralization coupled with opposition victories may create openings in the political opportunity structure that are especially important for the political participation and representation of low-income Mexicans.

The impact of municipal reforms on political activism should not be overstated, however. Despite more than a decade of efforts to decentralize and devolve power to state and local governments, analysts agree that relatively little municipal autonomy actually resulted. While federal and state transfers have strengthened the capacity of municipal governments in Mex-

Table 6.2. To What Level of Government Do You Petition (Percentage by Income)?

	Low income	Medium income	High income	Total
Federal	15.9	39.1	45.7	29.4
State	25.0	28.1	22.9	25.7
Local	51.1	23.4	31.4	38.0
Other	8.0	9.4	0.0	7.0
Total *n*	88	64	35	187

Source: CSES-CIDE 2003.

ico to carry out infrastructure projects, and while these funds have made local politics more relevant for citizens, it appears that the push to decentralize power away from the federal level in Mexico has benefited state governments much more than municipalities. From the perspective of citizens, this means that changes to state-level political opportunities are more important for political activity than local-level ones. My interviewees in both urban and rural areas recognize these limitations and are aware that most of the resources and much of the power remains in the hands of state and federal governments.

> Even if the local government has the best intentions, they still depend on the state government. You might want to change things, to work to improve your community, but if they want to, they simply deny you the resources at the state level and you are left right where you started.
>
> —TOMÁS, NEZACUBI

> Pretty much all [the mayor] can do for us is give us the signatures we need so that we can go and petition state agencies. But we don't petition him to help us, to help the poor. Where will he get the money? The municipal government does not have money for that . . . you have to contact the governor.
>
> —NORMA, LA CIÉNEGA

One of the perverse consequences of decentralization and democratization in Mexico has been the ability of PRI governors to use their increased discretionary power to hijack funds from opposition-controlled local governments and channel them instead to partisan municipal administrations. As a result, the democratizing potential of increased opposition victories at the local level has been checked. In a city like Oaxaca, where the PAN has been in power locally but state politics was still controlled by a powerful PRI political machine, the governor and the mayor compete against each other for votes. Each tries to recruit supporters by carrying out infrastructure projects and promising material rewards, but because states control the vast majority of resources coming from the federal government, this an unequal battle. Sometimes city residents are the winners of this intragovernmental competition, because they can play one administration against the other, but if they show their support for an opposition party, their situation often worsens.[10]

Oaxaca's PRI-governor at the time, José Murat (1998–2004), jockeyed with the mayor of the capital city for influence, often denying the city funds to which it was entitled. In other parts of the state, he used his power and abundant resources to consolidate control over his regional political machine by rewarding supporters in towns where the PRI won elections and punishing towns and neighborhoods that had voted for the opposition, or even those that had supported rival PRI factions. During the first five years of his administration, Murat suspended or removed municipal authorities in 140 of Oaxaca's 570 municipalities. According to Edward Gibson (2005, 116), the most politically significant interventions took place in urbanized municipalities controlled by the opposition. Beatriz Magaloni (2006) has referred to this political dynamic as a "punishment regime." Unlike governing parties in democratic settings that reward core supporters and swing voters with patronage, hegemonic parties facing electoral competition "react in an unforgiving fashion toward defectors by withdrawing funds from those municipalities that elect opposition representatives. In the context of Mexico's municipal elections, this means that the PRI should invariably punish municipalities governed by the opposition and simultaneously divert more funds to those loyal municipalities that are more vulnerable to opposition entry" (ibid., 124).

According to Magaloni (ibid., 65–72), these tactics are most often directed toward the poor because they are more vulnerable to punishment, because they value targeted side payments such as cash transfers and credit more, and because the price of buying them off is lower than for higher-income voters. This logic is consistent with the experiences of people in the four towns I studied. Teotitlán del Valle, for example, was one of the first towns in the central valleys of Oaxaca to defect from the PRI by supporting the PRD in the 1997 federal midterm elections. In the years after that election, residents were repeatedly punished by the state government, which withheld funds from local schools and for infrastructure projects. In contrast, La Ciénega, which had been a PRI stronghold but was increasingly in danger of falling into PRD hands, received relatively consistent streams of funding directed both at the town government and at residents in the forms of credits, subsidies, direct cash transfers, building materials, and large infrastructure projects.

Given the availability of detailed precinct-level electoral data available through the IFE and state electoral institutes, it is easy for autocratic governors to extend the punishment regime beyond the municipal level and apply it to smaller geographic units such as villages and even urban neighborhoods. Although the city of Oaxaca voted overwhelmingly for the PAN between 1992 and 2000, PRI officials knew exactly which neighborhoods in the city had supported the party and which had defected to the PAN. Both middle-class and low-income neighborhoods supported the PAN in the 1995 and 1998 mayoral elections, but the logic of vote buying under a statewide hegemonic party meant that lower-income neighborhoods, particularly squatter neighborhoods that depended the most on the state government for resources and services, suffered the most for backing the PAN. Nezacubi was one of these neighborhoods. Because it closely identified with the PAN, ADOSAPACO, the state-level water agency, dragged its feet in providing water service to the neighborhood long after neighboring *colonias*—all of which had supported the PRI in the most recent elections—had been hooked up to the system. Petitions, small protests, appeals to the mayor, negotiations with neighboring associations all proved ineffective when dealing with this state-level agency. Squatters knew they were being punished. "They told us to our face that they weren't going to give us water because we're PANistas," Edmundo, the president of Nezacubi's neighborhood association between 1996 and 1999, complained to me.

Where they operate, punishment regimes also create different perceptions of access and therefore different political behavior among opposition supporters and PRIistas. In general, supporters of opposition parties living in Nezacubi, Teotitlán del Valle, and Zimatlán—all of which had competitive local electoral systems—expressed a strong sense of empowerment when discussing local politics. But they acknowledged a great deal of cynicism and pessimism when discussing state and national politics. This difference in attitudes results from people's perceptions of access they have to local versus state and national government officials. As a result, they consider varied strategies for pressuring officials at different levels of government. Isabel, for example, thought that voting was an effective way to hold city officials accountable, but this sense of efficacy did not extend to higher levels of government:

Well, if you vote, you're still not sure whether they're going to do what they promise. But it's good to vote. Because now when you vote for the mayor, if in all these years he didn't do a thing, you didn't see any results, then you go vote for the other guy.

[Do you think there is any way to make the federal government pay more attention to people like you?]

It's unlikely they will take us into account, you can see it with all the things that have happened in Chiapas. For example, we heard now that the government has killed all of those poor indigenous people, poor just like us. So I think that people fight in small villages and resort to violence to get the attention of the President. But what does he care? He can't be bothered where he is. Here [in Oaxaca] if we want something it is easier that the mayor will know about it than for Zedillo to ever find out. All we have to do is go to the COMVIVE and they take my problem

to the authorities. If not, all of us from the neighborhood go the city hall, and that way they will pay attention to us.
—ISABEL, NEZACUBI

In contrast, because they understand the logic of participation under hegemonic parties very well, supporters of the PRI in Nezacubi did not see PAN victories locally as a political opportunity at all. In the past mayors have acted as important mediators between local groups and state and national government officials. But an opposition mayor cannot easily mediate with a PRI governor or PRI legislatures, so these people anticipated losing access to power brokers and streams of patronage. Of more immediate concern, PRI supporters expected, quite correctly as it turned out, that the neighborhood as a whole would be punished for supporting the PAN. This made it quite rational for squatters to continue supporting the PRI even though the party's economic and social policies implemented at the national level did not benefit them much. Tomás was one of the original settlers in Nezacubi and had participated in the land invasion that had established the neighborhood. He did not consider himself to be a political activist, but up until the mid-1990s, Tomás had voted regularly for the PRI and attended rallies and campaign events for PRI candidates whose names he scarcely knew. He does not agree with the neoliberal policies of the ruling party and is frustrated by its blatant corruption. Still, Tomás continues to support the party and its candidates, believing that it is his best chance for getting any assistance from the government.

We prefer the PRI because realistically there are more possibilities with the PRI because they have always been in charge in Oaxaca. If the mayor were still from the PRI, we would not face so many obstacles in getting water and other services. It would be easier for the mayor and the governor to talk. With a PAN mayor it is all much more difficult.
[If the governor were from the PAN, would you vote for the PAN?]
Yes, then it would be different, but I doubt the PAN will ever govern us.
—TOMÁS, NEZACUBI

The reaction of other PRI loyalists in Nezacubi was similar. Although they had been the most active residents when the PRI governed the city, they saw opposition victories in local government as a *closing* of opportunities for influence, so they participated much less than before. They stopped attending weekly *tequios*, where residents participated in community-improvement projects, and they no longer attended community assemblies held at least once a month. Many shifted their activism away from the neighborhood and local level to the state and national government officials, where they thought their efforts would be more successful. However, access to these levels is also difficult and costly, thus many PRIistas simply dropped out of politics temporarily, hoping for a PRI victory in future elections. Ironically, Oaxaca's local context, where a democratic city government coexists with an authoritarian provincial one, has created incentives for the poor to support the PRI because of, not in spite of, its strong authoritarian tendencies.

[Do you feel that the municipal or the state government has more legitimacy?]
    The state government, because that is where the important decisions are made. In the next elections it will be difficult for the PAN to win control over the municipal government. We have always been PRIistas, and we have seen that in the past two [PANista] administrations there has not been any real benefit. The state government has control over most of the resources, and they give it to the municipal government whenever they want to. So public works projects get backed up, the streets are not paved in time, we don't get water, and that is how the problems start. The state government will always favor its own . . . and they will hold out on the funding for the local government.
                                        —TOMÁS, NEZACUBI

    It is worth emphasizing that this dynamic operated primarily in states controlled by autocratic PRI governors. People living in states governed by the PAN face a very different set of incentives and opportunities for participation that should produce varied patterns of participation. Contrary to conventional wisdom, in those contexts local-level democratization may lower overall rates of participation, since the power of clientelist leaders to mobilize supporters is weakened. Like all political parties seeking supporters, the PAN is not shy about appealing to voters' pocketbooks, either by promising more economic development or by simply distributing their share of government pork. However, wherever the PAN is in control of state governments, politics tend to be more open and competitive, resembling more the political dynamics of established democracies (Beer 2003). In such circumstances voters, particularly low-income voters, are freer to support whichever party they choose in whatever way see fit; they are also freer to not participate at all.

Democratization and Political Participation across Mexico

These interviews and the case study analysis provide clues about Mexico's uneven and at times uncertain progress toward cleaner, more competitive, and more open politics and the effect it had on the political activism of Mexicans, primarily the poor. The partial institutional models presented in chapter 4 must be augmented with variables that capture key dynamics of Mexico's political process. I use OLS regression to assess the impact that public policies, cleaner elections, more party competition, and opposition party victories have on the political participation of Mexicans as a whole. Then I test the full institutional model separately for low- and higher-income groups. Finally, I test the same models for four different kinds of political activities: voting, campaign activities, political contacting, and protesting. The statistical analysis has two goals. The regression analysis tests my institutional explanation against the standard socioeconomic status and organizational theories common in the literature. If the institutional factors influence political participation after controlling for income, education, and membership in organizations, we have strong evidence in favor of an institutional explanation of political participation. The regression analyses also allow us to identify *which* institutional factors matter for which income groups and for what kinds of activities. That information provides insight into the key puzzle of why the poor tend to participate less than the affluent in Mexico.

To test the effect that cleaner elections and more democratic politics has on political participation, I added variables that measure people's perceptions of *fraud* and how *satisfied they are with democracy* in Mexico. These variables are based on questions included in the 2003 wave of the CSES surveys that asked respondents to evaluate on a five-point scale how clean the most recent federal elections were and on a four-point scale their satisfaction with the democratic process in Mexico. Given the evidence from my interviews and from previous studies, the effect of satisfaction with democracy should be positive, particularly on electoral forms of participation, whereas the effect of fraud should be more mixed. Although the literature consistently finds that perceptions of fraud depress turnout, we might expect the turnout of people enmeshed in clientelist networks to increase, since the prevalence of fraud suggests that old-style clientelist mobilization still operates. But the political participation of independent voters may suffer where elections are not clean, since the effectiveness of the vote in such circumstances is diminished. In the aggregate, these effects may cancel each other out, so the statistical analysis may not reveal any impact even though it exists.

The models contain several measures of both political party and intragovernmental party competition at the state level. I focus on the state level because this arena has gained immense importance as a result of decentralization reforms and increasing political competition. My interviews show that people have learned to distinguish between levels of government and, because of the enormous resources governors have at their disposal, state-level politics weighs heavily on people's minds when deciding whether and how to participate in politics. Moreover, there is a great deal of variation in the political opportunities across Mexican states, so measuring political competition and opposition party victories at this level captures much of that variation. To measure the effect of political party competition on political participation, I constructed two dummy variables that indicate whether the PRD (or a left-of-center party or coalition) or the PAN (or a right-of-center party or coalition) was competitive in the most recent gubernatorial elections. A state was classified as competitive if the PAN or the PRD won more than 25 percent of the vote in the most recent statewide elections. Although the literature generally has argued that greater electoral competition should bolster participation more or less uniformly across income groups, my interviews suggest that low-income people respond more favorably when the PRD is competitive and negatively or not at all when the PAN is competitive. Recall that Mexico's party system has three major parties competing at the national level but regionally usually only two of the three were competitive. This means that where the PAN was competitive, the PRD usually was not, especially before 2006. In such contexts the poor may feel like democratic politics offers them little choice and little chance to have their preferences represented.

Although political competition opens up opportunities for participation, people may care more about which party governs, since opposition party victories are clear evidence that local- and state-level politics are opening up. The statistical models in chapter 4 included two dummy variables that identified whether respondents lived in states governed by the PAN or the PRD. These variables should pick up some of the effect of intragovernmental party competition, since politics in states governed by the opposition should be less subject to the PRI's punishment regime and should see less of the autocratic political dynamics observed in Oaxaca. This would create more incentives and opportunities for citizens to participate in all kinds of activities, however. My interviews suggest that strong partisans react differently to political competition. If an individual's preferred party is competitive or in power, he or she is more likely to feel efficacious, be interested in politics, and become involved in the political life of the community. If the opposite is true, he or she is likely to feel shut out of politics and participate less. The statistical analysis should therefore pay attention to how political preferences and political contexts interact. To do this, I have added two variables that interact partisanship (whether someone is a PRD or a PAN supporter) with the dummy variables for political competition to produce two new variables: *PRDista with PRD competitive in state-level elections* and *PANista with PAN competitive in state-level elections.* If those interaction variables are significant and the dummy variables for political competition are not, it means that increased state-level political competition bolsters participation only among those who already have strong ideological commitments to opposition parties, whereas "independent" voters practice a "wait-and-see" strategy.

Partisans also care which party is in power at the state level. PRIistas may care the most, because they feel like they have the most access to policymakers and to government patronage when the PRI is in power, but they feel shut out when an opposition party governs. PRIistas should on the whole participate most when the PRI is in power and drop out of politics when it is not. To test if this is correct, I have added three other interaction variables that represent PRIistas living in states governed by each of the three main parties—the PRI, the PRD, and the PAN. The main expectation is for a PRI government to boost the participation of PRIistas, particularly in the electoral arena where recipients of PRI patronage are expected to deliver their support for the party.

Clientelism exerts a powerful influence on the political behavior of the poor. We should expect people subject to clientelist recruitment to participate more than independent voters for several reasons: (1) because people enmeshed in clientelist networks are more likely to be asked (even forced) to participate, (2) because they are more likely to receive information about candidates and government policies, and (3) because they are more likely to feel pressure from their peers to vote, attend rallies, and contact government officials. Measuring the impact of clientelism is difficult, but the 2003 CSES survey asked a battery of questions about the kinds of recruitment individuals received from political parties during elections, including visits in their home from campaign officials, whether campaigns offered them gifts, and whether they received campaign advertising in the mail. The first two are very personal kinds of political recruitment, often associated with clientelist mobilization strategies. To tap into the influence of political recruitment generally, and clientelist recruitment specifically, I have included an additive scale of the number of ways someone was recruited by political campaigns during an electoral cycle, ranging from 0 to 3.

Finally, if democratic politics is to draw people into the political arena, it needs to provide meaningful opportunities to choose among parties that represent people's political preferences. If people feel like the electoral process does not offer them sufficient choice among parties, they may feel like political activities such as voting or attending campaign rallies are simply not worth the effort. The 2003 survey asked respondents to evaluate, on a four-point scale, how well they thought Mexico's electoral process (campaigns and voting) ensures that members of congress will represent the views of voters (ELECREP). We can think of this question as measuring the expected utility individuals experience from voting and campaign activities, since elections that produce deputies that actually represent voters increase the likelihood that any kind of political activity, whether it be voting or contacting, will produce the desired policy outcome.

Table 6.3 reports the results of OLS regression analysis of the full model of political participation, where the dependent variable is the same additive index of political participation used throughout the book. The first column reproduces the partial institutional model from chapter 4 to facilitate the comparison of results, while columns 2, 3, and 4 reproduce the analysis for the full sample, for low-income and medium- and high-income respondents respectively. Focusing for now on the full institutional model, we can see that most of the variables included from the partial model continue to operate in the same way. The coefficient for education is once again both positive and statistically significant. Organizational membership, particularly in political organizations and labor unions, also matters for political participation. These results confirm the validity of standard explanations of political participation for the case of Mexico. However, the more theoretically interesting and important finding is that even after controlling for socioeconomic status and organizational factors, many of the institutional variables added to the full model also proved to be important explanations for who participates and how much.

Among the institutional variables included in the partial model, it is worth noting that union membership and receipt of government transfers through programs like Oportunidades have distinct class-based effects, with only government transfers boosting the poor's participation. Clientelist recruitment remains a powerful mechanism through which Mexicans come to participate in politics. Neither measure of intragovernmental competition—with the PRD or the PAN in power at the state level—had a statistically significant impact on activism when looking at the full sample; however, both factors provide a powerful boost to the political activity of medium- and high-income groups, thus contributing to the stratification of political par-

Table 6.3. Full Political Participation Models (OLS)

Variables	Partial institutional model (1)	Full institutional model (2)	Low-income respondents only (3)	Middle- and high-income respondents only (4)
INDIVIDUAL-LEVEL FACTORS				
Education	.04 (.02)**	.03 (.02)**	.02 (.02)	.04 (.02)
Income	.03 (.02)	.036 (.02)	−.01 (.09)	.03 (.04)
Male	.03 (.06)	.005 (.06)	.04 (.08)	−.04 (.09)
Age	.009 (.002)***	.007 (.002)***	.005 (.003)*	.01 (.004)***
ORGANIZATIONS				
Union member	.26 (.09)***	.25 (.10)***	.04 (.16)	.33 (.13)**
Political organization count	.39 (.05)***	.36 (.05)***	.29 (.07)***	.48 (.09)***
Nonpolitical organization count	.05 (.04)	.04 (.04)	.07 (.06)	−.03 (.06)
POLITICAL OPPORTUNITIES				
Efficacy	.04 (.008)***	.03 (.009)***	.02 (.01)**	.04 (.01)***
Receive government transfers	.19 (.07)***	.20 (.08)***	.22 (.09)**	.17 (.14)
Political recruitment	.28 (.03)***	.30 (.03)***	.26 (.04)***	.33 (.05)***
PRD in power at state level	.14 (.08)*	.14 (.14)	−.06 (.19)	.48 (.24)**
PAN in power at state level	.05 (.07)	.08 (.08)	.04 (.12)	.21 (.12)*
DEMOCRATIZATION				
Satisfaction with democracy	—	.04 (.04)	.02 (.05)	.08 (.06)
Past elections were clean	—	.009 (.02)	.006 (.03)	.01 (.03)

Table 6.3. Full Political Participation Models (OLS) *continued*

Variables	Partial institutional model (1)	Full institutional model (2)	Low-income respondents only (3)	Middle- and high-income respondents only (4)
DEMOCRATIZATION *(continued)*				
PRD competitive in state elections	—	-.18 (.12)	-.19 (.15)	-.28 (.22)
PAN competitive in state elections	—	-.34 (.12)***	-.41(.14)***	-.38 (.25)
PRDista with PRD competitive	—	.93 (.16)***	.88 (.21)***	.94 (.25)***
PANista with PAN competitive	—	.09 (.08)	.22 (.12)*	-.01 (.12)
ELECREP	—	.10 (.03)***	.14 (.05)***	.06 (.05)
INTRAGOVERNMENTAL COMPETITION				
PRIista w/ PRIGOV	—	.36 (.09)***	.38 (.11)***	.35 (.14)**
PRIista w/ PRDGOV	—	.19 (.25)	-.09 (.34)	.87 (.44)**
PRIista w/ PANGOV	—	.10 (.17)	.39 (.24)	-.03 (.24)
Constant	-.26 (.16)	-.16 (.22)	.17 (.32)	-.28 (.40)
	$R^2 = .156$	$R^2 = .200$	$R^2 = .194$	$R^2 = .242$
	$N = 1,551$	$N = 1,407$	$N = 754$	$N = 635$

Source: CSES-CIDE 2003.
Notes: * significant at 0.1 level   ** significant at 0.05 level   *** significant at 0.01 level

ticipation in Mexico. The coefficients for satisfaction with democracy and for clean elections were both positive, as expected, but neither was statistically significant. This is an unusual finding and merits some explanation.

Perceptions of fraud may increase the political activity of those enmeshed in clientelist networks while depressing the activism of others, so that the effects cancel each other out. Whether these variables are significant also depends on the model specification. I replicated the analysis with a model that included only demographic and organizational variables but excluded all other measures of institutional factors. In such a truncated model, the estimated coefficients of satisfaction with democracy and clean elections were positive and statistically significant. However, once I include variables that account for other features of Mexico's political environment—for example, whether the PRI governs at the state level, whether one's preferred party is competitive in state-level elections, or levels of efficacy—the effect of fraud and satisfaction with democracy disappears. Perceptions of fraud have a strong negative effect on individuals' sense of political efficacy (see chapter 4), so when efficacy is included in the model, it absorbs much of the effect that clean elections have on political participation. This does not mean that clean and fair elections do not boost political activity. On the contrary, it is evidence that clean elections boost political activism by making people feel like their activity can really make a difference. Where fraud is more common, efficacy drops, which in turn makes it less likely that individuals will engage in any kind of political activity. People's assessments of how well the democratic process functions are also skewed by political preferences and political contexts. Thus PRIistas living in states governed by the PRI may perceive elections to be fraudulent and may think Mexico is not yet very democratic, but nonetheless they turn out to support their preferred party.[11]

Curiously, all of the coefficients associated with measures of political party competition (PRD competitive and PAN competitive) are negative, indicating that Mexico's parallel two-party systems do not boost political activism as many would have expected. On the contrary, where the PAN competes with the PRI in statewide elections, the decline in political activism is relatively large and statistically significant. A glance at the coefficients for this variable across the models tells a more nuanced story: PAN-PRI competition at the state level depresses only the political activity of the poor, with no systematic effect on the affluent. This is likely because the poor feel like elections in which the PRD is not competitive do not offer them meaningful choices that reflect their preferences. The exception is among people who have strong partisan feelings: partisans of the PAN and the PRD, particularly low-income partisans, participate in politics more often when their preferred party is competitive. The political participation of PRI supporters also depends on which party is in power. PRIistas of all income levels participate more when the PRI is in power at the state level, while the presence of a PRD governor increases the activism only of high-income PRIistas.

My interviews suggest that perceptions of access explain the increase in political activity among partisans of parties in power or of parties that can credibly compete for power. We saw in the case of Oaxaca that when someone's preferred party was in power at the state or local level, perceptions of access increased *for that level of government only*. PRIistas in particular were very sensitive to which party was in power, generally feeling shut out where the opposition governed locally and much more engaged at the state level where the PRI was still dominant. Access matters because it increases the expected utility of political action, expands the opportunities citizens have for targeting governments, and, in time, builds political interest, engagement, and feelings of efficacy that support political activity into the future. Thus institutions that create new channels through which ordinary citizens can access state and government officials can have powerful positive effects on political participation.

Overall, the impact of democratization, cleaner elections, and party competition on political participation has been mixed, and is not altogether encouraging. Political competition boosts political activism only among supporters of Mexico's main political parties. However, the percentage of Mexicans who self-identify as independents is large and growing, while citizens' trust and identification with parties is declining (Klesner 2005 and Camp 2006). Indeed, public opinion polls conducted in recent years show that Mexicans are deeply dissatisfied with all of the major political parties, a trend that shows no sign of abating. Similarly, political participation increased the more respondents felt like the electoral process produced deputies that adequately represent constituents' interests (ELECREP). However, Mexicans appear increasingly disgruntled with the country's politicians, who appear more focused on their own careers and power games than on serving the people who elected them. According to the 2005 World Values Survey, well over 70 percent of Mexicans had little or no trust in Congress, including more than 75 percent of low-income Mexicans. This discontent with political parties and politicians bubbled over during the 2009 midterm elections when a well-organized protest campaign encouraged voters to nullify their ballots, either by voting for all candidates or by writing in the name of fictitious ones. Overall, about one in twenty ballots was deemed invalid,

Table 6.4 Political Participation Models for Electoral and Government-directed Activities (Logit)

Variables	Electoral activities		Government-directed activities	
	Voting	Campaign activities	Contacting	Protesting
INDIVIDUAL-LEVEL FACTORS				
Education		+	+	
Income	+		+++	
Male				
Age	+++			++
Union member	++			++
Political organization count	++	+++		
Nonpolitical organization count			+	
POLITICAL OPPORTUNITIES				
Efficacy	+++	+	++	
Receive government transfers			++	+
Political recruitment	+++	+++	+++	+++
PRD in power at state level				+
PAN in power at state level	+			
DEMOCRATIZATION				
Satisfaction with democracy				+++
Past elections were clean				

Table 6.4 Political Participation Models for Electoral and Government-directed Activities (Logit) *continued*

Variables	Electoral activities		Government-directed activities	
	Voting	Campaign activities	Contacting	Protesting
DEMOCRATIZATION (*continued*)				
PRD competitive in state elections				–
PAN competitive in state elections	+		– –	
PRDista with PRD competitive	+++	+++		
PANista with PAN competitive	++			
ELECREP	+++	+++		
INTRAGOVERNMENTAL COMPETITION				
PRIista with PRIGOV	+	+++	++	+
PRIista with PRDGOV				
PRIista with PANGOV	+			
	$LL = 1514.35$	$LL = 1024.60$	$LL = 889.05$	$LL = 726.68$
	$X^2 = 138.24$	$X^2 = 110.37$	$X^2 = 115.1$	$X^2 = 98.42$
	X^2 prob. $p \leq 0.000$	X^2 prob. $p \leq 0.000$	X^2 prob. $p \leq 0.000$	X^2 prob. $p \leq 0.000$
	$N = 1,427$	$N = 1,429$	$N = 1,424$	$N = 1,425$

Source: CSES-CIDE 2003.
Notes: The dependent variables are dichotomous variables indicating whether an individual undertook one of the political acts.
+ Positive effect at 0.1 level
++ Positive effect significant at 0.05 level

and in Mexico City more than 10 percent of ballots cast were nullified. If these trends continue, political participation, electoral participation in particular, will decline further.

We should not expect the same institutional factors to affect different modes of activism in the same way. For this reason table 6.4 uses logistic regression analysis to examine which factors influence four different kinds of activity: voting, attending campaign rallies, contacting government representatives, and protesting. Electoral activities were much more sensitive to institutional changes associated with Mexico's democratization, while government-directed activities depended almost exclusively on the activities of federal and state governments, either through the spending policies they pursued, or through the different governing styles of the parties in power at the state level. Breaking out the analysis by political acts sheds light on a paradoxical finding in table 6.3: that political competition tends to decrease overall levels of activism. Columns 1 and 4 of table 6.4 shows that political competition actually increases turnout (and campaign activities among partisans) but decreases the amount people protest. This means that where the PAN and the PRD compete effectively with the PRI, Mexicans protest less but protest the most where the PRI is still hegemonic. This makes sense: without opportunities to work for political change through electoral channels, people living in states governed by a dominant PRI political machine are more prone to protest.

The results also confirm that electoral activity depends not just on competition among political parties; rather, it is a function of both political competition and political partisanship. PRDistas in particular are more likely to vote and attend campaign rallies when the PRD has a credible chance of winning a statewide election, while PANistas are more likely to attend campaign events when their preferred party is competitive. People's perceptions that the electoral process produces deputies who represent their constituents' interests (ELECREP) have an especially strong effect on electoral activity but no systematic effect on contacting or protesting. Among the variables included in earlier models, organizational opportunities and explicit recruitment by political parties were powerful determinants of who participates in campaign rallies, although the political weakness of unions is evident. Being a member of a union makes someone more likely to protest but does not increase the likelihood someone will vote, attend campaign rallies, or contact politicians. The results confirm that government transfers create incentives for recipients to target governments directly with political activity—likely to protect their access to the benefits. However, government transfers do little to increase turnout or participation in campaign events. Because government-spending programs were used by the ruling party for political ends in the past, both to boost turnout and votes for the PRI (Magaloni 2006), the fact that receiving government benefits no longer increases electoral activism could be interpreted as evidence that the programs have been successfully protected from clientelist manipulation (Fox 2007).

The results provide some indirect evidence that clientelism continues to structure patterns of political participation in Mexico. The three independent variables with the most consistently positive effects on political participation are membership in political organizations, being targets of political recruitment by political campaigns, and being a PRIista living in a state with a PRI governor. Put together, these three variables create a profile typical of someone who belongs to a clientelist network. Particularly revealing is the impact that having a PRI governor as opposed to a PRD or PAN governor has on the activism of self-declared PRI supporters. States where the PRI has managed to hold on to power are typically (although not exclusively) states where governors have been able to rebuild and consolidate a regional political machine capable of mobilizing large numbers of people around elections. Thus the fact that PRIistas participate the most when the PRI is in power in their state is consistent with the results we would expect if statewide political machines were responsible for mobilizing people into politics.

Tables 6.5 and 6.6 break down the analysis even further to assess whether reforms to Mexico's political system had a differential impact on the political participation of low-income Mexicans. They examine the effect of institutional variables on the electoral and government-directed activities of individuals from different income groups. This analysis is particularly useful for identifying which independent variables contribute to the stratification of political participation in Mexico and which hold potential for reducing class-based differences. Focusing first on electoral activity, the results in table 6.5 yield three important conclusions. First, as noted in chapter 4, civil-society organizations contribute to the stratification of political participation in Mexico.

Unions in particular have a systematic *negative* effect on the campaign activities of the poor, while membership in political organizations boosts turnout among medium- and high-income Mexicans, with no systematic effect on the poor. The one exception might be membership in clientelist organizations, as evidenced by the strong positive effect of political recruitment on the likelihood poor Mexicans will vote. Second, political competition holds a great deal of potential for equalizing turnout rates across income classes

Table 6.5. Effect of Institutional Factors on Voting and Campaign Activity, by Income (Logit)

Variable	Voting		Campaign activities	
	Low income (2)	High income (3)	Low income (5)	High income (6)
INDIVIDUAL LEVEL				
Education				
Income				
Male				
Age	++	+++	+	
Union member			–	
Political organization count		+++	+++	++
Nonpolitical organization count				
POLITICAL OPPORTUNITIES				
Efficacy	++	+++		
Receive government transfers				
Political recruitment	+++		+++	+++
PRD in power at state level	–			
PAN in power at state level				
DEMOCRATIZATION				
Satisfaction with democracy				
Past elections were clean				

Table 6.5. Effect of Institutional Factors on Voting and Campaign Activity, by Income (Logit) *continued*

Variable	Voting		Campaign activities	
	Low income (2)	High income (3)	Low income (5)	High income (6)
DEMOCRATIZATION *continued*				
PRD competitive in state elections	+			
PAN competitive in state elections	+			
PRDista with PRD competitive	+++		+++	+++
PANista with PAN competitive	+++			
ELECREP	++	++	+++	+++
INTRAGOVERNMENTAL COMPETITION				
PRIista with PRIGOV			++	+++
PRIista with PRDGOV				
PRIista with PANGOV				
	$LL = 839.47$	$LL = 637.50$	$LL = 534.15$	$LL = 471.29$
	$X^2 = 73.05$	$X^2 = 88.00$	$X^2 = 68.93$	$X^2 = 55.60$
	X^2 prob. $p \leq 0.000$	X^2 prob. $p \leq 0.000$	X^2 prob. $p \leq 0.000$	X^2 prob. $p \leq 0.000$
	$N = 776$	$N = 634$	$N = 777$	$N = 635$

Source: CSES-CIDE 2003.
Notes: The dependent variables are dichotomous variables indicating whether an individual undertook one of the political acts.
+ Positive effect at 0.1 level
++ Positive effect significant at 0.05 level
+++ Positive effect significant at 0.01 level
– Negative effect at 0.1 level
LL = log likelihood

189

Table 6.6. Effect of Institutional Factors on Contacting and Protest Activity, by Income (Logit)

Variable	Contacting		Protesting	
	Low income (1)	High income (2)	Low income (3)	High income (4)
INDIVIDUAL LEVEL				
Education	+			+
Income	−	+		+
Male				
Age				++
Union member				+++
Political organization count		+	++	
Nonpolitical organization count				
POLITICAL OPPORTUNITIES				
Efficacy	++	+++		
Receive government transfers	+++	+++	+++	+++
Political recruitment		++		
PRD in power at state level				
PAN in power at state level				
DEMOCRATIZATION				++
Satisfaction with democracy				
Past elections were clean			−	
PRD competitive in state elections				

Table 6.6. Effect of Institutional Factors on Contacting and Protest Activity, by Income (Logit) *continued*

	Contacting		Protesting	
Variable	*Low income (1)*	*High income (2)*	*Low income (3)*	*High income (4)*
DEMOCRATIZATION *(continued)*				
PAN competitive in state elections	– –		– – –	
PRDista with PRD competitive				
PANista with PAN competitive				
ELECREP		–		
INTRAGOVERNMENTAL COMPETITION				
PRlista with PRIGOV	+		+	
PRlista with PRDGOV				
PRlista with PANGOV				
	$LL = 397.32$	$LL = 447.99$	$LL = 367.24$	$LL = 324.30$
	$X^2 = 45.11$	$X^2 = 81.34$	$X^2 = 68.40$	$X^2 = 62.11$
	X^2 prob. $p \leq 0.003$	X^2 prob. $p \leq 0.000$	X^2 prob. $p \leq 0.000$	X^2 prob. $p \leq 0.000$
	$N = 774$	$N = 633$	$N = 773$	$N = 635$

Source: CSES-CIDE 2003.

Notes: The dependent variables are dichotomous variables indicating whether an individual undertook one of the political acts.

+ Positive effect at 0.1 level

++ Positive effect significant at 0.05 level

+++ Positive effect significant at 0.01 level

– Negative effect at 0.1 level

– – Negative effect significant at 0.05 level

– – – Negative effect significant at 0.01 level

LL = log likelihood

in Mexico. Competitive statewide elections boosted turnout only among the poor, with particularly significant effects among poor partisans of both the PAN and the PRD. This confirms impressions that emerged from my interviews that poor Mexicans look consistently to the electoral process for opportunities to make their voices heard and to support candidates they think will represent their interests. If they find such candidates, they are encouraged and participate more; however, if elections provide few choices that reflect their preferences, then these individuals are likely to drop out.

Changes in Mexico's democratic political process also affected contacting and protest activity. The activities of organizations tend to widen the participatory gap between the rich and the poor. Both unions and political organizations mobilize medium- and high-income citizens to protest, which helps explain why, contrary to conventional wisdom, the poor are the least likely to protest in Mexico. The one partial exception to this pattern is non-political organizations, which have a positive effect on the contacting activity of the affluent but appear to be more effective at mobilizing the poor to protest. The effect of political competition on government-directed activity is almost the opposite of the effect it has on electoral activity. Where the PRD is in power at the state level, political contacting increases among the more affluent, with no effect on the poor. In contrast, where the PRD is competitive in statewide elections, the poor are *less* likely to protest. This may not be all bad, since it may signal greater satisfaction with political outcomes, but nonetheless viable PRD candidacies tend to depress government-directed activism among the poor.

More troubling from a normative perspective is the consistently negative impact that PAN candidacies at the state level have on the poor's contacting and protest activity. Not even PAN or PRD partisans participate more in government-directed activities where their preferred party has a credible chance of winning elections. Because the PRI is the comparison group for these variables, the negative sign on the coefficients means that participation rates among the poor may be highest where the PRI preserves its hegemonic hold over state politics. This hypothesis receives further confirmation by the positive sign on the coefficient for PRIista with PRIGOV for low-income respondents. Poor PRIistas participate the most in government-directed activities where the governor is from their preferred party for several reasons: (1) perhaps because they feel like they have more access to policymakers under those circumstances, (2) perhaps because they are mobilized by PRI political machines, or (3) perhaps because of a combination of these reasons. Whatever the grounds, the conclusion is the same: competitive PAN or PRD candidacies in gubernatorial elections reduce the income gap in electoral activities but increase the gap for contacting and protest activities.

The analysis of interview and survey evidence did not find a single cause of the income gap in participation; rather, we can point to many causes. Lower levels of income and education do contribute to the participation gap, primarily regarding relatively costly activities like contacting government officials. Organizations in civil society tend to mobilize middle- and upper-class Mexicans into politics more consistently and effectively than the poor, so that growing organizational pluralism contributes to political inequality in Mexico rather than reducing it. For better or worse, clientelist organizations and networks may be the exception. Where they survive and strengthen, they tend to boost the political activity of members, who usually come from lower-income groups. This suggests that where provincial autocracies endure, political participation rates may be more equalized because political machines tend to target the poor for mobilization. However, this kind of participation does not produce greater voice, representation, or accountability. Receiving government transfers is the one variable that consistently boosted the poor's political activity and engagement. This is a hopeful conclusion as long as the Mexican government can continue to increase the coverage and benefits of such antipoverty programs as Oportunidades. There are reasons to suspect that it will not, though, especially in a neoliberal context that demands balanced budgets even in times of major economic crises.

The findings show that democratization in Mexico has created new opportunities for participation, but it has also introduced constraints. State and local political dynamics exert a powerful influence on patterns of political participation. If politics at the state and local levels are open, competitive, and fair, political efficacy and activity increases. But where politics are dirty, authoritarian, or offer voters little choice, the positive impact of free, fair, and competitive national elections is diminished. Public opinion surveys in Mexico consistently report that poor Mexicans are more likely to perceive elections to be fraudulent. Thus the uneven spread of democratic practices in Mexico tends to widen the engagement and activism gap between the poor and the rich. Political competition has a mixed effect on political participation. Where the PRD competes effectively and wins important offices, it boosts turnout only among poor Mexicans, helping to narrow Mexico's participatory gap. However, where party competition is between the PAN and the PRI, the political activity of the poor declines, especially with regards to government-directed activity.

The exception to these patterns is that political party competition by either the PAN or the PRD boosts the political involvement of partisans, especially among poor supporters of the PAN. Thus competitive elections in Mexico boost the political activity of the poor only if they feel like the elections offer them a real choice between parties and candidates who represent their interests. Overall, the PAN has had considerably more electoral success than the PRD, especially at the national level, where it has won the presidency twice in a row and held the largest number of seats in both houses of congress until 2009. On balance, then, increasing party competition and opposition party victories tend to dampen the participation of the poor, especially in states where the PRD does not compete effectively.

CHAPTER 7

POLITICAL EQUALITY AND
DEMOCRACY IN MEXICO

Whether in Chile's exclusionary military regime or Mexico's one-party electoral dictatorship, growing citizen political activism was a crucial factor in weakening authoritarian governments and ushering in democratic transitions throughout the 1980s and 1990s across Latin America. Both the rich and poor, college graduates and the uneducated, joined in peaceful and violent protests, organized marches and strikes, voted in referenda, joined grassroots organizations, and participated in countless other ways while struggling for democracy. Sometimes, as in the case of Chile, it was the poor who, despite precarious living situations and real threats to their lives, were the catalysts for their country's democratic transition (Garretón 1989, Oxhorn 1995, and Roberts 1999). Today, the consolidation of democratic governments in the region means that citizen political participation is more important than ever for selecting political leaders, deciding on public policies, and ensuring governmental accountability, legitimacy, and responsiveness.

Have the poor been able to maintain their activism under democratic political regimes? Across Latin America the answer seems clear: no. Expectations that democratic governments would institutionalize the political participation of the popular groups active during the transition and give voice

196 □   Political Equality and Democracy in Mexico

to the demands and preferences of the region's poor have not been realized. Rather, popular movements have splintered and floundered in most countries, political participation is increasingly atomized and limited to voting in elections, and participatory inequalities appear to be growing (Dietz 1998, Kurtz 2004, Levine 2006, Levine and Romero 2004, Oxhorn 1994, Oxhorn and Ducatenzeiler 1998b, Posner 2008, Roberts 1999, and Weyland 1996). In many Latin American countries today the urban and rural poor participate much less often and in fewer political activities than the more affluent. To the extent that the region's severe socioeconomic inequalities—which are among the worst in the world—are reflected in patterns of political participation, the quality and perhaps the long-term stability of democratic governments will be in jeopardy.

During the past two decades Mexico has undergone a dramatic transformation from a one-party authoritarian regime to a multiparty competitive democracy. Economically it has undergone just as radical a transformation from a state-led development model to a free-market model emphasizing free trade, reduced government spending, and diminished state regulation over the economy. During this same period overall levels of political engagement have declined, with the sharpest drops occurring among low-income Mexicans. This has produced a stratified pattern of political participation that mirrors more and more Mexico's severe socioeconomic inequalities. Although it is tempting to conclude that this stratified pattern in Mexico (and Latin America) is merely mirroring patterns in such advanced democracies as the United States, or are signs of a "normalization" of democratic politics, these conclusions are misleading. There is a causal relationship between these big structural reforms and the political behavior of ordinary citizens.

While much of the political participation research has emphasized the importance of individual resources such as income, skills, and education, as well as individual political attitudes, I have used a variety of methodological strategies and data to show that in Mexico, these tell only part of the story. To fully understand who participates, when they do so, and in what kind of activities, we need to pay attention to the political opportunities and constraints people face locally and nationally. The specific institutions that matter for political activity vary from case to case, but in Mexico the scope and design of antipoverty programs, the features of the party system, the prevalence of fraud and clientelist practices, and the nature of party competition can enhance or dampen the political participation of citizens above and beyond what might be expected from their income and education levels alone. Moreover, political institutions do not have uniform effects across income groups: the same institutional context can send very different signals to the rich and the poor about how open the political system is to political pressure from below. Sometimes public policies and political party competition open up opportunities for participation among the poor that encourage greater interest and engagement with politics and equalize levels of activism. At other times they create obstacles to participation that magnify the demobilizing effect of low resource levels.

Which institutional factors contribute to the stratification of political participation in Mexico and which help to equalize the political voice of Mexican citizens? Among institutional factors, neoliberal reforms narrowed opportunities for political action and created powerful disincentives that discouraged the poor from participating in Mexico's political process. The switch from a development strategy characterized by heavy state intervention in the economy to a free-market model centralized policymaking decisions in a few ministries in Mexico City; institutionalized the use of predetermined formulas to determine spending levels for education, health care, and poverty-alleviation programs; and reduced the size and scope of state activities. These changes had a devastating impact on poor people's political activism by making income and organizations more important for political participation while making the distribution of these resources more unequal in society. Just as damaging has been the declining relevance of government policy in the lives of the poor. As recently as the 1980s, it made sense for people in Mexico to turn to the state to satisfy needs as diverse as affordable housing, better pay, lower prices for food, subsidies for inputs for farmers, for land, for jobs, for health care, for titles to land, and for water, sewage, and other services. But now, because the state has dismantled most of its subsidy and large-scale economic development programs, the poor simply have less stake in the political system and fewer reasons to target the state to satisfy their needs.

The shift to more targeted and technocratic poverty-alleviation programs was a particularly important institutional innovation that affected the poor more than middle- and higher-income groups. The initial shift from PRONASOL to PROGRESA was excruciatingly slow, so that for a few years, millions of Mexicans stopped receiving government transfers. Once in place, PROGRESA and its successor Oportunidades grew quickly in scope, but coverage in urban areas remains low. Actual benefits are too small to bring the resources of the poor above participatory thresholds, while the program's top-down and technocratic design does not create many opportunities or incentives for recipients to become more politically active. Nonetheless, the evidence shows quite clearly that poor recipients of government transfers feel more efficacious and on average contact government officials more than those who do not receive any government benefits. The boost in activism does not extend to voting or other kinds of political acts, but it does speak to the potential that government programs have for alleviating political inequality, especially if greater attention is placed on program design and funding levels (Campbell 2003).

The transition to democracy has not solved these problems of political equality or representation; instead, it has created a complicated set of opportunities and constraints that simultaneously include some people in the political process while continuing to exclude others. Increased political competition has not provided poor Mexicans with the kinds of incentives or opportunities that would draw them consistently into politics. On the contrary the left is frequently too dysfunctional and divided to provide the poor with credible candidates in local and national elections, while competition between the PRI and the PAN tends to demobilize the poor. At times it seems like the PRI's state-level political machines still provide low-income Mexicans with the most consistent opportunities and motivation for political action, albeit in activities that do not necessarily give them real voice.

Cleaner elections, where they exist, boost levels of political efficacy and activity among all income groups. However, progress toward the elimination of fraud has been uneven in Mexico. Analysts agree that the safeguards implemented by the Federal Electoral Institute (IFE) make it virtually impossible for any party or organization to carry out large-scale fraud in national elections, but incidents of vote buying, coercion, and manipulations of ballots still occur in many urban and rural areas. State and local elections, which are not administered by the IFE, are especially rife with electoral mischief that is widespread and systematic enough to alter election results. Aggregate and individual-level evidence shows that the poor are more likely to live in states where elections are dirty, thus they are more likely to perceive fraud to be widespread. To the extent that fraud dampens people's engagement with politics, its prevalence contributes to the participation gap in Mexico.

The strength, number, and autonomy of organizations are important factors that influence overall levels of political participation, especially among the poor, who have fewer resources of their own with which to participate. The growing organizational pluralism and autonomy of civil society has been justly celebrated as an important societal check on abuses of power by government officials and as vehicles for greater citizen involvement in the political lives of their communities. However, I found that the positive effects of a stronger civil society on political participation, representation, and accountability are concentrated among middle- and upper-income Mexicans, so that civil society tends to translate socioeconomic hierarchies into political ones (see also Fox 2007 and Shefner 2008). The reason is not because poor Mexicans are not joiners. Survey evidence from the 2003 wave of the CSES shows that if we exclude unions, the poor are just as likely to be members of organizations as the rich. But organizations, especially political ones, have strong incentives to focus their energies on mobilizing higher-income members who can donate more money, may be more likely to vote, are easier to contact, and are less likely to raise divisive policy issues during elections (Piven and Cloward 1979 and 1997b). In addition, poor people's organizations tend to be weak, fragmented, and too resource-poor to mobilize members into politics with any consistency or long-term autonomy. Thus the organizational arena is another place where the new political environment in Mexico systematically transforms economic inequalities into political ones.

Two institutional factors hold the most promise for boosting the political participation of the poor in Mexico. Although the shift from PRONASOL to PROGRESA and Oportunidades initially created new obstacles for the poor to become involved, today those receiving government transfers feel more efficacious and participate more often in politics, especially in government-directed activities. The expansion of benefits and coverage of Oportunidades has the potential not only to alleviate poverty, but also to create a new kind of engaged, participatory citizen much like Social Security did among the elderly in the United States. However, the expansion of antipoverty programs in Mexico is always contingent on sustained economic growth, especially under a neoliberal paradigm that makes it almost impossible for Mexican governments to engage in deficit spending. Recurrent economic crises in the past have forced well-intentioned administrations to slash antipoverty spending, with inevitable negative consequences to poor people's standards of living *and* political engagement. President Felipe Calderón, elected in 2006, promised to continue to increase the scope of antipoverty programs like Oportunidades. The global economic crisis that devastated Mexico's economy in 2008 and 2009 may force his administration to do the opposite.

A strong left capable of mobilizing voters on a national scale and offering them credible candidates at the local level could draw the poor away from clientelist networks and generate more interest in politics—and eventually also more opportunities for them to become politically involved. Sometimes a strong left has preformed that role, galvanizing voters to challenge the PRI in 1988, the PAN in 2006, and to win control of Mexico City's government since 1997. However, it also has had trouble making inroads among its natural constituency—the urban and rural poor. Although the PRD had its best showing ever in 2006, winning sixteen states and barely losing out on the presidency, by 2009 many of the states and municipalities that had voted for the PRD's presidential candidate switched back to the PRI. In Oaxaca the PRD's vote share dropped from 42 percent to less than 16 percent in 2009, while the PRI's increased from 34 percent to almost 44 percent, reestablishing its dominant position in the state. Currently the PRD is the weakest of the three major parties, unable to compete consistently for national-level offices, with little or no organizational capacity outside of its regional strongholds, and devastated by internal factional conflict. Until that changes, incentives and opportunities for the poor to participate in politics will continue to be limited.

Four Questions Revisited

In chapter 2, I posed four questions that a theory of political participation needed to answer to make sense of patterns of political participation in Mexico and elsewhere. Ultimately, the utility of the framework I've developed depends on its ability to provide better and more complete answers to these questions than current socioeconomic, attitudinal, and mobilizational models alone. Next we compare how well the main theories of political participation answer each of these four questions to better see where the value of an institutional approach to political participation lies.

Why Do the Poor Sometimes Participate More and Sometimes Less Than Individuals with Larger Personal Resource Endowments?

A snapshot of political participation in Mexico today would show that as individuals' income and education levels increase, so too does their political involvement. This relationship between socioeconomic status and political activism holds true for most kinds of political activity, including voting, contacting government representatives, joining political organizations, protesting, and volunteering for political campaigns. Moreover, people's interest in politics and overall feelings of political engagement also increase with their socioeconomic status. It would be very tempting indeed to conclude that in Mexico, as in the United States, socioeconomic status is the most important factor explaining patterns of political participation. This would be a serious yet common mistake. Given the standard model's status as a dominant para-

digm, researchers too often stop looking for other causes of political participation once they find a strong relationship between resources and political
activism. However, a fundamental weakness of standard socioeconomic status and attitudinal models is that they frequently underpredict the political
participation of low-income actors and cannot explain situations in which
the poor participate more than the affluent.

Despite the popular image of poor Mexicans as "parochial," cynical, and
uninvolved in politics, the urban and rural poor in Mexico have a long history of activism, the rhythms of which have varied in concert with the actions and policies of the Mexican state. Throughout the twentieth century,
peasants interacted constantly with the state, their benefactor and landlord,
in cycles of protest and revolt interspersed with periods of real and feigned
submission (A. Bartra 1985 and 1996). Workers and the urban poor have at
times been among the most active segment of the population, participating in strikes, protests, and land invasions as well as a constant stream of
personal contacting and voting. Of course, a great deal of this political activity was mobilized by and channeled through the PRI's corporatist organizations; this created a political situation in which the poor often voted,
participated in campaign events, and contacted government officials with
greater frequency than unincorporated and disaffected middle- and upper-
class citizens. Once neoliberal reforms and democratization diminished the
mobilizing power of the PRI's corporatist organizations, the pattern became
inverted, with the affluent outparticipating the poor.

Although socioeconomic status theories can explain Mexico's current
stratified pattern of political participation, they cannot explain the ebb and
flow of participation over time, or why the poor's activism surges at times
and recedes at others. The answer is well-known to Mexicanists: throughout
the PRI's reign the state and the ruling party in Mexico exerted a powerful influence over the poor's political activity, alternatively opening and closing opportunities for action, mobilizing and demobilizing whole groups and
communities according to the interests of the governing elite. This is clearly
an institutionalist explanation that, while not ignoring the relevance of individual resources, finds the causes of the correlation between socioeconomic
status and political activity in the actions of the state, not in the attributes of
individuals. Looking at the opportunities and obstacles created by the political environment, how these opportunities and obstacles have changed over
time, and which groups have been most affected by these institutional features gives us the analytical leverage to explain both poor people's activism
and their quiescence. The ability to explain why the poor sometimes partici-

pate more and sometimes less than the rich is one of the primary advantages of a focus on political institutions.

Why Do Actors Choose the Political Activities That They Do?

Resource models of political participation do provide some leverage in explaining which political activities individuals are more likely to choose. Each kind of political act imposes a different cost and demands a different set of resources and skills from potential participants. For example, voting is a relatively costless activity that demands some cognitive skills, particularly if we assume people put some thought into their voting decision, but otherwise requires few if any socioeconomic resources. In contrast, donating money to political candidates and parties requires significant monetary resources from actors, writing letters to representatives requires writing skills and perhaps some self-confidence, while participating in a protest or march often requires a significant outlay of both money and time (particularly if the protest is out of town). We might expect, therefore, actors who have these resources in abundance to engage in these activities more often that people with little money, education, or time.

However, as Steven Rosenstone and John Hansen have observed (1993), attention to resources, skills, interests, and beliefs tells only half the story. By opening and closing opportunities for certain actions rather than others, and by shaping the expected costs and benefits of different kinds of acts, political institutions channel political behavior toward certain acts and away from others. Stated simply: people choose the political acts that give them the most bang for their buck. It is apparent that authoritarian systems constrain political behavior in powerful ways, perhaps allowing voting in officially sanctioned elections but outlawing any kind of collective challenge to the state. Democracies also shape behavior by constraining people's choice over possible modes of political action so that not all kinds of political acts are available to all individuals in all locations. Until the 1960s blacks living in the northern United States could vote more or less freely, but blacks living in the south did not have that activity available to them. Registration laws, campaign finance laws, the timing of elections and legislative sessions, labor policy, the repressive capacity of the state, and other features of the institutional context determine which political acts are available to individuals and groups at any given time. In Mexico it is relatively easy to register to vote and to cast a ballot, but in many locations political and civil rights are not effectively enforced, making autonomous voting extremely risky. Choice is restricted by local- and state-level autocracies where fraud is common and neither the PAN nor the PRD compete effectively.

Over time institutions affect behavior by shaping people's preferences and ideas about what is politically desirable and possible. If these institutions are stable over time, individuals develop well-practiced repertoires of action—activities they feel comfortable and confident pursuing without much planning or forethought. Quite often, they will come to value the activity itself and prefer it to other acts that are also available to them. Voting because one feels it is a civic obligation or participating in a strike as a union member are two examples of how stable institutions create repertoires of action. In Mexico one of the consequences of decades of PRI rule and the clientelist links it encouraged with the poor was the development of a strong preference by the poor for direct personal contact with political leaders. They came to prefer political contacting not only because it was an effective strategy, but because it had become an "appropriate" one. In contrast, political contacting is much less common among the poor in the United States, who never had many incentives or opportunities to target government officials. A corollary of this is that the exclusionary nature of Mexico's current political environment may over time produce feelings of powerlessness and learned apathy among the poor, which creates a preference for inaction. As John Gaventa (1980, 255) wrote: "Continual defeat gives rise not only to the conscious deferral of action but also to a sense of defeat, or a sense of powerlessness, that may affect the consciousness of potential challengers about grievances, strategies, or possibilities for change. Participation denied over time may lead to acceptance of the role of nonparticipation."

Why Do People Move in and out of the Political Arena over Time? Why Do Overall Levels of Political Participation in a Country Increase or Decrease over Time?

Because individual and societal resources are relatively stable once acquired, the dominant socioeconomic status and attitudinal models are unable to answer either of these questions satisfactorily. In reality, the political participation of individuals, activists included, is quite fluid. Habitual voters sometimes choose not to vote, people who have never thought of writing a letter to a representative suddenly feel compelled to do so, and people join political movements that engage them for months or even years, only to suddenly drop out of politics altogether. Mexican citizens, like citizens in all countries, are attentive to the opportunities and obstacles their political system presents them. They engage or disengage depending on the choices and incentives they are offered. This is no less true for low-income actors. The poor experiment constantly with different strategies—political and nonpolitical, formal and informal, collective and individual—to satisfy their most immediate needs and to improve the situation of their families. If one set of strategies fails or becomes impractical, they quickly shift to a different mode with greater promise. Sometimes this means temporarily exiting the political system. But such quiescence is usually transitory and ends when new opportunities arise in the political system that make political action worthwhile again.

At the aggregate level, regional and national levels of political participation also change over time, albeit more slowly. Analysts have been lamenting for decades the decline in turnout in the United States, and Mexico seems to be following the example of its northern neighbor. Although I have emphasized the declining political participation among the poor, in fact the political activity of all Mexicans has declined since the implementation of democratic reforms. Whatever the explanation for the decline in the United States, political scientists agree that it is not the result of dropping income or educational levels. Some have pointed to declining overall levels of interest in politics, efficacy, and partisanship, but ultimately the drop in these political attitudes is due to changing features of the political process (for example, increased corruption, partisan gridlock, the decline in face-to-face campaigning in favor of media-driven campaigns), not to essential attributes of citizens. Similarly in Mexico, declining turnout, activism, and political engagement have their roots in the political and electoral dynamics of Mexico's imperfect democracy and in changing state-society relationships that have made certain acts like contacting government offices and protesting more difficult and costly.

These findings go a long way toward establishing the institutional origins of political participation and suggest a need to reinterpret the standard socioeconomic status and resource explanations of political participation. One important conclusion is that we should not be too quick to blame the poor if we observe lower levels of political participation among them. Instead, we should look to the powerful ways that institutions constrain the choices available to them for participation and influence. The literature commonly blames the poor for their low levels of political engagement and activism. In fact, all of the resource models of political participation—including Sidney Verba, Kay Lehman Schlozman, and Henry Brady's (1995) civic voluntarism model—have assumed that political actors operate within an institutional context that is neutral in its effects on people from different income groups.

The unstated assumption is that opportunities for participation are equally available to all, and that everyone who desires to participate can (Leighley 1995). From this perspective inaction either results from consensus or some cultural, attitudinal, or resource deficiency of the nonparticipants themselves (Gaventa 1980, 7–8). This is patently wrong. Although income and education certainly matter for participation in Mexico, as in the United States, they matter because the institutional environment *makes* them matter. Similarly, while measures of political efficacy and political engagement help predict who is most likely to participate, these attitudes are themselves the result of learned experiences with the political process—not deeply felt norms (Dennis 1991). Rather than seeing them as measures of individual psychological predispositions, they should be seen as measures of political reality.

When the poor participate less in politics than the rich, it is a clue that institutional factors are working *against* the inclusion of the poor in the political process. Low incomes matter most when the institutional context places a high monetary cost on participation. If political activity is easy, requiring small investments in time and money, or is subsidized by political organizations and interest groups, then even low-income and resource-poor actors are able to engage in a wide variety of acts. It is not a coincidence that income and education are so important for political participation in the United States, because restrictive registration laws, weak unions, expensive media-driven campaigns, and complicated policymaking processes place a premium on money and education for most kinds of meaningful political activities. By contrast, in countries with universal registration, stronger unions, and lower thresholds for the creation, survival, and success of small parties, income and education tend to matter less. So income and education matter, but they do not matter equally everywhere, and this difference can be explained by paying attention to political institutions. In Mexico the reforms of the state required by Mexico's shift from a state-led to a neoliberal development model have raised the cost of petitioning, protesting, participating in campaigns, and organizing collective actions against the state. This places much political activity beyond the reach of a majority of the population who live near or below the poverty line.

A similar lesson is that people cannot be described as "active" or "passive," "citizens" or "subjects," "radicals" or "clients" in any absolute sense.[1] Many of the people I interviewed behaved like clients in one context (uninterested in politics, cynical, participating only when mobilized by a local leader, in ways that reinforced power imbalances) but as radical citizens in another (participating autonomously and confidently in elite-challenging ways). The reason for this is that all individuals, rich and poor alike, college graduates and high school dropouts, have the capacity to learn relatively quickly and efficiently how to participate in democracy or in whatever kind of political system they find themselves (Anderson and Dodd 2005). They can also learn the rules of different political games operating simultaneously at the local, state, and national level and adjust their behavior and beliefs according to the opportunities they perceive for action at each level. In Mexico, however, overlapping democratic and authoritarian contexts make this kind of political learning more difficult, because citizens are constantly receiving conflicting signals about how the political system really works. Nonetheless they are learning and adjusting their behavior and beliefs.

Another general conclusion is that while all political systems create opportunities *and* obstacles for participation, these do not have uniform effects on people from different social and economic groups. Indeed, institutional features that create opportunities for some may be perceived as obstacles by others. A good example of this is the candidacy and electoral victory of blacks to important political positions in the United States. Studies show that increasing minority office-holding, a feature of the political opportunity structure, depresses the activism of whites while often increasing the activism of African Americans (Bobo and Gilliam Jr. 1990 and Gay 2001). Similarly, increasing representation of women in important political positions enhances the political engagement and the political activity of women in the United States, with little or no impact on men (Burns, Schlozman, and Verba 2001). In Mexico electoral competition between the PRI and the PAN offered adequate choice for middle- and upper-class citizens, but the poor (who were looking for more nationalistic economic policies and a greater emphasis on poverty alleviation rather than economic growth) felt justifiably unrepresented.

Studying Political Participation

Surveys are the overwhelming method of choice used by political scientists interested in explaining political behavior. But because survey methods are not well suited to studying institutions, they have severe limitations when it comes to explaining human behavior. In particular, surveys are not very effective at establishing the links between macrovariables and microlevel decisions about action. For this reason alone, most survey researchers do not design studies that measure the impact of political variables on political participation, skewing their findings in the process. In the introduction to their study of mass political action in five Western democracies, Samuel Barnes and Max Kaase (1979, 16) admit as much: "The 'assessment of the state of mind' of a people is among the procedures at which survey research excels. Thus, the overwhelming importance of individual level factors in explanations of political participation is due in great part to the overwhelming use of survey methods to study the phenomena. Different methods, better suited to uncovering contextual factors could—and have—enrich our understanding of the causes of citizen activism."[2]

Attention to political opportunities requires an eclectic use of methods capable of uncovering the links between institutions, rules, norms, and individual behavior. These should include creative combinations of comparative case studies, participant observation, in-depth interviewing, oral histories, and ethnographic fieldwork (see, for example, Gutmann 2002). The value added by these approaches is that they allow researchers to search for and uncover the mechanisms through which institutions affect behavior and identify which institutional features have this effect. Seeing politics from the ground up, from the perspective of "the people," tells us a lot about how the specific political systems work. These approaches tell us why people are engaged or detached, what would have to change for them to become active, and why they choose one activity over another. A promising strategy is to combine qualitative case-study research with survey work that is informed by the findings of fieldwork. Surveys can be designed to tap into some institutional factors, and doing so successfully can yield great insight into the interrelationship between political opportunities, psychological factors, and political participation. This requires a self-conscious effort on the part of the researcher to include measures of institutional factors into the survey design and to formulate questions that tap into the full array of choices— political and otherwise—available to individuals when pursuing their goals. However, without prior fieldwork researchers may not know which questions to ask.

The most interesting and promising applications of an institutionalist framework do not lie in studying single cases, but in comparing political activity across geographical units and social groups within the same political context. Our understanding of the causes of political participation has been limited by the excessive focus on politics in advanced industrial democracies and may very well be an artifact of the cases studied and the method used. In particular, our understanding of political participation has been unduly influenced (I would even say biased) by findings from the United States, which by all accounts is rather unique when it comes to citizen participation in politics (Dalton 1996 and Verba, Nie, and Kim 1978). Such single-country national-level samples hold institutions constant, making it impossible to observe the influence of institutional variables because they are effectively controlled for by the research design. This has inhibited the development of a truly comparative theory of institutional effects on political behavior.

When we think of comparative research, we often turn to cross-national comparisons in the tradition of the work of G. Bingham Powell Jr. (1986) and of Sidney Verba, Norman Nie, and Jae-On Kim (1978). Much can also be learned from comparisons across subnational units within a single country by exploiting within-country variation in institutional contexts. Two examples are Steven Rosenstone and Raymond Wolfinger's (1978) study of the effect of registration laws across counties on the voting behavior of different groups of citizens and Nancy Burn's analysis of political representation across states (Burns, Schlozman, and Verba 2001). Their research also exemplifies how individual-level data from survey research can be analyzed in conjunction with macrolevel features of the institutional environment to enrich our understanding of political behavior.

Longitudinal studies that compare changes in political activity over time in a single setting—whether a neighborhood, city, or country—also hold much promise for theory building. My work approximates a longitudinal design by collecting political oral histories from citizens, relying on their recollections and reports about how changes in the institutional context have impacted their participatory strategies. Susan Stokes's *Cultures in Conflict* (1995) is another example of how such a longitudinal study could be carried out by mixing archival research with qualitative research and surveys. Other notable examples of longitudinal studies that have contributed to our understanding of how changing political contexts affect political participation include Henry Dietz's (1998) study of political participation in urban Lima between 1970 and 1990; Samuel Eldersveld and Bashiruddin Ahmed's (1978) study of changes in patterns of political participation in India after independence; and Steven Rosenstone and John Hansen's (1993) longitudinal analysis of existing survey data in the United States.

Implications for Political Equality and the Quality of Democracy

Twenty years after governments across Latin America began implementing neoliberal reforms in earnest, there is today growing concern about the impact these reforms are having on the quality of democracy in the region. The idea of the "quality of democracy" is a bit vague, and scholars disagree on what its most important indicators are. Nonetheless, because the intrinsic equality of each citizen is a fundamental assumption of democracies, any assessments of the quality of democracy must consider the equality of political voice—that is, whether a political system provides citizens with more or less equal opportunities for effective political participation and political access to decision makers during and in between elections (Dahl 1989 and Verba, Schlozman, and Brady 1995). Any differences in the opportunity or capacity of citizens to voice their preferences in the political arena, especially systematic inequalities that overlap with social cleavages (income, gender, religion, and so on), damage democracy by affecting the messages that politicians hear. This diminishes the incentives politicians have for responding to the needs and preferences of certain groups.

It is tempting to assume, as many have done, that a transition from authoritarianism to democracy creates political openings and opportunities to participate for all citizens, regardless of their income, where they live, or what their political beliefs are. But as I have emphasized throughout, there are good theoretical and empirical reasons to expect the opposite; that is, that a transition to democracy will not create uniform political opportunities for all (see also Dahl 2006 and Verba, Nie, and Kim 1978). This means that it is important to distinguish between formal or de jure restrictions to participation (of which there are few in countries like Mexico) and de facto restrictions and obstacles (of which there are many). Although income and resource inequalities are partly responsible for the existence of political inequalities in democracies, ultimately inequalities in voice and participation result from the formal and informal rules of the political game that create unequal opportunities for political activity. If the poor vote less, protest and petition less, we can assume that they face restrictions to participation that more affluent citizens do not.

Active political participation by the lower class is of special importance in Latin America not just because the poor make up more than half of the population in many countries, but also because their voice is most easily silenced in democratic systems. In this regard, neoliberal reforms were doubly pernicious to the quality of democracy. Not only did the reforms fail to reduce poverty levels or ease socioeconomic inequalities in the short term, because neoliberal reforms were often implemented in an authoritarian context, citizen participation lags even after greater openings of the political system were achieved. As Philip Oxhorn and Graciela Ducatenzeiler (1998a, 10) have observed: "The resultant political regimes are characterized by a number of authoritarian aspects that can begin to blur the distinction between democratic and authoritarian regimes." The effect of this political exclusion of citizen voices is most pronounced among the poor, who are least able to organize within a neopluralist context and who have the least resources with which to attempt increasingly costly political activities. This lack of political equality makes, according to some, the consolidation of representative democracies in the region impossible (Oxhorn 1998 and Weffort 1998).

From the perspective of citizen voice, an assessment of the quality of Mexico's democracy is not encouraging.[3] Only a few years since the end of the "perfect dictatorship," many Mexicans, in particular Mexico's poor, already seem disenchanted with democratic politics. Poor Mexicans are skeptical about the ability of elections to give them power over their leaders, they are voting less than before, and they seem resigned to having little say in the political process. The poor also participate less in government-directed political activity than the more affluent. When they do participate, they tend to do so in activities that send little information to or put little pressure on government officials. The danger is that this inequality in the voices that are heard in the corridors of power produce a systematic bias in policymaking, leading to policies that do not take into account the needs and preferences of well over half of the country's population.

Although social divisions in political participation are important, *how* citizens participate in politics is just as important as *who* participates for evaluating the quality of democracy. Some political acts, such as protesting or the direct contacting of legislators, put a lot of pressure on political leaders and convey detailed information about the needs and preferences of citizens. Other acts, such as voting, do not. Political acts serve different purposes within the political process. Some forms of political participation, such as elections and referenda, provide opportunities for citizens to decide on collective decisions, while others are more important for placing issues on the decision-making agenda or for influencing the content of policies (Davis and Brachet-Marquez 1997). Distortions of the principle of political equality also arise, therefore, when some social and economic groups are better able to participate in activities that convey detailed information about policy matters and place significant pressure on politicians, even if they vote little or not at all. A full assessment of citizen voice, and therefore of the quality of democracy in Mexico, needs to consider not just the differences in levels of participation across groups but also variations in the kinds of political activities participants attempt.

Voting and Campaign Activity

The establishment of regular, competitive elections in most Latin American countries in recent decades has been justly celebrated because most authoritarian rulers during the 1960s, 1970s, and 1980s governed by excluding large sectors of the population from the political process. Even in countries such as Mexico, where elections occurred regularly (and often), electoral fraud and clientelist mobilization practices meant that voting served more to legitimize the regime than to transmit information about citizen preferences to political leaders. Voting is now the most common political activity for Mexican citizens (even in 2003, when turnout reached historic lows) and is now meaningful because it provides a credible mechanism for removing incumbents from power. However, compared with other kinds of electoral and government-directed activities, voting has little capacity to convey detailed information about preferences and even less capacity to put pressure on policymakers. The vote is on the whole a weak tool for influencing the decisions of policymakers.[4] Although available to all, unless votes are organized in large, disciplined blocks around policy issues, elections convey little information to elected officials and exert even less pressure on their decisions (Piven and Cloward 1997, 281). We might therefore think of a political system that relies primarily on voting as a means to ensure government responsiveness and accountability as a "thin democracy," because there will be few opportunities for citizens to put pressure on government officials in between elections (Davis and Brachet-Marquez 1997).

Campaign activity—such as attending rallies, volunteering for political candidates, or donating money—hold more potential for citizen voice than voting alone. Although citizen participation in electoral campaigns has always been important in Mexico, given how expensive, sophisticated, and organizationally complex electoral campaigns have become, candidates depend more than ever on citizen support to run successful campaigns.[5] Volunteering for campaigns or donating money to candidates gives participants multiple opportunities to meet with political candidates and their advisers. In turn, candidates have more incentives to listen and respond to the messages they hear from these activists. Just as important, campaign activity, unlike voting, can be multiplied in frequency and intensity, so that citizen inputs are not counted or weighed equally. The clearest example of this are campaign donations, which, despite ceilings on the amount that can be donated by any individual, can be multiplied in size in ways that are not possible with other forms of activity. This means simply that by augmenting the volume of campaign activity, individuals and groups can put greater pressure on policymakers to respond to their interests (Verba, Schlozman, and Brady 1995, 45–46). In Mexico the affluent are about twice as likely to participate in campaign activities as the poor (see chapter 1), and they much more likely to donate money to campaigns. This creates the potential for severe inequalities in voice that overlap with Mexico's severe income inequalities, producing candidates that are less responsive and accountable to the poor. Unless the poor are able to participate in other ways that send clear messages to government officials and put more pressure on them in between elections—by contacting them directly or carrying out protests and marches—they may have little voice in policymaking.

Petitioning and Contacting Activity

Like campaign activity, the petitioning of government officials and the participation in protests can be used by individuals to send precise messages about their needs and opinions about issues. These actions can be multiplied in ways that increase the pressure individuals place on policymakers. These characteristics make such activities powerful vehicles for citizen voice that can be used by the poor to mitigate the class biases generated by the electoral process. Petitioning party and government officials for assistance has been one of the most common and meaningful forms of participation for Mexico's poor. Although it is a strategy that reflects the clientelist relationship between political leaders and the poor, and as such it tends to reinforce power asymmetries, the poor still view it as necessary to secure their share of government spending. However, petitioning among the poor has declined since the democratic transition, so that now they petition much less frequently than before and about half as often as the most affluent (Holzner 2007a).

The root of this decline can be traced to the devastating impact neoliberalism has had on the poor's capacity and incentives to contact government officials. On the one hand, contacting government officials has become an increasingly costly and ineffective strategy, requiring a significant investment in time, money, and lost wages. On the other, during the 1990s policy and distributional decisions became more centralized in distant ministries, while many budgetary decisions are now insulated from political pressures from below by using fixed formulas to determine spending levels for education, health care, and poverty-alleviation programs. To be effective, contacting activities require the support of important allies within government ministries and from local organizations that subsidize the cost of travel or whose leaders carry out the petitioning activity on behalf of local groups. However, traditional worker and peasant organizations have been severely weakened as a result of economic crises and free-market policies that reduced their access to government patronage. Many new independent organizations now populate Mexico's civil society, but these too are small, weak, and fragmented (Olvera 2004). While it is true that clientelist and corporatist organizations during the PRI's rule tended to demobilize popular groups by fragmenting them and forcing them to compete against each other for patronage, civil society in Mexico today is no less fragmented. Organizations face different but strong pressures to compete against each other for resources and access (Kurtz 2004). Although the rise of independent organizations certainly means that the poor have gained a measure of political autonomy, the inability of these organizations to aggregate interests effectively means that the poor have lost a measure of political voice.

Protests and Strikes

Faced with little access to government officials, with familiar clientelist and corporatist strategies rendered ineffective by top-down, hierarchical, and technocratic policymaking practices, the poor are left with few options to participate in formal political activity. We might expect that because of worsening grievances and the closing of conventional channels of access, there would be an increase in protest activity. However, many if not most of Mexico's poor see protest as a risky, dangerous, and not very effective strategy, to be attempted only after all other options have been exhausted (Holzner 2004). This should not be interpreted, as some have argued, as an attitude rooted in a political culture characterized by deference to authority (Almond and Verba 1963 and Stokes 1995). Rather, it is rooted in a clear recognition of the risks, difficulties, and unlikelihood of success of protest activity. In fact, because of the centralization of policymaking in Mexico, protest campaigns must target the highest levels of government over a sustained period of time to be successful. These are the kinds of protests that are most visible and receive the greatest media coverage, but they are practically impossible for increasingly unorganized and resource-poor actors to undertake. Given that the affluent are nearly twice as likely to attempt protests in Mexico, we would be right to suspect that they are better able to bear the risks and costs of protesting. Thus they have more opportunities to pressure the state than the poor.

Informal Politics and Exit Strategies

Although many of Mexico's poor vote less often, attend fewer political rallies, and disdain protests, declining efficacy and exit from the formal political arena do not mean that they have stopped looking for ways to improve their situation. Citizens do not pursue their interests through the formal political arena alone but also through community organizing, cooperative problem solving, and other informal activities that do not target the state directly (Booth and Seligson 1978 and Dietz 1998). These kinds of self-help activities are important survival strategies for resource-poor actors who use them to provide for themselves the goods they no longer receive from the state. In addition to these informal political strategies, the poor also choose private exit strategies—such as working harder, sending more family members into the workforce, and even crime—instead of state-directed activities to fulfill their needs (Huntington and Nelson 1976).[6] Joining nongovernmental organizations and other kinds of grassroots organizations that provide access to credit and income-generating opportunities have become appealing alternatives to formal political participation for the poor since the late 1990s. Labor migration to urban areas or to the United States is also a common exit strategy pursued by Mexico's poor (and not so poor).[7]

Although they are different in many ways, what migration, joining local organizations, and self-help strategies have in common is that they communicate little or no information to political leaders. Rather than put pressure on the state, they let it off the hook. Because these strategies are a form of exit rather than voice, these activities do not increase the political power of the poor, nor do they enhance the responsiveness and accountability of local and national governments (Hirschman 1970). Again, it would be wrong to interpret this upsurge in exit strategies as evidence of a cynical or apathetic political culture among the poor. Instead, this energy directed toward informal and community politics is indicative of poor people's awareness that despite the political openings that democratization might produce, participation in state-directed activities is often not an effective strategy for achieving their main objectives of food, economic security, housing, and a better life for their children.

What does this all mean for the quality of democracy in Mexico? The signing of NAFTA in 1994 and the defeat of the PRI in the 2000 presidential elections were regarded by many as sure signs that a modern democratic system was taking hold in Mexico. A closer look reveals a citizenry deeply disillusioned with key political institutions—namely, with political parties and the congress, although not yet with democracy itself. Many are losing interest in electoral politics that they see as corrupt, as having little influence on what happens in their daily lives, and that offer few palatable choices at the ballot box. Without firm party loyalties to anchor their behavior, voters are flip-flopping from party to party, depending on which candidate they find more appealing. This of course has created a great deal of electoral volatility in both national and local elections (Camp 2006). The clearest example of this occurred in 2009, when the PRI resurrected itself after a disastrous showing in 2006 to once again become Mexico's largest party. As impressive as its recovery was, the PRI owes its recent success much more to the failings of the PAN and the PRD than to its own platforms or record of good governance.

While Mexico's imperfect democracy discourages, its free-market policies exclude—not through the threat of force or sanctions, as authoritarian regimes might do, but by making mobilization and demand making more difficult and costly or by channeling discontent into such arenas as local governments or neighborhood councils that have relatively little power. Although much of the poor's demobilization occurs at the level of groups, affecting their capacity to undertake collective action, the voice of the poor is silenced just as much by the cumulative effect of individual decisions to simply drop out of politics. As Matthew Gutmann (2002, 88) has noted: "One noteworthy feature of NAFTA-era popular nationalism in Mexico is the heightened conviction on the part of many that they are unable to influence national politics. . . . They grow less and less optimistic about Mexico's political future and increasingly disillusioned about the nature and import of democracy in their country. . . . The reality, most feel, is that only rarely are they able to politically control their own daily lives, and even less frequently can they influence any political process that might conceivably be regarded as democratic self-determination in Mexico." As a consequence, the voice of the poor in Mexico is heard neither loudly nor clearly, and certainly not equally, impoverishing democracy as a result.

Appendix A. Survey Questions and Variables

The majority of the statistical analysis in this book relies on the results of the 2003 Mexico wave of the CSES survey (see http://www.cses.org). In addition to the standard CSES survey questions, which are the same for every country, each country collaborator can add additional questions to the end of the questionnaire. For all the regression analysis and much of the rest of the statistical analysis, I rely on the full Mexico version of the 2003 CSES survey which is housed at the CIDE's library (Centro de Investigación y Docencia Económica), which I refer to as CSES-CIDE 2003 (the datasets for 2000, 2003, 2006 can be accessed free of charge at http://www.biiacs.cide.edu/consulta).The principal advantage of this version is that it has a much richer set of political participation questions than the standard CSES questionnaire and than the 2006 CIDE version. Some of the analysis, particularly in chapter 4, used four additional datasets: the 1990–2005 Mexico waves of the World Values Survey, and the standard CSES dataset for Mexico from 1997 and 2000 (referred to as CSES 1997 and CSES 2000). This appendix contains descriptions of all of the variables used in the analysis for this book. In some cases I provide the exact wording of the survey question, and in others I describe how the variables were constructed. Unless otherwise noted, the variables were taken from the CSES-CIDE 2003 dataset.

Political Participation

1. *Voting.* "Did you vote in the past elections held on July 6 for federal deputies?"
2. *Campaign activity.* "I am going to read a few activities that people do during elections. Please tell me if you did any of these activities during the

past elections: Did you show support for a party or candidate by attending meetings or campaign rallies, distributing posters or bumper stickers, or in any other way?"

3. *Political contacting.* "During the past five years, have you have you contacted any politician or government official in person, by writing a letter or in any other way?"

4. *Protest.* "Please tell me if during the past five years you've participated in any manifestation, protest or march?"

5. *Overall activity index.* For 2000 data the political participation index is an additive scale of fifteen different political acts: voting in the 2000 elections, contacting a congressional representative, signing a petition, organizing a complaint or petition against the government, protesting, participating in a sit-in, occupying government offices, participating in land invasions, blocking streets or roads, participating in an armed uprising against the government, distributing campaign propaganda, attending a campaign meeting or rally, donating money to a political party or candidate, working for a political campaign, party or candidate, and trying to persuade others to vote for a party or candidate. One point was given for each act; the scale runs from 0 to 15 (Cronbach alpha = 0.6797).

For analyses using 2003 data, the political participation index is an additive scale of eight different acts: persuading others to vote for a party or candidate, voting in 2003 elections, participating in campaign activities or events, participating in marches or protests, contacting government officials, organizing informally with others to solve a common problem, occupying government offices, blocking roads or highways. One point was given for each act; the scale runs from 0 to 8. (Cronbach alpha = 0.556)

Demographic Variables

1. *Income.* The WVS measures income on a 10-point scale, with monetary values varying across waves. In all cases, I coded those who reported incomes ranging from 1 to 3 points as low income, 4–6 points as middle income, and those reporting incomes ranging from 7 to 10 points as high income. Though not identical, the coding of income categories for all datasets turned out to be quite consistent. The CSES-CIDE 2000 and 2003 coded household income according to multiples of the monthly Mexican minimum wage, with the following frequency distributions:

In addition, I divided individuals into three income categories:

Table A.1. Frequencies for Household Income Categories, 2000

Values	Frequency	Percentage
1 times the minimum wage ($1,128 per month)	166	11.2
2 times the minimum wage	403	27.2
3 times the minimum wage	312	21.1
4 times the minimum wage	176	11.9
5 times the minimum wage	98	6.6
5–7 times the minimum wage	125	8.4
7–10 times the minimum wage	88	5.9
10–30 times the minimum wage	96	6.5
30+ times the minimum wage	17	1.1
Total	1,481	100

Source: CSES 2000 survey.

Table A.2. Frequencies for Household Income Categories, 2003

Values	Frequency	Percentage
0–1 times the minimum wage ($0–1,310 per month)	372	20.1
1–3 times the minimum wage ($1,131–3,930)	720	39.0
3–5 times the minimum wage ($3,931–6,550)	427	23.1
5–7 times the minimum wage ($6,551–9,170)	131	7.1
7–10 times the minimum wage ($9,171–13,100)	98	5.3
10–30 times the minimum wage ($13,101–39,300)	89	4.8
30+ times the minimum wage ($39,301+)	9	0.5
Total	1,846	100

Source: CSES 2003 survey.

Low income = 1 to 3 times minimum wage ($0–$3,930 for 2003)

Middle income = 4 to 7 times minimum wage ($3,931–$9,170 for 2003)

High income = 7+ times minimum wage ($9,171 + for 2003)

Where I report results for only low- and high-income groups, as I do in the regression analysis, Low Income is defined as above, while High Income includes both Middle and High Income groups.

Table A.3. Frequencies for Education Levels

	2000		2003	
Values	*Frequency*	*Percentage*	*Frequency*	*Percentage*
No schooling	87	4.9	119	6.0
Incomplete elementary	258	14.6	343	17.3
Finished elementary	336	19.0	365	18.4
Incomplete middle school (*secundaria*)	106	6.0	147	7.4
Finished middle school	317	18.0	355	17.9
Incomplete high school	116	6.6	163	8.2
Finished high school	252	14.3	228	11.5
Incomplete university	146	8.3	125	6.3
Finished university and more	148	8.4	142	7.2
Total	1,766	100	1,988	100

Source: CSES-CIDE 2000–2003 survey.

2. *Education.* "What is the highest grade level you have completed?" ("¿Hasta qué año escolar estudió usted?")

3. *Age.* What is your current age? (¿Cuántos años cumplidos tiene usted?")

4. *Male.* Dichotomous variable designating respondents' sex: 1 = Male, 0 = Female.

Attitudinal Variables

1. *Political efficacy.* The political efficacy index was constructed using four questions from the CSES survey: "Some people say that no matter who people vote for, it won't make a difference to what happens. Others say that who people vote for can make a difference to what happens. Using the scale on this card, where ONE means that voting won't make a difference to what happens and FIVE means that voting can make a difference, where would you place yourself?" (VOTEMAT). "Some people say that members of Congress know what ordinary people think. Others say that members of Congress don't know much about what ordinary people think. Using the scale on this card, where ONE means that the members of Congress know what ordinary people think, and FIVE means that the members of Congress don't know much about what ordinary people think, where would you place yourself." (REPSCARE). This scale

was inverted in the analysis so that 1 = don't know much about what ordinary people think and 5 = know what people think.

"Some people say it makes a difference who is in power. Others say that it doesn't make a difference who is in power. Using the scale on this card, where ONE means that it makes a difference who is in power and FIVE means that it doesn't make a difference who is in power, where would you place yourself?"(POWERMAT). This scale was inverted in the analysis.

"Some people say that political parties in Mexico care what ordinary people think. Others say that political parties in Mexico don't care what ordinary people think. Using the scale on this card (where ONE means that political parties care about what ordinary people think, and FIVE means that they don't care what ordinary people think, where would you place yourself? (PTYCARE). This scale was inverted in the analysis. Each component has a value that ranges from 1 to 5, (Low to High) so the efficacy scale runs from 4 to 20, which was rescaled to range from 0 to 16 (Cronbach alpha = 0.5533).

2. *Party identification.* Party identification was constructed using two follow-up questions in the CSES survey. "Do you usually think of yourself as close to any particular party?" If yes, respondents were asked: "Which party is that?" If no, they were asked: "Do you feel yourself a little closer to one of the political parties than the others?" If yes, they were asked: "Which party is that?" Adding these two responses together produced a party identification for each respondent. I then constructed three dummy variables: PANista (n = 485, 27.5 percent), PRIista (n = 405, 22.9 percent) and PRDista (n = 177, 10 percent).

3. *Satisfaction with democracy.* "On the whole are you very satisfied, fairly satisfied, not very satisfied, or not at all satisfied with the way democracy works in Mexico." The scale was inverted in the analysis so that 1 = not at all satisfied, 4 = very satisfied.

4. *National economic situation.* "What do you think about the state of the economy these days in Mexico? Would you say that the state of the economy is very good, good, neither good nor bad, bad, or very bad. The scale was inverted in the analysis so that 1 = very bad, 5 = very good.

5. *HUMRTS.* How much respect exists for individual liberties and human rights in Mexico? (1 = no respect at all, 4 = a lot of respect).

6. *CORRUPT.* How extensive do you think corruption is among politicians in Mexico? (1 = there is almost no corruption, 4 = very extensive).

7. *ELECREP.* How much does the electoral process in Mexico (campaigns and elections) assure that members of Congress will represent the opinions of voters? (1 = not at all, 4 = very much).

Organizational Variables

1. *Union.* "Do you belong to a union or labor organization?" (Where 1 = belong; 0 = does not belong).

2. *Political and nonpolitical organization index.* The CSES survey asks a number of questions about organizational membership. The distinction between political and nonpolitical organizations is not always clear cut. Following Verba et al. 1995, I defined nonpolitical organizations are those voluntary organizations that do not take stands on politics as a regular part of activity, and political organizations as those that potentially could, as part of their activities, take stands on politics (with the exception of union membership, which I consider separately).

   The political organization index is an additive scale that measures the number of political organizations to which an individual belongs. It consists of the following organizational types: *ejido*, farm, business, neighborhood, and ecological. One point was given for each membership. The scale ranges from 0 to 5 (Cronbach alpha = 0.46).

   The nonpolitical organization index is an additive scale that measures the number of nonpolitical organizations to which an individual belongs. It consists of the following organizational types: religious, professional, sports, women's, and charity. One point was given for each membership. The scale ranges from 0 to 5 (Cronbach alpha = 0.41).

Political Recruitment (POLREC)

The Mexico version of the CSES questionnaire contained the following questions used to construct the political recruitment index:

To make themselves known, some candidates send letters, give out gifts, and canvass houses and neighborhoods. Did any campaign organizations for presidential candidates

a. visit your house to encourage you to vote?
b. Send you campaign propaganda by mail?
c. Give you a gift?

One point was given for each time a respondent was recruited by a campaign or candidate producing an additive scale that ranged from 0 to 3.

Political Opportunity Variables

1. *Fraud.* "In some countries, people believe their elections are conducted fairly. In other countries, people believe that their elections are conducted unfairly. Thinking of the last election in Mexico, where would you place it on this scale of one to five, where ONE means that the last election was not clean and FIVE means that the last election was clean?"

2. *Government assistance.* "Do you or any member of your family receive any type of assistance from a federal or state government program, such as *Leche, Oportunidades,* PROCAMPO, etc.? Yes = 426 (21.5 percent); No = 1553 (78.5 percent).

3. *Political competition.* A party or coalition was considered to be competitive if it received at least 25 percent of the vote in the most recent gubernatorial election. This may seem like a rather low threshold for competitiveness, but it is appropriate because at the time many gubernatorial elections in Mexico had three or more parties splitting the vote, so that the winner frequently obtained less than an absolute majority of the vote. In addition, political competition is important for political participation primarily because it signals to voters that their preferred political party or candidate has a credible chance of winning. In elections with three or more parties, a 25 percent threshold is reasonable because, though not usually enough to win an electoral contest, it is enough to signal a credible candidacy. In cases where the PAN and the PRD were in a coalition together, the election was coded according to candidate's party affiliation.

   The *Left Competitive in State* is a dichotomous variable indicating whether a leftist party or coalition was competitive in the most recent gubernatorial election. In all cases the leftist party or coalition always involved the PRD. The *Right Competitive in State* is a dichotomous variable indicating whether a right-of-center party or coalition was competitive in the most recent gubernatorial election. In all cases the party or coalition always involved the PAN.

4. *Party in power at the state level.* PRIGOV (PRI in power at the state level) is a dichotomous variable indicating whether or not the PRI controlled the executive branch of respondents' state government at the time the survey was conducted (n = 961, 54.4 percent). PRDGOV (PRD in power at the state level, or in Mexico City) is a dichotomous variable indicating whether or not the PRD controlled the executive branch of respon-

dents' state government at the time the survey was conducted (n = 401, 22.7 percent). PANGOV (the PAN in power at the state level) is a dichotomous variable indicating whether or not the PAN controlled the executive branch of respondents' state government at the time the survey was conducted (n = 449, 25.4 percent).

Appendix B. Regression Results

Table B.1. Political Participation Models for Electoral and Government-directed Activities (Logit Regression Results for Table 4.5)

Variables	Electoral activities		Government-directed activities	
	Voting	Campaign activities	Contacting	Protesting
INDIVIDUAL LEVEL				
Education	.03 (.03)	.07 (.04)	.09 (.05)*	.10 (.05)*
Income	.13 (.05)***	-.02 (.06)	.18 (.06)***	.01 (.07)
Male	-.04 (.12)	-.08 (.16)	.03 (.18)	.12 (.20)
Age	.03 (.005)***	.012 (.006)**	.01 (.006)**	.007 (.007)
Union member	.23 (.22)	-.13 (.25)	.14 (.25)	.62 (.25)**
Political organization count	.21 (.12)*	.50 (.12)***	.15 (.14)	.51 (.13)***
Nonpolitical organization count	.05 (.09)	.04 (.10)	.24 (.11)**	.11 (.12)
POLITICAL OPPORTUNITIES				
Efficacy	.09 (.02)***	.08 (.02)***	.05 (.02)**	.02 (.03)
Receive government transfers	.19 (.16)	.12 (.20)	.42 (.21)**	.27 (.24)
Political recruitment	.18 (.07)***	.34 (.08)***	.57 (.08)***	.40 (.10)***
PRD in power at state level	.006 (.17)	-.11 (.23)	.33 (.22)	.24 (.26)
PAN in power at state level	.47 (.16)***	-.04 (.20)	-.24 (.24)	-.14 (.27)
Constant	-2.1 (.36)***	-4.1 (.49)***	-5.1 (.54)***	-4.2 (.58)***
	LL = 1738.92	LL = 1144.38	LL = 975.84	LL = 816.71
	X^2 = 108.28	X^2 = 60.81	X^2 = 108.1	X^2 = 69.38
	X^2 prob. $p \leq 0.000$	X^2 prob. $p \leq 0.000$	X^2 prob. $p \leq 0.000$	X^2 prob. $p \leq 0.000$
	N = 1,574	N = 1,574	N = 1,574	N = 1,574

Source: CSES-CIDE 2003.
Notes: The dependent variables are dichotomous variables indicating whether an individual undertook one of the political acts.
$* p < 0.1$ $** p < 0.05$ $*** p < 0.01$
LL = log likelihood

Table B.2. Political Participation Models for Voting and Contacting by Income (Logit Regression Results for Table 4.6)

Variables	Voting		Contacting government officials	
	Low income	High income	Low income	High income
INDIVIDUAL LEVEL				
Education	.04 (.05)	.02 (.06)	.11 (.08)	.05 (.07)
Income	.03 (.17)	.14 (.09)	-.47 (.28)*	.20 (.11)*
Male	.05 (.16)	-.11 (.19)	.09 (.27)	-.002 (.25)
Age	.02 (.006)***	.05 (.009)***	.01 (.009)	.01 (.009)
Union member	.10 (.32)	.23 (.31)	.34 (.44)	.12 (.32)
Political organization count	.01 (.14)	.84 (.29)***	.16 (.19)	.06 (.22)
Nonpolitical organization count	.14 (.12)	-.08 (.14)	.11 (.16)	.33 (.14)**
POLITICAL OPPORTUNITIES				
Efficacy	.08 (.02)***	.11 (.03)***	.03 (.04)	.08 (.04)**
Receive government transfers	.19 (.18)	.20 (.30)	.59 (.28)**	.18 (.34)
Political recruitment	.20 (.09)**	.16 (.11)	.41 (.13)***	.72 (.12)***
PRD in power at state level	-.14 (.23)	.19 (.28)	-.35 (.44)	.72 (.29)**
PAN in power at state level	.52 (.22)**	.53 (.23)**	-.08 (.38)	-.27 (.32)
Constant	-.14 (.55)***	-.29 (.66)***	-3.6 (.90)***	-.55 (.82)***
	LL = 1014.56	LL = 694.94	LL = 454.80	LL = 486.62
	X^2 = 41.90	X^2 = 79.47	X^2 = 27.33	X^2 = 77.44
	X^2 prob. $p \leq 0.000$	X^2 prob. ≤ 0.000	X^2 prob. $p \leq 0.007$	X^2 prob. $p \leq 0.000$
	N = 885	N = 676	N = 882	N = 674

Source: CSES-CIDE 2003.

Notes: The dependent variables are dichotomous variables indicating whether an individual undertook one of the political acts.

* $p < 0.1$ ** $p < 0.05$ *** $p < 0.01$

LL = log likelihood

Table B.3. Political Participation Models for Electoral and Government-directed Activities (Logit Regression Results for Table 6.4)

Variables	Electoral activities		Government-directed activities	
	Voting	Campaign activities	Contacting	Protesting
INDIVIDUAL LEVEL				
Education	.03 (.04)	.08 (.05)*	.09 (.05)*	.09 (.06)
Income	.10 (.05)*	-.03 (.07)	.19 (.06)***	.07 (.08)
Male	-.07 (.13)	-.05 (.17)	-.001 (.19)	.00 (.21)
Age	.03 (.005)***	.008 (.006)	.008 (.007)	.005 (.008)
Union member	.28 (.24)	-.27 (.27)	.14 (.26)	.61 (.27)***
Political organization count	.33 (.14)**	.44 (.13)***	.15 (.14)	.32 (.15)***
Nonpolitical organization count	.05 (.10)	.03 (.11)	.19 (.11)*	.18 (.13)
POLITICAL OPPORTUNITIES				
Efficacy	.07 (.02)***	.05 (.03)*	.06 (.03)**	.00 (.03)
Receive government transfers	.12 (.17)	.16 (.21)	.45 (.22)**	.45 (.25)*
Political recruitment	.20 (.07)***	.35 (.08)***	.63 (.09)***	.44 (.10)***
PRD in power at state level	-.42 (.32)	-.32 (.43)	.54 (.43)	.79 (.47)*
PAN in power at state level	.33 (.19)*	-.002 (.25)	-.11 (.30)	-.02 (.35)
DEMOCRATIZATION				
Satisfaction with democracy	-.02 (.08)	.08 (.10)	.07 (.11)	.33 (.13)***
Past elections were clean	.01 (.04)	-.05 (.06)	.04 (.06)	.02 (.07)
PRD competitive in state elections	.35 (.28)	-.13 (.35)	-.21 (.38)	-.72 (.4)*

Table B.3. Political Participation Models for Electoral and Government-directed Activities (Logit Regression Results for Table 6.4) *continued*

Variables	Electoral activities		Government-directed activities	
	Voting	*Campaign activities*	*Contacting*	*Protesting*
DEMOCRATIZATION *(continued)*				
PRDista with PRD competitive	1.47 (.48)***	1.62 (.39)***	.04 (.43)	.56 (.45)
PANista with PAN competitive	.39 (.19)**	.27 (.23)	.31 (.25)	-.31 (.33)
ELECREP	.27 (.08)***	.41 (.10)***	-.14 (.10)	.03 (.12)
INTRAGOVERNMENTAL COMPETITION				
PRIista with PRIGOV	.34 (.19)*	.90 (.22)***	.53 (.26)**	.51 (.28)*
PRIista with PRDGOV	-.61 (.56)	.56 (.74)	.74 (.65)	-.17 (.91)
PRIista with PANGOV	.85 (.45)*	.006 (.49)	.12 (.56)	.26 (.62)
Constant	-2.78 (.50)***	-4.80 (.65)***	-4.35 (.68)***	-3.76 (.74)***
	LL = 1514.35	LL = 1024.60	LL = 889.05	LL = 726.68
	X^2 = 138.24	X^2 = 110.37	X^2 = 115.1	X^2 = 98.42
	X^2 prob. p $\leq$ 0.000	X^2 prob. p $\leq$ 0.000	X^2 prob. p $\leq$ 0.000	X^2 prob. p $\leq$ 0.000
	N = 1,427	N = 1,429	N = 1,424	N = 1,425

Source: CSES-CIDE 2003.
Notes: The dependent variables are dichotomous variables indicating whether an individual undertook one of the political acts.
* p < 0.1   ** p < 0.05   *** p < 0.01
LL = log likelihood

Table B.4. Effect of Institutional Factors on Voting and Campaign Activity by Income (Logit Regression Results for Table 6.5)

Variable	Voting		Campaign activities	
	Low income	High income	Low income	High income
INDIVIDUAL LEVEL				
Education	.01 (.05)	.04 (.06)	.08 (.07)	.05 (.07)
Income	.11 (.19)	.08 (.10)	.22 (.27)	-.09 (.12)
Male	.07 (.18)	-.20 (.21)	-.14 (.24)	-.03 (.25)
Age	.02 (.007)**	.05 (.01)***	.014 (.008)*	.004 (.01)
Union member	.13 (.36)	.25 (.33)	-.86 (.48)*	-.05 (.34)
Political organization count	.15 (.16)	.90 (.31)***	.54 (.17)***	.44 (.21)**
Nonpolitical organization count	.12 (.13)	-.06 (.15)	.13 (.15)	-.04 (.17)
POLITICAL OPPORTUNITIES				
Efficacy	.07 (.03)**	.08 (.03)***	.05 (.04)	.05 (.04)
Receive government transfers	.02 (.21)	.35 (.32)	.29 (.26)	-.03 (.39)
Political recruitment	.28 (.10)***	.11 (.11)	.31 (.12)***	.42 (.13)
PRD in power at state level	-.78 (.41)*	.70 (.57)	.38 (.61)	-.82 (.66)
PAN in power at state level	.31 (.27)	.39 (.27)	-.04 (.35)	-.01 (.37)
DEMOCRATIZATION				
Satisfaction with democracy	-.10 (.11)	.14 (.13)	.04 (.14)	.13 (.15)
Past elections were clean	.01 (.06)	.03 (.07)	-.08 (.08)	-.06 (.09)
PRD competitive in state elections	.60 (.34)*	-.65 (.52)	-.63 (.49)	.30 (.55)

Table B.4. Effect of Institutional Factors on Voting and Campaign Activity by Income (Logit Regression Results for Table 6.5)

continued

Variable	Voting		Campaign activities	
	Low income	High income	Low income	High income
DEMOCRATIZATION *(continued)*				
PAN competitive in state elections	.52 (.28)*	-.30 (.59)	-.08 (.42)	-.35 (.62)
PRDista with PRD competitive	1.6 (.62)***	1.25 (.81)	1.57 (.53)***	1.62 (.63)***
PANista with PAN competitive	.78 (.28)***	.10 (.26)	.52 (.32)	.03 (.35)
ELECREP	.26 (.10)**	.27 (.12)**	.44 (.14)***	.40 (.15)***
INTRAGOVERNMENTAL COMPETITION				
PRIista with PRIGOV	.36 (.25)	.27 (.32)	.77 (.31)**	1.11 (.33)***
PRIista with PRDGOV	-.78 (.78)	.06 (.97)	-.34 (1.12)	1.56 (1.00)
PRIista with PANGOV	.99 (.65)	.90 (.75)	.14 (.75)	.05 (.66)
Constant	-2.25 (.71)***	-3.04 (.95)***	-5.33 (1.00)***	-3.97 (1.09)***
	LL = 839.47	LL = 637.50	LL = 534.15	LL = 471.29
	X^2 = 73.05	X^2 = 88.00	X^2 = 68.93	X^2 = 55.60
	X^2 prob. $p \leq 0.000$	X^2 prob. $p \leq 0.000$	X^2 prob. $p \leq 0.000$	X^2 prob. $p \leq 0.000$
	N = 776	N = 634	N = 777	N = 635

Source: CSES-CIDE 2003.

Notes: The dependent variables are dichotomous variables indicating whether an individual undertook one of the political acts.

* $p < 0.1$ ** $p < 0.05$ *** $p < 0.01$

LL = log likelihood

Table B.5. Effect of Institutional Factors on Contacting and Protest Activity by Income (Logit Regression Results for Table 6.6)

Variable	Contacting		Protesting	
	Low income	High income	Low income	High income
INDIVIDUAL LEVEL				
Education	.14 (.08)*	.03 (.07)	.03 (.09)	.16 (.09)*
Income	-.58 (.30)*	.23 (.11)*	.02 (.33)	.26 (.14)*
Male	.05 (.29)	-.02 (.26)	.39 (.30)	-.39 (.32)
Age	.004 (.10)	.01 (.01)	-.001 (.01)	.016 (.012)
Union member	.26 (.48)	.21 (.34)	.29 (.45)	.77 (.37)**
Political organization count	.09 (.20)	.12 (.22)	.06 (.20)	.65 (.24)***
Nonpolitical organization count	.03 (.18)	.26 (.16)*	.39 (.17)**	-.13 (.21)
POLITICAL OPPORTUNITIES				
Efficacy	.02 (.04)	.10 (.04)***	.008 (.05)	-.01 (.05)
Receive government transfers	.67 (.30)**	.25 (.36)	.40 (.31)	.55 (.45)
Political recruitment	.48 (.14)***	.75 (.13)***	.46 (.14)***	.41 (.16)***
PRD in power at state level	-.94 (.81)	.142 (.70)**	.51 (.71)	.73 (.81)
PAN in power at state level	.12 (.49)	-.22 (.38)	-1.25 (.83)	.73 (.45)
DEMOCRATIZATION				
Satisfaction with democracy	.09 (.17)	.06 (.16)	.26 (.18)	.40 (.19)**
Past elections were clean	.07 (.10)	.03 (.09)	-.05 (.10)	.08 (.12)
PRD competitive in state elections	-.10 (.50)	-.68 (.69)	-.95 (.50)*	.07 (.81)

Table B.5. Effect of Institutional Factors on Contacting and Protest Activity by Income (Logit Regression Results for Table 6.6)

continued

Variable	Contacting		Protesting	
	Low income	*High income*	*Low income*	*High income*
DEMOCRATIZATION *(continued)*				
PAN competitive in state elections	-1.10 (.45)**	-.88 (.66)	-1.69 (.42)***	-.34 (.80)
PRDista with PRD competitive	.48 (.76)	-.12 (.57)	.56 (.69)	.32 (.64)
PANista with PAN competitive	.05 (.45)	.39 (.32)	-.19 (.52)	-.35 (.45)
ELECREP	.05 (.17)	-.26 (.15)*	-.005 (.17)	.13 (.18)
INTRAGOVERNMENTAL COMPETITION				
PRIista with PRIGOV	.66 (.35)*	.32 (.40)	.67 (.36)*	.44 (.47)
PRIista with PRDGOV	1.62 (1.17)	.92 (.92)	-5.4 (13.7)	.55 (1.03)
PRIista with PANGOV	.29 (.89)	.11 (.76)	1.44 (1.24)	.06 (.75)
Constant	-2.93 (1.10)***	-4.50 (1.13)***	-2.59 (1.14)**	-6.92 (1.47)***
	$LL = 397.32$	$LL = 447.99$	$LL = 367.24$	$LL = 324.30$
	$X^2 = 45.11$	$X^2 = 81.34$	$X^2 = 68.40$	$X^2 = 62.11$
	X^2 prob. $p \leq 0.003$	X^2 prob. $p \leq 0.000$	X^2 prob. $p \leq 0.000$	X^2 prob. $p \leq 0.000$
	$N = 774$	$N = 633$	$N = 773$	$N = 635$

Source: CSES-CIDE 2003.
Notes: The dependent variables are dichotomous variables indicating whether an individual undertook one of the political acts.
* $p < 0.1$ ** $p < 0.05$ *** $p < 0.01$
LL = log likelihood

Notes

Chapter 1. The Return of Institutions

1. Civil and political liberties are still not protected in Mexico as consistently as many would like. Repression of protests and strikes by local and national governments occurred with some frequency between 2000 and 2006. Police forces are notorious for violating human rights.

2. For a more thorough review of recent research on the quality of democracies, see Levine and Molina 2007.

3. The three principal corporatist organizations were the CTM (Confederación de Trabajadores Mexicanos), which represented labor; the CNC (Confederación Nacional Campesina), which represented peasants; and the CNOP (Confederación Nacional de Organizaciones Populares), which grouped together urban settlers, professionals, and government employees.

4. In addition to periodic outbursts of armed resistance. See Bartra 1996 and Harvey 1998 for more information on important guerilla movements in Guerrero and Chiapas.

5. There are, however, a number of very good regional studies of political participation carried out during the 1960s and 1970s. See Craig and Cornelius 1980 for a review of this literature.

6. Although much attention has been paid to political participation of the urban poor (see, for example, Cornelius 1975, Eckstein 1977, Vélez-Ibañez 1983, and Cross 1998), the 1970s saw a sharp increase in political mobilization in rural areas as well. See, among many other works, Grindle 1986, Fox 1993, A. Bartra 1985 and 1996, and Harvey 1998.

7. After aggregating individual political acts into a single scale that ranges from 0 to 5, on average low-income Mexicans performed 0.17 acts, while medium- and high-income Mexicans performed 0.24 acts.

8. I use this scale as the principal measure of political participation in subsequent chapters. Its components are described more fully in Appendix A.

9. It should be noted that, as with all surveys, the figures for voter turnout are exaggerated. The actual turnout rate in the 2000 election was about 64 percent, more than twenty points lower than reported by the survey. It is difficult to know whether the poor are more or less likely to overreport their voting behavior than more affluent individuals,

but evidence from other public opinion polls confirms that the poor do indeed vote less frequently than the rich.

10. For additional perspectives on the differences between formal and informal modes of political participation, see Booth and Seligson 1978; Huntington and Nelson 1976; Milbrath and Goel 1977; Nelson 1994; Verba, Nie, and Kim 1971; and Verba, Nie, and Kim 1978.

11. See Bobo and Gilliam 1990; Gay 2001; and Verba, Nie, and Kim 1978 for examples. For more general discussions of how democratic politics excludes the voices of the poor, see, among other works, Bacharach and Baratz 1962, Gaventa 1980, and Schattschneider 1960.

12. There are certainly important exceptions, particularly in studies of voting behavior (see Aldrich 1993; Crotty 1991a; Jackman 1987; Powell 1986 and 1993; and Rosenstone and Wolfinger 1978) and of protests and similar forms of contentious collective action (see Jenkins 1983; Jenkins and Klandermans 1995; McAdam 1982; McAdam, McCarthy, and Zald 1996; Tarrow 1998; and Tilly 1978), but the literature's overwhelming focus on individual constraints has drawn analytic attention away from the influence of political and institutional factors and places the blame on individuals if they fail to exercise their political voice.

13. I also returned for follow-up trips during the summers of 2003, 2004, and 2005. Oaxaca is one of the two or three poorest states in Mexico. Approximately half of the population live in rural areas, and close to one-third of residents belong to an indigenous ethnic group. Local politics in Oaxaca are unique because 418 of its 570 municipal governments are governed by *usos y costumbres*, or customary law. However, three towns included in this study have normal party systems that represent the range of contexts occurring across Mexico, which allows me to make useful comparisons across the cases while controlling for many potentially confounding factors. During most of my research, the PRI (Partido Revolucionario Institucional) and the right-of-center PAN (Partido de Acción Nacional) competed in a two-party system in the state capital (Oaxaca); Zimatlán has a competitive two-party system in which the left-of-center PRD (Partido de la Revolución Democrática) and the PRI have alternated in power; finally, La Ciénega is an example of old-style Mexican electoral politics in which the PRI enjoys a local electoral hegemony.

14. See chapter 5 for a description of the social and political context in each of these towns.

15. Listening to the poor is not easy. It requires long hours, dusty travels, patience, and the persistence to make repeated visits to find respondents. It can be exhausting and frustrating, but such persistence is necessary and ultimately very rewarding. Winning the trust of respondents is crucial for this kind of research, and I worked hard to win their trust and confidence. As a matter of course, I never interviewed anyone the first time I met them. Usually I requested permission to interview someone only after having informal conversations with them on several occasions. My participation in regular meetings and activities of these organizations made members comfortable with my presence and gave us the opportunity to have conversations in informal settings. Maintaining a regular presence in these organizations was a logistical nightmare, sometimes requiring multiple trips to different field sites on the same day. I typically spent two days per week in each field site, but quite often I would visit three organizations on

the same day. My almost daily presence in the organizations and my efforts to win the trust of members were richly rewarded, both in the time people were willing to take to answer my questions and in the richness of the stories they shared. The questionnaires were lengthy, probably too long, but I had developed enough rapport with most people that they answered my questions patiently for more than two hours. The shortest interview lasted approximately eighty minutes, while the longest lasted more than ten hours and required four separate visits. The names of people interviewed are all pseudonyms.

16. There are other excellent survey studies of Mexico carried out during this period, most notably the World Values Survey (WVS) and the Mexico 2000 and 2006 Panel Studies, but none of these combine the detailed information about political activity and institutional factors my analysis required. Even the most recent wave of the CSES survey in Mexico carried out in 2006 asks a much more limited number of political participation questions. For most analyses of CSES data, I used the full Mexico dataset housed at the Centro de Investigación y Docencia Económicas (CIDE) library in Mexico City, available online at http://www.biiacs.cide.edu.

17. Nancy Burns, Kay Lehman Schlozman, and Sidney Verba (2001, 48–50) used separate regressions for men and women in their examination of gender differences in political participation for precisely the same reasons.

Chapter 2. Toward an Institutional Theory of Political Participation

1. The cisterns were built by the residents themselves, with no help from the government.

2. Another reason for their refusal was that this policy was most likely to keep the squatters dependent on and therefore voting for the PRI.

3. Lack of running water and indoor plumbing is not simply an inconvenience. Poorly dug latrines and the shortage of water and sewage facilities combine to create a dangerous public health problem in squatter neighborhoods.

4. For example, according to the Latin American Public Opinion Survey carried out in 2004, only about 7 percent of low-income Mexicans reported having ever participated in a protest (compared with about 12 percent of high-income individuals), whereas about 28 percent reported contacting their local government, more than a third had worked with neighbors to solve a community problem, and more than half had voted in most elections.

5. The truth is, most individual-level models of political participation were developed by studying the United States, a unique case by most any standard, suggesting that standard models are strongly biased by domestic politics in the United States.

6. For example, almost all research on political participation being carried out in Latin America today is based on public opinion surveys that import independent variables from standard U.S.-based models of political participation.

7. See, among many others, Almond and Verba 1963; Barnes and Kaase 1979; Burns, Schlozman, and Verba 2001; Milbrath and Goel 1977; Verba, Nie, and Kim 1971; and Verba, Schlozman, and Brady 1995.

8. Verba, Nie, and Kim's (1978) seven-nation study of political participation and Rosenstone and Hansen's (1993) longitudinal study of political participation in the United States are classic studies that critique the SES model on empirical grounds.

9. The literature is extensive. Some representative examples include Beck and Jen-

nings 1975 and 1982; Burns, Schlozman, and Verba 2001; Campbell et al. 1960; Huck-feldt 1979; Jennings and Niemi 1968 and 1981; Langton and Jennings 1968; Langton and Karns 1969; Lipset 1981 [1960]; Miller and Shanks 1996; Percheron and Jennings 1981; and Verba, Schlozman, and Brady 1995. Numerous studies have also examined period effects to explain changes in political attitudes, such as interest in politics and partisanship (Beck and Jennings 1991 and Jennings and Niemi 1975). For recent stud-ies on how political attitudes, particularly partisanship, have become much more fluid in Mexico since 1994, see Moreno 2003, McCann and Lawson 2003, and the essays in Domínguez and Poiré 1999.

10. For example, Verba, Nie, and Kim 1978 (71) argues that "education and income should lead to greater interest in and concern for political matters, just as they lead to greater political activity."

11. Though a rich literature has demonstrated that political engagement and politi-cal participation are reciprocally related (see, among many others, Finkel 1985, Finkel 1987, and Pateman 1970), by and large studies deal with this issue of reciprocal causation by simply assuming the direction of causality goes in only one direction, from attitudes to activism. Inserting political engagement models into regression models without ac-counting for the possibility of reciprocal causation produces estimates of the effect of political attitudes that are biased upward, overstating their impact on political participa-tion (Leighley 1995). See Verba, Brady, and Schlozman 1995; and Verba, Schlozman, and Brady 1995 for a discussion of statistical techniques that deal with reciprocal causation between dependent and independent variables.

12. Although there is some debate in the literature about whether measures of politi-cal engagement tap into properties of individuals or of the political system, particularly regarding measures of internal and external efficacy, in practice most studies assume these measures tap into individual-level attributes. An exception is Ruy Teixeira's *The Disappearing American Voter* (1992). For discussion of this literature, see Abramson 1983, Balch 1974, Craig and Maggiotto 1982, Crotty 1991a, and Petrocik 1991.

13. Indeed Bobo and Gilliam Jr. (1990) find the existence of a black mayor increases political activism of African Americans through their effects on political engagement, which they find to be more closely related to local political opportunities than income, education, or prior socialization experiences. See also Gay's 2001 study of the differen-tial influence of black congressional representation on the political engagement of blacks and whites.

14. See especially chapters 4, 11, and 13 in Burns, Schlozman, and Verba 2001.

15. Similarly, research has shown that high levels of political engagement and efficacy among the elderly in the United States (Campbell 2003) and among African Americans living in cities governed by black mayors (Bobo and Gilliam Jr. 1990) is the result of pub-lic policies and a relatively receptive political context—not income, education, family, or prior experiences with nonpolitical organizations.

16. It is worth noting that even Gabriel Almond and Sidney Verba, whose seminal 1963 study of the effect of political attitudes on political participation and on the stabil-ity of political systems in five countries is responsible for much of the interest in po-litical attitudes, were keenly aware of the powerful effects that politics has on citizen attitudes: "Our findings will show that the civic orientation is widespread in Britain and the United States and relatively infrequent in the other countries, but we would be most

hesitant to attribute these gross differences in political culture to the relatively slight differences in childhood socialization brought to light in our findings. *They seem more clearly to be related to characteristics of the social environment and patterns of social interaction, to specifically political memories, and to differences in experience with political structure and performance*" (ibid., 35, emphasis mine). More specifically, Almond and Verba attribute differences in levels of civic obligation and political efficacy to the degree to which local structures foster citizen participation and provide meaningful opportunities for influence (ibid., 164).

17. Nonparticipation or abstention is usually assumed to be costless, although some models consider the possibility that actors may regret not participating if their actions could have made a difference in the outcome (Ferejohn and Fiorina 1974).

18. See Whiteley 1995 for a lengthier discussion and critique of these and similar kinds of models.

19. Indeed, in several empirical tests of this choice model of voting, the D term proved to be the strongest predictor of political activity. See Aldrich 1993 and chapter 4 of Verba, Schlozman, and Brady 1995 for a discussion of these studies.

20. Although Verba, Nie, and Kim (1978) say that they are interested in examining the broad impact of "institutions" on political participation, in practice, they focus more narrowly on political parties and voluntary organizations.

21. A great deal of research has shown that often asking is not enough; how people are asked is the most important factor in political recruitment. Face-to-face contacting, which is more likely to occur among members of organizations, is much more effective than recruitment by mail, and even more effective than telephone contacting (Blydenburgh 1971; Caldeira, Clausen, and Patterson 1990; Gerber and Green 2000; Huckfeldt and Sprague 1992; Kramer 1970; Leighley 1995; Lupfer and Price 1972; Patterson and Caldeira 1983; Pollock III 1982; and Wielhouwer and Lockerbie 1996).

22. There are also numerous case studies of political participation in Chile (Oxhorn 1995 and Schneider 1991), Egypt (Singerman 1995), Mexico (Cornelius 1975 and Eckstein 1977), Peru (Collier 1976 and Dietz and Palmer 1978), and elsewhere that take the role of the state seriously. Many, if not most, of these studies examined the state's role in authoritarian or semiauthoritarian settings, where the state's impact on political activity is magnified precisely because of the state's explicit efforts to control, regulate, and limit political participation. Although states in democratic systems also try to control, regulate, and limit political participation, so that these case studies could teach us a lot about the logic of participation in democratic settings from the perspective of ordinary citizens, the two literatures have largely developed on parallel paths, intersecting only rarely.

23. Although the dependent variable in these studies is related to citizen activism, and is useful for understanding some ways that the state might influence political activity, they are not themselves studies of political participation.

24. The one exception is the voting behavior literature, but it focuses narrowly on a rather unique type of political activity and a relatively narrow range of institutional variables.

25. The one exception, again, is legal and constitutional restrictions on suffrage.

26. This is not to say it is not important. By intimidating citizens, enforced restrictions on freedom of speech and organization can produce dramatic demobilizing effects on individuals and groups.

27. See, for example, John C. Cross's 1998 analysis of how state structures and actions shaped, and were in turn influenced by, informal street vendors' organizations.

28. Although the prevalence of fraud could be thought of as a feature of the political process, the occurrence of fraud ultimately depends on the capacity and willingness of the state to enforce electoral laws. Elections during 2008 in Kenya and Zimbabwe provide tragic examples of how weak states hinder the democratic process and influence people's decisions about whether to vote, protest, or riot.

29. See also Susan Stokes's *Cultures in Conflict* (1995) for another analysis of the impact of the actions of the Peruvian state on the political activity of the urban poor.

30. Stokes (1995) has analyzed a similar process in the case of Peru.

31. For example, in her study of the effect of black congressional representation on political participation, Claudine Gay (2001, 600) has found that "black electoral success can have a measurable but strikingly asymmetric effect on political behavior, both engaging (some black) and disengaging (many white) constituents in the electoral process."

32. Something like this may already be happening in places like Peru, where the urban poor, frustrated by repeated economic crises and the incapacity of the state to do anything meaningful to ease their plight, are increasingly choosing what Dietz (1998) has called "exit strategies," abandoning formal politics and focusing instead on self-help activities or voting for antiestablishment candidates. See also Gutmann 2002, especially chapters 6 and 10.

Chapter 3. Neoliberal Reforms, the State, and Opportunities for Political Participation

1. Wolfinger and Rosenstone (1980) make a similar argument for voting behavior in the United States (see page 79).

2. The average household income of the people I interviewed was US$250 per month, but many earned less than US$150. Even public-sector employees with college degrees in the city of Oaxaca could not expect to earn more than US$400 per month. These salaries did not allow for any savings and very little discretionary spending on nonessential items.

3. This is true regardless of how poverty is measured (see Boltvinik 2003, 404–5).

4. Certainly the economic crisis in 1982 and the exhaustion of the ISI model had a negative impact on the living standards of the poor, while the economic crisis in 1995 devastated people's incomes. It is possible that poverty levels and income distribution would have been worse in the absence of structural reforms. However, we do not know what poverty and inequality levels would be in the counterfactual—that is, if a different basket of policies had been chosen. Nonetheless, the evidence is quite strong that in the short and medium term, free-market reforms and structural adjustment policies did redistribute income away from the poor without significantly increasing their income or reducing their poverty.

5. Indigence rates have improved recently, dropping from 22 percent in 1996 to 11.7 percent in 2004 (ECLAC 2006).

6. This perspective is similar to Amartya Sen's capabilities approach, in which poverty is seen not simply as people's lack of income, but as their lack of freedom to do and choose things to help themselves and influence the world around them (see Sen 1999, especially chapters 1 and 4).

7. CONAPO is the government agency in charge of collecting demographic informa-

tion. The poorest states as well as the most marginal municipalities are concentrated in southern Mexico, in the states of Chiapas, Guerrero, Oaxaca, and Veracruz. Oaxaca ranks third from last among states, ahead of only Guerrero and Chiapas. By comparison, Mexico City and the state of Nuevo León have the lowest marginalization scores (CO-NAPO 2004). Overall 1,292 (53 percent) of Mexico's 2,443 municipalities suffer from high or very high levels of marginalization. Of these, 64 percent are located in the five poorest states. Oaxaca alone accounts for 35 percent of Mexico's poorest municipalities, where 458 of 570 municipalities suffer from high or very high levels of marginalization.

8. CONAPO's IM rates geographical units—states, municipalities, towns, and neighborhoods—according to a five-point scale: very low marginalization, low marginalization, moderate marginalization, high marginalization, and very high marginalization. This scale is based on marginalization scores calculated using nine socioeconomic indicators of human development collected during the 2000 census. These scores range from –2.56 to 3.94, where higher scores indicate a greater degree of deprivation. Detailed information on how CONAPO calculates the index is available on CONAPO's Web site at http://www.conapo.gob.mx.

9. For example, between 1990 and 2000 the percentage of people without electricity dropped from 13 percent to 4.8 percent, and the percentage of people without sewage service was halved from 21.5 percent to 9.9 percent; during the same period the illiteracy rate dropped from 12.5 percent to 9.5 percent and the percentage of people who did not complete the sixth grade dropped from 37.1 percent to 28.5 percent (CONAPO 2004, 35).

10. It is important to remember, however, that there exists a wide range of conditions within Oaxaca city as in most urban centers in Mexico. Conditions in squatter settlements such as Nezacubi, which lack many basic services, may be just as bad or worse than in rural towns such as Zimatlán or Teotitlán del Valle.

11. In fact, the strongest predictor of poverty and income inequality levels during the period is economic growth: during periods of negative growth, such as 1995–1996, poverty levels increased sharply, only to decline again once economic growth resumed in 1997. Increasing remittances from abroad also helped reduce poverty levels, mainly in rural areas, while poverty-alleviation programs seemed to have had relatively little impact before 2000.

12. Inflation declined significantly during the Salinas administration, reaching a low of 7 percent in 1994. Inflation once again became a problem after the 1995 crisis, when it peaked at 52 percent, but it declined rapidly thereafter. At the time of my interviews, annual inflation rates were once again at historic lows, between 12 percent and 15 percent annually.

13. A recent study by the World Bank estimates that the food expenses account for nearly half of total spending by the urban and rural poor in Mexico, compared with only 24 percent and 32 percent of expenses for the nonpoor in urban and rural areas respectively (World Bank 2005, 8–11). In fact, results from the 2000 wave of the CSES survey conducted in Mexico show that low-income groups perceived inflation to be a bigger problem than high-income groups: 72 percent of low-income respondents thought inflation had increased compared with only 54 percent of high-income groups.

14. Labor income accounts for 57 percent of the total income for urban households from the two lowest-income quintiles; the rural poor, though, receive a larger share of their income from remittances and government transfers (World Bank 2005, 11–12).

15. Current debates about migration describe it as a form of economic exit, in which people leave their home in search for more jobs, better wages, or both. Migration is also a classic form of political exit, in which actors leave a political unit in search of greater security, protection from state repression, or greater political rights (see, for example, Herbst 1990). In the case of Mexico, there is growing evidence "exit" can be a first step toward "voice," as organized migrants to the United States use remittances, government programs that match, and transnational networks to increase their voice and participation in local affairs. However, recent evidence suggests that the vast majority of Mexicans living in the United States pay little attention to politics in their home country, did not vote in the 2006 presidential elections, and do not otherwise participate in politics back home (McCann, Cornelius, and Leal 2006). For an introduction to this literature, see Fitzgerald 2004, and Fox 2007 (chapter 10). I would like to thank an anonymous reviewer for reminding me of this point.

16. However, whenever this kind of formal incorporation failed to produce material benefits or effective representation, as often happened, members usually became politically apathetic (Eckstein 1977).

17. See Houtzager and Kurtz 2000 for similar arguments about the effect of neoliberal policies on popular mobilization in Chile and Brazil, and Cross 1998 for a study of the informal sector in Mexico that emphasizes the ability of street vendors to organize and influence state policies.

18. In Mexico the percentage of people employed in the formal sector declined from 63 percent to 47 percent by 1998, whereas petty entrepreneurs and informal workers made up nearly 40 percent of the workforce (Portes and Hoffman 2003, 56–57; and Salas and Zepeda 2003).

19. For prospects of party representation for informal workers, see ibid., especially pages 75–76; for a discussion of party representation for peasants under neoliberalism, see Kurtz 2004.

20. See also Durand Ponte 1994a and 1994b and Middlebrook 1995. Although this exclusionary process has been particularly marked in Mexico, it is a common characteristic of neoliberal reform processes in other Latin American countries. According to Judith Teichman (2001, 8), "institutionalized links providing real access to the policy process exist for the private sector, but personalized inroads to the policy process are more important, and even institutionalized ones tend to be highly personalized. Such links for other groups, such as labor, rural workers, small farmers, and small business are either weak or absent, raising the specter that policy formulation will likely ignore the interests of these groups."

21. An anonymous reviewer pointed out that because the International Labour Organization (ILO) collects its information on strikes from the Mexican government, and the Mexican government has the power to declare strikes "nonexistent" (or illegal), this data may only be counting strikes acknowledged and reported by the government. As the reviewer pointed out, the decline in strikes may reflect as much declining support of the government toward labor as actual declines in activity.

22. Mark Eric Williams (2001) has argued that the decline in strikes does not necessarily reflect labor union weakness relative to a strong state; rather, it is the result of unions adjusting their strategies as they learned how best to deal with privatizations.

23. The 1980s saw a proliferation of independent urban and rural movements as well

as the defection of groups that traditionally had been loyal to the ruling party. Cuauhtémoc Cárdenas and a group of left-leaning members of the PRI left the party in 1987 and launched an independent presidential campaign to challenge the PRI and its neoliberal turn. Many members of autonomous (and official) labor unions and peasant organizations joined this political movement to voice their opposition to the PRI's aggressive gutting of the state and its social-spending programs (Aguilar García 1992, Arroyo 1992, Paré Ouellet 1992, and Ramírez Sáiz 1992).

24. Organizations achieved significant gains at the local level, in part due to increasing electoral competition and in part due to decentralization policies that granted municipal and state governments more control over financial resources (Shefner 2008). However, policymaking continued to be centralized in the federal government, where organizations had little access.

25. Oaxaca lacks a significant industrial base, so labor union penetration outside of the service sector—especially education—is minimal. However, because most of the state's rural towns and communities are governed by customary law, residents, especially males, have the opportunity and obligation to serve on multiple committees designed to provide for and manage such key services as irrigation, security, road building, and education.

26. See Holzner 2002 and Stephen 1991 for more detailed descriptions of the town's rather unique system of governance based on a traditional cargo system.

27. Centéotl, which operates projects in Zimatlán and La Ciénega, has a budget that easily exceeds US$200,000 annually, dwarfing the budgets of most rural municipalities. For many in its service area, targeting local and state governments for benefits has simply become irrational.

28. Weaving rugs is not only very labor intensive, it also requires significant investments in raw materials, such as wool and dyes, and a large initial investment in a loom.

29. Needless to say, this means that now there are many more organizations competing with each other over a finite and not necessarily growing set of resources.

30. The exchange rate at the time of my interviews hovered around ten pesos to one U.S. dollar.

31. See Shefner 2008 for an excellent ethnographic account of the opportunities and challenges the urban poor face when trying to organize.

32. For example, the executive committee of Nezacubi's neighborhood association met Saturday nights between nine and eleven because it was the only time members were sure not to be working.

33. It is difficult to generalize across poor neighborhoods in Mexico, because local conditions are so different. Other scholars studying organizing in poor neighborhoods in places like Guadalajara, Mexico City, and Monterrey found higher levels of social solidarity than I did in Oaxaca (Alonso 1986 and 1988, Farrera Araujo 1994, Shefner 2001 and 2008, and World Bank 2005).

34. The few teachers that lived in Nezacubi were members of a teachers union; taxi drivers were also typically members of drivers associations; but the self-employed, those who worked in restaurants or in construction, were the least likely to have other organizational options.

35. These processes of fragmentation and atomization are made worse by neoliberal politics which, according to Marcus Kurtz (2004, 164), has "induced massive social dif-

ferentiation, recreated powerful economic vulnerabilities for peasants relative to local elites, and dismantled the institutional structures that were the historic foundations of broadly shared peasant 'interests' across the breadth of the countryside."

36. See also Portes and Hoffman's (2003, 66–74) discussion on alternative strategies to political participation.

37. This predilection for such informal activities is evident in figure 1.2, which shows that, besides voting, working with neighbors to solve a community problem is the most common activity in which the poor engage.

38. Sam Dillon and Julia Preston (2000) have provided salacious details of many of these authoritarian practices in Puebla, Tabasco, and elsewhere, which contrasted with the national-level march toward democratic rule.

39. Felipe Calderon's alliance during the 2006 presidential election with Elba Esther Gordillo, a former PRI senator and the powerful leader of the largest teachers union in Mexico (Sindicato Nacional de Trabajadores de la Educación, SNTE), is also a sign that the PAN is recruiting leaders of established clientelist networks to secure electoral victories.

40. See Magaloni 2006 and Greene 2007 for an elaboration of the reasons hegemonic parties seek to win elections by overwhelming margins.

41. This is not to say that popular groups never behaved autonomously or showed their dissatisfaction with the regime. On the contrary, dissent was common among peasants, labor, and urban popular groups, especially when these groups were able to establish independent organizations outside of the PRI structure (Hellman 1994, Hernández and Fox 1992, and Ramírez Sáiz 1986).

42. In 2000 total government spending amounted to about 23 percent of GDP, a sharp decline from 1987, when it accounted for 41.5 percent of GDP. The sharpest drop in government spending came during the Salinas administration (1988–1994), when the GDP share of public spending was reduced from 37.3 percent to 23.6 percent in only four years (Giugale, Lafourcade, and Nguyen 2001).

43. This expectation is based on research into the impact of Social Security on the political activity of seniors in the United States. In *How Policies Make Citizens*, Andrea Louise Campbell (2003, 55) found that low-income seniors, "who are more dependent on Social Security, participate at higher rates vis-à-vis the program than affluent seniors, the opposite of the usual income-participation relationship in the United States." Of course, many middle-class Mexicans, especially those employed by the state, also depended on government policies and expenditures for their livelihood. However, government-spending programs often matter more to the poor because the benefits make up a larger share of poor people's overall income.

44. Of course, the expansion of the state in the form of new rural development programs such as PIDER-COPLAMAR was in part the result of, not merely the cause of, increased peasant militancy. For a more detailed discussion on the reciprocal influence of state expansion and peasant mobilization, see Fox 1993.

45. This election was marred by massive amounts of electoral fraud, without which, many analysts have argued, the PRI would have lost the election.

46. See especially *Transforming State-Society Relations in Mexico* (Cornelius, Craig, and Fox 1994). On the political manipulation of Solidarity spending, see *Voting for Autocracy* (Magaloni 2006), and *Poverty, Vote Buying and Democracy* (Diaz-Cayeros, Estevez, and Magaloni forthcoming).

47. Between 1998 and 1999 public social spending accounted for 9.2 percent of Mexico's GDP, compared with 20.9 percent for Argentina, 19.3 percent for Brazil, 14.3 percent for Chile, and 13.7 percent for Colombia.

48. PROGRESA and its successor, Oportunidades, were the government's flagship antipoverty programs after PRONASOL was dismantled in 1994. The government established PROCAMPO in 1993 to compensate producers of such basic grains as corn, beans, and wheat for the loss on input subsidies, price supports, and import protection. By 2000 its budget approached US$1 billion and provided cash payments to more than 2.6 million farmers, most of them *ejidatarios*. Although PROCAMPO is not technically a poverty-alleviation program in that it does not target poor farmers specifically, it is a progressive program that provides cash transfers to the vast majority of poor farmers, at a rate of about US$80 to US$90 per hectare per season (World Bank 2005).

49. An expected utility (E(U)) function usually takes the form of $E(U)=pB-C$, where B represents the benefits, C the costs, and p the probability of actually receiving the benefits by undertaking the activity.

50. See especially Fox 1994b, 184–88; and Lustig 1994, 83–88.

51. In that way it resembles other entitlement programs, such as a government pension program that provides direct cash transfers to beneficiaries, which they are then free to spend as they see fit.

52. The expansion was slowed due to a freeze in new enrollments six months before the 2000 presidential elections. This decision to freeze enrollments was made to avoid the impression of electoral manipulation, which was important for opposition parties, particularly the PAN, to buy into the program. However, it also created the impression among the poor that the government's commitment to expanding the program was lukewarm at best.

53. In fact, a recent study by the World Bank and the International Bank for Reconstruction and Development estimated that Mexico's urban poor receive only about 3.5 percent of their income from government transfers, mostly in the form of pensions, compared with the rural poor, who receive 18 percent of their income from transfers, mostly from PROGRESA-Oportunidades. By contrast, PRONASOL spent as much as half of its budget in urban areas.

54. Between 1995 and 1998 the Zedillo administration sharply reduced or eliminated generalized subsidies on bread and tortillas, subsidies that had been in place for as long as thirty years.

55. PRONASOL's budget in dollar terms was about the same in 1992 (US$2.3 billion) (Graham 1994, 321) as the budget for Oportunidades more than a decade later (US$2.8 billion in 2005).

56. With the exception of targeted programs like PROGRESA-Oportunidades and PROCAMPO, and spending on primary education, social spending in Mexico tends to be slightly regressive (World Bank 2005). Even today, most of the urban and rural poor have very low participation rates in Mexico's formal welfare systems, with little or no access to social security, public health care, or pensions (World Bank 2004 and 2005).

57. Actual payments depend on the size and composition of households. Families with school-age children and pregnant and nursing women tend to receive more, although benefits are capped at about US$150 per family per month.

58. This is so at least in the short run. At their core PROGRESA and Oportunidades

are programs designed to promote investment in human capital (health, nutrition, and education) by the poor. Its central effects will occur gradually through the accumulation of human capital in younger generations who will be better positioned to earn higher incomes and break out of the intergenerational cycle of poverty (Levy 2006, 48).

59. See Shefner 2008 for a detailed account of these marketing efforts in Guadalajara.

60. The candidate, Luis Donaldo Colosio, would almost certainly have succeeded Salinas as president of Mexico, but he was assassinated during a campaign rally in Tijuana in March 1994. Salinas then selected Ernesto Zedillo, who was Colosio's campaign manager, to replace him as the PRI's candidate.

61. This program, known by the acronym FOBAPROA, was implemented after the 1994–95 economic crisis that forced millions of individuals and businesses to default on their loans. Banks, burdened by debts that could not be collected, turned to the government for help. Under FOBAPROA, which became the IPAB (Instituto Para la Protección al Ahorro Bancario) under the Fox administration, the state took on the bank's debt obligations at the taxpayers' expense. More recent estimates place the total cost of the bank bailout at more than $100 billion, or around 20 percent of GDP (*La Jornada*, March 20, 2007).

62. Although it is undeniable that much of the mobilization was channeled through clientelist channels, PRONASOL was also responsible for stimulating significant amounts of organizational pluralism and for giving autonomous organizations the resources with which to grow (Fox 1994b and Haber 1994).

63. This dynamic is not limited to the Mexican case but is a common effect of neoliberal policies. For example, Kurtz (2004) found exactly the same dynamic of fragmentation and atomization in Chile, which had a more repressive political system at the time free-market reforms were implemented. Nevertheless, he concludes that the results of neoliberal reforms were essentially the same despite a more open political system in Mexico: "What the Mexican case shows is that free market policies can induce atomized politics even where they are implemented gradually in a comparatively politically open environment" (ibid., 203).

64. Here I am focusing on policymaking at the federal level. Decentralization reforms implemented between 1994 and 2000 significantly increased the funds available to local and state governments to carry out infrastructure projects and promote economic growth. There is evidence that decentralization has increased political participation directed at local governments (Holzner 2007a), but a detailed analysis of its effect is beyond the scope of this book.

65. In a perverse reciprocal chain of influence, the decline in poor people's political activity caused by neoliberalism is one of the reasons successive Mexican governments have been able to impose free-market reforms on a majority of citizens that opposed those policies (Kurtz 2004 and Oxhorn and Ducatenzeiler 1998b).

Chapter 4. Political Institutions, Engagement, and Participation

1. It is also possible that if the PRD's electoral victories were the result of clientelist mobilization of supporters, then it is the clientelist relationships, not ideological positions and policy proposals, that stimulate political action.

2. In *The Private Roots of Public Action*, Nancy Burns, Kay Lehman Schlozman, and Sidney Verba (2001, 48–50) have used separate regressions for men and women in

their examination of gender differences in political participation for precisely the same reasons.

3. The literature is extensive. Some representative examples include Beck and Jennings 1975 and 1982; Burns, Schlozman, and Verba 2001; Campbell, Converse, Miller, and Stokes 1960; Huckfeldt 1979; Jennings and Niemi 1968 and 1981; Langton and Jennings 1968; Langton and Karns 1969; Lipset 1981 [1960]; Miller and Shanks 1996; Percheron and Jennings 1981; and Verba, Schlozman, and Brady 1995. Numerous studies have also examined period effects to explain changes in political attitudes, such as interest in politics and partisanship (Beck and Jennings 1991, and Jennings and Niemi 1975). For recent studies on how political attitudes, particularly partisanship, have become much more fluid in Mexico since 1994, see Moreno 2003, McCann and Lawson 2003, and the essays in Domínguez and Poiré 1999.

4. For example, Sidney Verba, Norman Nie, and Jae-On Kim (1978, 71) have argued that "education and income should lead to greater interest in and concern for political matters, just as they lead to greater political activity."

5. Again, although Verba, Nie, and Kim have argued that institutions have a direct and independent effect on political activity, they are not willing to allow that institutions may also affect political engagement. According to them, psychological involvement in politics differs from political activity in that "it should be less susceptible to the intervening effects of political institutions" (ibid.).

6. In addition to helping us avoid issues of reciprocal causation between political participation and political preferences. One common criticism of using political attitudes to explain political participation is that it is not attitudes that cause participation, but political participation experiences that create greater engagement with politics. If experiences with political institutions impact both political attitudes and political participation, we can begin to escape this chicken-and-egg problem.

7. See also the other essays in Domínguez and Lawson 2004.

8. There was no reason to think otherwise in 2000, but that changed by 2006, when many low-income Mexicans became disillusioned with electoral politics after the PRD's presidential candidate failed to win the presidential election. This was also not the case as the limitation of decentralization reforms—for funding infrastructure projects, for giving municipalities political autonomy from higher levels of government, and for reducing crime and insecurity—became more and more apparent.

9. See Appendix A for more detail on how the scale was constructed.

10. Notably, the World Values Surveys do not ask questions about political efficacy, while the CSES surveys do not ask questions about interest in politics.

11. The dependent variable in this analysis is the overall scale of political efficacy discussed earlier.

12. Union membership and receiving government assistance are dichotomous variables; NATECON is measured on a four-point scale from 1 ("Economy did not improve at all") to 4 ("Economy improved a lot").

13. These are all ordinal variables ranging from 1 to 4 in the case of ELECREP and 1 to 5 for FRAUD, CORRUPT, and HUMRTS. For FRAUD the values range from 1 ("Elections are not clean at all") to 5 ("Elections were clean"); for CORRUPT from 1 ("Not much corruption") to 5 ("Corruption very extensive"); for HUMRTS from 1 ("Not much respect for rights") to 5 ("A great deal of respect").

14. GINIAVG is a dichotomous variable, from 0 ("The state has below-average levels of inequality) to 1 ("The state has above-average levels of inequality").

15. A similar model tested on the 2000 data without the government assistance variable produced similar results. I also tested other specifications of the model that included impressions about whether inflation or crime had gotten worse, level of marginality in the state where respondents lived, region of residence, but no other variables proved significant or altered the substantive results when included in the model.

16. Perhaps more accurately, we have ready-made measures of people's perceptions of how the political system works. Perception is not reality, but when it comes to political participation, actors have to perceive political opportunities as such to undertake political action (Gamson and Meyer 1996).

17. For more points of view on such a use of measures of political orientations, see Leighley 1995; Balch 1974; Clarke and Acock 1989; Craig and Maggiotto 1982; Niemi, Craig, and Mattei 1991; Dennis 1991; and Morrell 2003.

18. Increased political competition in state and local elections, efforts to decentralize fiscal powers away from Mexico City, and concerted efforts by both Presidents Zedillo and Fox to give up some of the informal powers of the presidency have contributed to this dynamic. Although local governments have been able to increase their powers significantly, the consensus among analysts is that governors have been the main beneficiaries of this devolution of power away from the federal government (Díaz-Cayeros 2004 and Rodríguez 1997).

19. See Beatriz Magaloni's insightful discussion on the logic of vote buying under electoral hegemonies in *Voting for Autocracy* (2006).

20. The mean number of political acts is calculated using an additive scale in which each of the following counts as one act: voting in the 2003 midterm elections, trying to persuade someone to vote for a particular candidate, supporting a candidate during an election campaign, contacting a government official, participating in a protest or march, organizing with others on an issue, occupying public buildings, and blocking streets or freeways. The scale takes on values from 0 to 8.

21. This discussion draws heavily from Burns, Schlozman, and Verba 2001, 2–3.

22. Andrea Campbell (2003) found a similar dynamic among recipients of Social Security benefits in the United States; see particularly chapters 2 and 3.

23. The core dependent variable is the same additive scale of political participation used in tables 4.3a and 4.3b, with values that range from 0 to 8. The analysis uses 2003 CSES data to explain the stratification of political participation at the time of the democratic transition. It would also be desirable to use data from the 2000 Mexico wave of the CSES survey; however, that data lacks information about government-spending programs. I replicated the analysis using the 2000 data and report the results in Appendix B. The results are substantively similar, although not entirely comparable because the models are not identical and because the two surveys asked slightly different political participation questions. As a result, the dependent variables in each model are not equivalent. Some readers may be curious about more recent patterns of political participation. Unfortunately, the 2006 Mexico wave of the CSES survey dropped most political participation questions and several measures of key independent variables, making it impossible to replicate the analysis for that year.

24. It can be difficult to distinguish between political and nonpolitical organizations. For this analysis I categorized organizations as "political" if they are likely to take political stands on issues or function as interest groups. They include *ejido* and farmers' organizations, business organizations, neighborhood organizations, and ecological organizations. The list of nonpolitical organizations includes charity groups, religious organizations, professional organizations, sports groups, and women's groups.

25. Wayne Cornelius (2004) used very similar measures taken from the Mexico 2000 Panel Study to study the incidence of vote buying, coercion, and other forms of mobilized voting in the 2000 elections.

26. For a sample or research from Latin America and elsewhere, see Collier and Collier 1991; Cook 1996; Leighley and Nagler 2004; Leighley 2007; Tanaka 1995; and Verba, Nie, and Kim 1978.

27. For detailed and instructive discussions on differences across political acts, see chapter 2 of Verba, Schlozman, and Brady 1995 and chapter 4 of Verba, Nie, and Kim 1978.

28. This is so at least in state and national elections, where there are usually thousands if not millions of other votes cast. In local elections, where the total turnout is in the hundreds, every individual vote not only counts but also matters.

29. For other essays and studies that examine specific weaknesses of Mexican civil society, particularly when it comes to representing the interests of the poor and holding the state accountable, see Fox 2007; Fox et al. 2007; and the essays in Cornelius and Shirk 2007.

30. There are, however, other ways that political bosses ensure clients do not defect or shirk. See Holzner 2004 for more details.

Chapter 5. Uneven and Incomplete Democratization in Mexico

Epigraph: Gay 2001, 590.

1. Turnout was low by Mexican standards: about 45 percent, with just over 5 percent of ballots invalidated. By comparison, only about 2.2 percent of ballots were soiled in the 2006 presidential election.

2. Because of the PRI's practice of inflating voter rolls or sending teams of supporters to vote multiple times in different locations, the party sometimes won with more than 100 percent of the vote. See Preston and Dillon 2004 for anecdotal descriptions of these practices and Molinar Horcasitas 1987 for a more systematic analysis of fraud in the 1986 gubernatorial election in Chihuahua.

3. For more details on the election system and electoral competition before 1946, see Crespo 2004 and González Casanova 1965 and 1985.

4. This SMSP system is more commonly known as a winner-take-all system or a first-past-the-post system, which is similar to the electoral system in the United States. In such a system candidates compete for a single seat in each of the federal districts. The candidate with the most votes, even if it is less than an absolute majority, wins the seat. It is a system that favors large, well-organized parties that can field candidates in all districts and tends to produce fewer parties than proportional representation systems.

5. See Magaloni 2006, chapters 4 and 8, for an analysis of the circumstances under which autocratic regimes rely on fraud to win elections and why they might at some point choose to forgo the use of fraud.

6. The TFE was replaced by the TEPJF (Federal Tribunal of the Federal Judicial Branch, Tribunal Electoral del Poder Judicial de la Federación) in 1996.

7. See Wayne Cornelius's discussion on this in *Mexican Politics in Transition* (1996, 57–58).

8. A reform implemented in 1963 allocated thirty to forty seats to minority party candidates on the basis of their national vote totals, but it was not a proportional representation system. For more detail on these reforms and their consequences, see the essays by Kevin Middlebrook, Wayne Cornelius, and Juan Molinar Horcasitas in Drake and Silva 1986.

9. The 1977 reforms made it possible for the left to reorganize and compete again in national elections. Between 1977 and 1985, the PSUM (Partido Socialista Unificado de México, Mexico's United Socialist Party), the PMT (Partido Mexicano de los Trabajadores, the Mexican Workers' Party), the PRT (Partido Revolucionario de los Trabajadores, the Revolutionary Workers' Party), and the PST (Partido Socialista de los Trabajadores, the Socialist Workers' Party) all formed and achieved a national registry. In addition, the conservative PDM (Partido Demócrata Mexicano, the Mexican Democratic Party) gained legal status.

10. See Rodríguez 1997 for further elaboration of the capacities of local governments in Mexico during the 1970s and 1980s.

11. This was especially true if they were able to win control over state governments.

12. It is also directly related to the degree of democratization achieved in a political system. If indeed the uncertainty of electoral outcomes is a hallmark of democracy (Przeworski 1991), and if party turnover is necessary for the consolidation of democratic transitions, then party competition without opposition victories is something less than a full democracy.

13. This changed in the 2006 elections, when many more states and districts were contested between the PRD and the PAN. See Klesner 2005 and 2007 for useful discussions of recent changes in Mexico's party system.

14. The PRD received 35.3 percent of the national vote in 2006, but only 12.2 percent in the 2009 midterm elections.

15. My own experience with the IEEO (the State Electoral Institute of Oaxaca) has been mixed. Up until 2001 it was easy to access electoral results, and the staff was universally helpful. When I returned in 2005 after the contentious statewide elections the previous year that were marred by widespread allegations of fraud, attitudes had changed and transparency suffered. Although the staff was still willing to grant me access to electoral results, which are a matter of public record, the new administrative council was less accommodating. I was required to make a formal written request for the documentation, but when I went to pick up the information a few days later, I was told that, upon orders from the president of the state electoral institute, they were not to hand out any information. I later received an official letter stating that due to "computer malfunctions," they regretted not being able to provide me with the information I requested. I later obtained the official data from one of the staff members who resented these stonewalling tactics by the council.

16. There is significant amount of variation within states as well. For example, within the state of Mexico, Mexico's most populous, perceptions of fraud ranged from a low of 26 percent to nearly 80 percent in some municipalities.

17. A study commissioned by the IFE of electoral fraud in the 2000 presidential elections revealed that 28 percent of respondents (in a sample of twelve hundred) experienced some kind of election-day violation of ballot secrecy or attempts to coerce or induce them to vote for a certain party. These attempts to manipulate people's votes were much more common in rural areas, in small towns, and among people with low levels of education. Interestingly, both the PAN and the PRI were identified just as often (47 percent versus 42 percent, respectively) as the party responsible for election-day irregularities, together accounting for 90 percent of reports (del Pozo and Aparicio 2001).

18. It is likely that many of these were PRD supporters from Mexico City. Roderic Ai Camp (2006) has reported that 81 percent of López Obrador supporters considered the 2006 elections dirty, compared with 93 percent of Calderón supporters who considered them clean.

19. *Dedazo* refers to the practice common in Mexico during PRI rule in which an incumbent politician designates his or her successor in office.

20. This has been with mixed success. When it has relied on authoritarian leaders or tactics too overtly, voters have tended to punish it, most notably in the 2006 elections.

21. Steven Wuhs (2008) described one PAN strategy of recruiting influential local leaders with close connections to civil society organizations to run as candidates in local elections, whether or not they had close ties to the party. Although he argues that the PAN struggled to avoid entering into clientelist dynamics typical of the PRI, they were not always successful.

22. See Wuhs 2008 and Shirk 2005 for discussions of other goals political party elites may pursue in addition to electoral victories.

23. On changing candidate selection strategies, see Langston 2006, Wuhs 2006 and 2008, and Shirk 2005.

24. A key part of its electoral strategy throughout the 1990s was to reserve as many as 50 percent of its candidacies to "outsiders" (Bruhn 1997 and 1999). The PAN did not reach out aggressively to external independent candidates until after its disappointing showing in the 2003 congressional elections (Wuhs 2008), but it has come to rely on this strategy much more since then.

25. In each of these cases, the winning PRD candidate split from the PRI only months before the election after the party denied them the nomination and managed to win the election even though the PRD had little or no presence in those states. In fact, much of the electoral growth at the local, district, and state levels during the 1990s happened due to elite defections from the PRI, not because of ideological or organizational innovations. For more on the dynamics of electoral splits, see Magaloni 2006, 44–54, and Bruhn 1997.

26. Such was the case with the 2004 gubernatorial election in Oaxaca, in which Convergencia's candidate, Gabino Cué Monteagudo, a PRI dissident, challenged and almost defeated the PRI's candidate, Ulíses Ruíz. See Gibson 2005 for more details.

27. Indeed, according to James Scott (1969), political machines develop only where some basic conditions of democratic politics are met, such as the selection of leaders through mass elections (usually universal suffrage), and a relatively high degree of electoral competition.

28. In fact, the biggest threat to the PRI's hegemony in the state has not come from

the PAN or the PRD, but from an elite split within the party that saw a powerful faction of the PRI defect to the Convergencia Party. See Gibson 2005 for more details.

29. The inability of the local electoral system to produce political change and give the opposition an institutional voice is an important factor behind the violent protests that shook the state's capital for several months during 2006.

30. Mexico has more than twenty-four hundred municipalities distributed over thirty-one states. Although the state has only about 3 percent of the national population, it contains almost 24 percent of the country's municipal governments.

31. On August 30, 1995, the state legislature approved an amendment to the state's electoral law that recognized the validity of indigenous customary law (usos y costumbres) for local governance. According to the statute, municipalities had the choice of electing their municipal leaders through conventional party competition or through usos y costumbres. Wherever communities chose customary law, political parties are prohibited from participating in any way in municipal politics, but residents still participate normally in state and national elections. A total of 418 of the state's 570 (73 percent) municipalities are governed by usos y costumbres (Gobierno del Estado de Oaxaca 1998).

32. It appears, however, that conflicts within municipalities ruled by usos y costumbres have been made worse by the penetration of political parties into local affairs and an increase in electoral competition (Eisenstadt 2007).

33. Much has been written about the modes of political control and participation in the ejido sector, but studies by Wayne Cornelius and David Myhre (1998) and by Alain de Janvry, Gustavo Gordillo, and Elisabeth Sadoulet (1997) provide a good description of the original structure of the ejido sector and how political and economic reforms since 1990 have transformed the relationship between peasants and the state.

34. The comisariado ejidal refers to the ejido's executive committee.

35. According to official election results, 58 percent of voters in La Ciénega supported PRI congressional candidates in the 1997 federal elections and 54 percent supported José Murat, the PRI's candidate for governor, in the 1998 state elections (IEE–Oaxaca 1998 and IFE 1997). Support dropped for the PRI in the 2000 presidential elections, when only 44 percent of residents voted for the PRI, compared with 29 percent for the PAN and 22 percent for the PRD. In 2006 residents voted for the PRD over the PRI (48 percent versus 29 percent) but shifted back to the PRI in 2009 (52 percent versus 23 percent).

36. The PRD candidate received 51 percent of the vote to the PRI's 49 percent, winning by a margin of only 60 of 3,022 votes. The right-of-center PAN is an absolute nonfactor in local elections.

37. Before 1995, the PAN had never won more than six municipal elections (or about 1 percent) and had never achieved more than 3 percent of the statewide vote in municipal elections (Díaz Montes 1994).

38. After consecutive losses in 1995 and 1998, one of the local PRI factions defected and joined the nascent Convergencia party. Convergencia's mayoral candidate, Gabino Cué Monteagudo, benefited from the political and financial support of Diódoro Carrasco, a former governor of the state and former minister of the interior under Zedillo. See Gibson 2005 for more detail on the meteoric rise of Convergencia in Oaxaca.

39. According to a 1995 census by the Instituto Nacional Estadística y Geografía (INEGI), more than 80 percent of the municipality's fifty-three hundred residents speak Zapotec as a first language.

40. Teotitlán del Valle may be unique in another way. Todd Eisenstadt's (2007) research found that postelectoral conflicts have increased in many communities governed by *usos y costumbres* in Oaxaca, but politics in Teotitlán del Valle has remained peaceful.

Chapter 6. Democratization, Political Competition, and Political Participation

1. Polling booths in Mexico are designed to serve a thousand or fewer voters, a number small enough to infer how neighborhoods or even small villages have voted.

2. Thanks to Luis Miguel Rionda of the University of Guanajuato for this insight.

3. A recent analysis of nationwide public opinion data by Andreas Schedler (1999) confirms that trust in elections has declined in Mexico since 1997, reaching levels of distrust comparable to 1988, when a majority of citizens were skeptical of election results.

4. A few even moved away from the neighborhood.

5. It is telling that three states with the highest turnout rates in the 2006 presidential election—Tabasco, the Federal District (Mexico City), and Yucatán—all have powerful and well-entrenched regional and local political machines.

6. In the 1995 municipal elections, the PRD defeated the PRI by a mere sixty votes of more than three thousand cast.

7. *Tequio* is a tradition common to indigenous communities in Oaxaca, where households are required to participate in such community-improvement projects as grading roads, repairing irrigation canals or sewage pipes, and building water tanks. Although the tradition is less common in urban areas, the *tequio* is a key practice that allows squatter neighborhoods to build infrastructure and provide important services that neither the local or the state government provides.

8. An opposition party is considered competitive if it wins at least 25 percent of the statewide vote. In 2003 there were very few states where *both* the PRD and the PAN were competitive.

9. Many of the people I spoke with became much more interested in the 2006 election once it became clear that López Obrador was a viable candidate and that they did not have to vote for the PAN to unseat the PRI. Nationally, the percentage of low-income Mexicans (those earning under four thousand pesos a month) who claimed they followed the presidential election jumped sixteen percentage points between October 2005 and July 2006, according to data from the 2006 Mexico Panel Study.

10. This has occurred in other parts of Mexico as well. One of the most publicized cases was in Puebla, where the governor, Manuel Bartlett, refused to fairly allocate funds under his control to local governments in the state. Instead, he favored rural municipalities controlled by the PRI and withheld funds from PAN-controlled governments, including the capital city. See Magaloni 2006 for more details on this dynamic.

11. In fact, a certain amount of fraud and electoral manipulation may be tolerated by citizens as part of the clientelistic bargain—as long as the party or faction they are associated with benefits from the cheating.

Chapter 7. Political Equality and Democracy in Mexico

1. The terms "citizen" and "subject" were used by Gabriel Almond and Sidney Verba (1963) to describe different political cultures in Mexico, whereas "radical" and "client" were used by Susan Stokes (1995) to describe the bifurcated political cultures she found in Lima's shantytowns.

2. Joan Nelson (1994) has made a similar point: "Survey based, cross-national research has taught us a great deal. . . . It does not detract from these contributions to note that a good deal remains unexplained regarding differences in individual levels and patterns of participation. . . . Much of the impetus to political action flows from contextual or situational factors that are difficult to capture through this kind of research and are better reflected in sociological and anthropological descriptions at the level of neighborhoods, villages, and other 'micro' settings."

3. This section draws from Holzner 2007b.

4. This of course does not mean that voting is not a potentially powerful tool for holding political leaders accountable, as recent electoral battles in Bolivia, Mexico, Peru, and Venezuela have shown.

5. This is so even if only to ritualistically confirm the legitimacy of the electoral process (Adler Lomnitz, Lomnitz Adler, and Adler 1993).

6. See also Alejandro Portes and Kelly Hoffman's (2004, 66–74) discussion on alternative strategies.

7. Although the international migration is usually interpreted as an economic strategy, Jonathan Hiskey and Daniel Montalvo (2008) have argued that emigration from Latin America is increasingly a political exit strategy pursued by individuals frustrated by underperforming political systems.

Bibliography

Abramson, Paul R. 1983. *Political Attitudes in America: Formation and Change*. San Francisco: Freeman.

Adler Lomnitz, Larissa, Claudio Lomnitz Adler, and Ilya Adler. 1993. "The Function of the Form: Power Play and Ritual in the 1988 Mexican Presidential Campaign." In *Constructing Culture and Power in Latin America*. Edited by D. H. Levine. Ann Arbor: University of Michigan Press.

Agüero, Felipe, and Jeffrey Stark, eds. 1998. *Fault Lines of Democracy in Post-transition Latin America*. Miami: North-South Center Press.

Aguilar García, Javier. 1992. "El estado mexicano, la modernización, y los obreros." In *El nuevo estado mexicano: Estado, actores y movimientos sociales*. Edited by J. Alonso, A. Azis, and J. Tamayo. Mexico City: Nueva Imagen.

Aldrich, John H. 1993. "Rational Choice and Turnout." *American Journal of Political Science* 37 (1): 246–78.

Almond, Gabriel Abraham, and Sidney Verba. 1989. *The Civic Culture Revisited*. Newbury Park: Sage Publications.

Almond, Gabriel, and Sidney Verba. 1963. *The Civic Culture: Political Attitudes and Democracy in Five Nations*. Princeton: Princeton University Press.

Alonso, Jorge, ed. 1986. *Los movimientos sociales en el Valle de México*. 2 vols. Vol. 1. Mexico City: Centro de Investigaciones y Estudios Superiores en Antropología Social, Ediciones de La Casa Chata.

———. 1988. *Los movimientos sociales en el Valle de México*. 2 vols. Vol. 2. Mexico City: Centro de Investigaciones y Estudios Superiores en Antropología Social, Ediciones de La Casa Chata.

———, Alberto Azis, and Jaime Tamayo, eds. 1992. *El nuevo estado mexicano: Estado, actores y movimientos sociales*. Vol. 3. Mexico City: Nueva Imagen.

Ames, Barry. 1970. "Bases of Support for Mexico's Dominant Party." *American Political Science Review* 64 (1): 153–67.

Anderson, Leslie E., and Lawrence C. Dodd. 2005. *Learning Democracy: Citizen Engagement and Electoral Choice in Nicaragua, 1990–2000*. Chicago: University of Chicago Press.

Arroyo, Alberto. 1992. "El estado mexicano de los años ochenta y sus trabajadores." In *El nuevo estado mexicano: Estado, actores y movimientos sociales*. Edited by J. Alonso, A. Azis, and J. Tamayo. Mexico City: Nueva Imagen.

Bacharach, Peter, and Morton S. Baratz. 1962. "Two Faces of Power." *American Political Science Review* 56 (December): 947–52.

Balch, George I. 1974. "Multiple Indicators in Survey Research: The Concept 'Sense of Political Efficacy.'" *Political Methodology* 1: 1–43.

Banfield, Edward C., and James Q. Wilson. 1965. *City Politics*. Cambridge: Harvard University Press.

Barnes, Samuel H., and Max Kaase. 1979. *Political Action: Mass Participation in Five Western Democracies*. Beverly Hills: Sage Publications.

Bartra, Armando. 1985. *Los herederos de Zapata: Movimientos Campesinos Posrevolucionarios en México*. Edited by Era, Los Problemas de México. Mexico City: Ediciones Era.

———. 1996. *Guerrero Bronco: Campesinos, ciudadanos y guerrilleros en la Costa Grande*. Mexico City: Ediciones Sinfiltro.

Bartra, Roger. 1975. *Caciquismo y poder político en el México rural*. Mexico City: Siglo XXI Editores.

Bates, Robert. 1981. *Market and States in Tropical Africa: The Political Basis of Agricultural Policies*. Berkeley: University of California Press.

Beck, Paul Allen, and M. Kent Jennings. 1975. "Parents as 'Middle Persons' in Political Socialization." *Journal of Politics* 37 (1): 83–107.

———. 1982. "Pathways to Participation." *American Political Science Review* 76 (1): 94–108.

———. 1991. "Family Traditions, Political Periods, and the Development of Partisan Orientations." *Journal of Politics* 53 (3): 742–63.

Beer, Caroline C. 2003. *Electoral Competition and Institutional Change in Mexico*. Notre Dame: University of Notre Dame Press.

Beltrán, Ulises, et al. 2006. *Estudio Comparativo de Los Sistemas Electorales (CSES)—2006*. Distributed by Banco de Información para la Investigation Aplicada en Ciencias Sociales and Centro de Investigación y Docencia Económicas. Available online at http://hdl.handle.net/10089/3715.

Blydenburgh, John C. 1971. "A Controlled Experiment to Measure the Effects of Personal Contact Campaigning." *Midwest Journal of Political Science* 15: 36–81.

Bobo, Lawrence, and Franklin D. Gilliam Jr. 1990. "Race, Sociopolitical Participation, and Black Empowerment." *American Political Science Review* 84 (2): 377–93.

Boltvinik, Julio. 2003. "Welfare, Equality, and Poverty in Mexico, 1970–2000." In *Confronting Development: Assessing Mexico's Economic and Social Policy*. Edited by K. J. Middlebrook and E. Zepeda. Palo Alto: Stanford University Press.

Booth, John A., and Mitchell A. Seligson. 1984. "The Political Culture of Authoritarianism in Mexico: A Reexamination." *Latin American Research Review* 19 (1): 106–24.

———, eds. 1978. *Political Participation in Latin America: Citizen and State*. Vol. 1. New York: Holmes and Meier.

Bruhn, Kathleen. 1997. *Taking on Goliath: The Emergence of a New Left Party and the Struggle for Democracy in Mexico*. University Park: Pennsylvania State University.

———. 1999. "The Resurrection of the Mexican Left in the 1997 Elections." In *Toward*

Mexico's Democratization: Parties, Campaigns, Elections, and Public Opinion. Edited by J. Domínguez and A. Poiré. New York: Routledge.

Burns, Nancy, Kay Lehman Schlozman, and Sidney Verba. 2001. *The Private Roots of Public Action: Gender, Equality, and Political Participation.* Cambridge: Harvard University Press.

Cabrero Mendoza, Enrique. 1995. *La nueva gestión municipal en México: Análisis de experiencias innovadoras en gobiernos locales.* Mexico City: Miguel Angel Porrúa.

———. 1998. *Las políticas descentralizadoras en México, 1983–1993: Logros y desencantos.* First edition. Mexico City: CIDE / Miguel Angel Porrúa.

———, ed. 1996. *Los dilemas de la modernización municipal: Estudios sobre la gestión hacendaria en municipios urbanos de México.* Mexico City: Miguel Angel Porrúa.

Caldeira, Gregory A., Aage R. Clausen, and Samuel C. Patterson. 1990. "Partisan Mobilization and Electoral Participation." *Electoral Studies* 9: 191–204.

Caldeira, Gregory A., and Samuel C. Patterson. 1982. "Contextual Influences in U.S. State Legislative Elections." *Legislative Studies Quarterly* 7 (3): 359–81.

Camp, Roderic Ai. 2003. "Learning Democracy in Mexico and the United States." *Mexican Studies/Estudios Mexicanos* 19 (1): 3–28.

———. 2004. "Citizen Attitudes toward Democracy and Vicente Fox's Victory in 2000." In *Mexico's Pivotal Democratic Election.* Edited by Jorge I. Domínguez and Chappell Lawson, 25–46. Palo Alto: Stanford University Press.

———. 2006. "Democracy Redux: Mexico's Voters and the 2006 Presidential Race?" Available online at http://web.mit.edu/polisci/research/mexico06/Papers.html.

Campbell, Andrea Louise. 2003. *How Policies Make Citizens.* Princeton, N.J.: Princeton University Press.

Campbell, Angus, Philip E. Converse, Warren Miller, and Donald Stokes. 1960. *The American Voter.* New York: Wiley. 1976, reprint. Chicago: University of Chicago Press.

Catterberg, Gabriela, and Alejandro Moreno. 2005. "The Individual Bases of Political Trust: Trends in New and Established Democracies." *International Journal of Public Opinion* 18 (1): 31–48.

Centro de Investigación y Docencia Económicas (CIDE). 2000. *Estudio Comparativo de los Sistemas Electorales (CSES)—2003.* Mexico City: Banco de Información para la Investigación Aplicada en Ciencias Sociales / CIDE. Available online at http://hdl.handle.net/10089/3550.

———. 2003. *Estudio Comparativo de los Sistemas Electorales (CSES)—2003.* Mexico City: Banco de Información para la Investigación Aplicada en Ciencias Sociales / CIDE. Available online at http://hdl.handle.net/10089/3687.

Chalmers, Douglas A., Carlos Vilas, et al., eds. 1997. *The New Politics of Inequality in Latin America: Rethinking Participation and Representation.* Oxford: Oxford University Press.

Chubb, Judith. 1981. "The Social Bases of an Urban Political Machine: The Christian Democratic Party in Palermo." In *Political Clientelism, Patronage, and Development.* Edited by S. N. Eisenstadt and R. Lemarchand. London: Sage Publications.

Clarke, Harold S., and Alan C. Acock. 1989. "National Elections and Political Attitudes: The Case of Political Efficacy." *British Journal of Political Science* 19 (4): 551–62.

Clemens, Elizabeth S. 1996. "Organizational Form as Frame: Collective Identity and Political Strategy in the American Labor Movement, 1880–1920." In *Comparative*

Perspectives on Social Movements: Political Opportunities, Mobilizing Structures, and Cultural Framings. Edited by D. McAdam, J. D. McCarthy, and M. N. Zald. Cambridge: Cambridge University Press.

Collier, David. 1976. *Squatters and Oligarchs: Authoritarian Rule and Policy Change in Peru.* Baltimore, Md.: Johns Hopkins Press.

Collier, Ruth Berins, and David Collier. 1991. *Shaping the Political Arena: Critical Junctures, the Labor Movement, and Regime Dynamics in Latin America.* Princeton: Princeton University Press.

Consejo Nacional de Polacion (CONAPO). 2004. *Índices absolutos de marginación, 1990–2000.* Mexico City: CONAPO.

Cook, Maria Lorena. 1990. "Organizing Opposition in the Teacher's Movement in Oaxaca." In *Popular Movements and Political Change in Mexico.* Edited by J. Foweraker and A. L. Craig. Boulder, Colo.: Lynne Rienner Publishers.

———. 1996. *Organizing Dissent: Unions, the State, and the Democratic Teachers' Movement in Mexico.* University Park: Pennsylvania State University Press.

Cornelius, Wayne A. 1975. *Politics and the Migrant Poor in Mexico City.* Palo Alto: Stanford University Press.

———. 1996. *Mexican Politics in Transition: The Breakdown of a One-Party-Dominant Regime.* La Jolla: Center for U.S.–Mexican Studies at the University of California San Diego.

———. 1999. "Subnational Politics and Democratization: Tensions between Center and Periphery in the Mexican Political System." In *Subnational Politics and Democratization in Mexico.* Edited by Wayne A. Cornelius, Todd A. Eisenstadt, and Jane Hindley. La Jolla: Center for U.S.–Mexican Studies at the University of California San Diego.

———. 2004. "Mobilized Voting in the 2000 Elections: The Changing Efficacy of Vote Buying and Coercion in Mexican Electoral Politics." In *Mexico's Pivotal Democratic Election: Candidates, Voters, and the Presidential Campaign of 2000.* Edited by J. Domínguez and C. Lawson. Palo Alto: Stanford University Press.

———, and Philip L. Martin. 1993. "The Uncertain Connection: Free Trade and Rural Mexican Migration to the United States." *International Migration Review* 27 (3): 484–512.

———, and David Myhre. 1998. *The Transformation of Rural Mexico: Reforming the Ejido Sector, U.S.-Mexico Contemporary Perspectives Series; 12.* La Jolla: Center for U.S.–Mexican Studies at the University of California San Diego.

Cornelius, Wayne A., and David A. Shirk, eds. 2007. *Reforming the Administration of Justice in Mexico.* Notre Dame: University of Notre Dame Press.

Cornelius, Wayne A., Ann L. Craig, and Jonathan Fox, eds. 1994. *Transforming State-Society Relations in Mexico: The National Solidarity Strategy.* San Diego: Center for U.S.–Mexican Studies at the University of California San Diego.

Cornelius, Wayne A., Todd A. Eisenstadt, and Jane Hindley, eds. 1999. *Subnational Politics and Democratization in Mexico.* La Jolla: Center for U.S.–Mexican Studies at the University of California San Diego.

Cox, Gary W., and Michael C. Munger. 1989. "Closeness, Expenditures, and Turnout in the 1988 U.S. House Elections." *American Political Science Review* 83: 217–31.

Craig, Ann L., and Wayne A. Cornelius. 1980. "Political Culture in Mexico: Continuities and Revisionist Interpretations." In *The Civic Culture Revisited*. Edited by G. Almond and S. Verba, 325–93. Boston: Little, Brown.

Craig, Stephen C., and Michael A. Maggiotto. 1982. "Measuring Political Efficacy." *Political Methodology* 8: 85–109.

Craig, Stephen C., Richard G. Niemi, and Glenn E. Silver. 1990. "Political Efficacy and Trust: A Report on the NES Pilot Study Items." *Political Behavior* 12 (3): 289–314.

Crespo, José Antonio. 2004. "Party Competition in Mexico: Evolution and Prospects." In *Dilemmas of Political Change in Mexico*. Edited by K. J. Middlebrook. London: Institute of Latin American Studies / Center for U.S.–Mexican Studies.

Cross, John C. 1998. *Informal Politics: Street Vendors and the State in Mexico City*. Palo Alto: Stanford University Press.

Crotty, William, ed. 1991a. *Political Participation and American Democracy*. New York: Greenwood Press.

———. 1991b. "Political Participation: Mapping the Terrain." In *Political Participation and American Democracy*. Edited by W. Crotty, 1–22. New York: Greenwood Press.

Dahl, Robert A. 1989. *Democracy and Its Critics*. New Haven: Yale University Press.

———. 2006. *On Political Equality*. New Haven: Yale University Press.

Dalton, Russell J. 1996. *Citizen Politics: Public Opinion and Political Parties in Advanced Western Democracies*. Chatham: Chatham House Publishers.

Davis, Charles L. 1983. "Political Regimes and the Socioeconomic Resource Model of Political Mobilization: Some Venezuelan and Mexican Data." *Journal of Politics* 45 (2): 422–48.

Davis, Diane, E., and Viviane Brachet-Márquez. 1997. "Rethinking Democracy: Mexico in Historical Perspective." *Comparative Study of Society and History* 39 (January): 86–119.

de Janvry, Alain, Gustavo Gordillo, and Elisabeth Sadoulet, eds. 1997. *Mexico's Second Agrarian Reform: Household and Community Responses, Ejido Reform Research Project*. La Jolla: Center for U.S.–Mexican Studies at the University of California San Diego.

del Mercado, Salvador Vázquez. 2007. "As Parties Compete for Votes (by Buying Them): Gifts and Votes in Mexico." Paper presented at the annual meeting of the American Political Science Association, August 30–September 2, Chicago.

del Pozo, Blanca Elena, and Ricardo Aparicio. 2001. *Estudio sobre la participación ciudadana y las condiciones del voto libre y secreto en las elecciones federales del año 2000: Una aproximación a la magnitud de la inducción y coacción del voto*. Mexico City: Facultad Latinoamericana de Ciencias Sociales (FLACSO) and IFE.

Dennis, Jack. 1991. "Theories of Turnout: An Empirical Comparison of Alienationist and Rationalist Perspectives." In *Political Participation and American Democracy*. Edited by W. Crotty. New York: Greenwood Press.

Díaz-Cayeros, Alberto. 2004. "Decentralization, Democratization, and Federalism in Mexico." In *Dilemmas of Political Change in Mexico*. Edited by K. J. Middlebrook. London: Institute of Latin American Studies / Center for U.S.–Mexican Studies.

———. 2005. Endogenous Institutional Change in the Mexican Senate. *Comparative Political Studies* 38: 1196–1218.

———, Federico Estevez, and Beatriz Magaloni. Forthcoming. *Poverty, Vote Buying, and Democracy: Strategies of Electoral Investment in Mexico*.

Díaz Montes, Fausto. 1994. "Elecciones Municipales en Oaxaca 1980–1992." *Cuadernos del Sur* 3 (6–7): 93–110.

Dietz, Henry. 1998. *Urban Poverty, Political Participation, and the State*. Pittsburgh: University of Pittsburgh Press.

Dietz, Henry A., and David Scott Palmer. 1978. "Citizenship Participation under Military Corporatism in Peru." In *Political Participation in Latin America: Citizen and State*. Edited by J. A. Booth and M. A. Seligson. New York: Holmes & Meier.

Dillon, Sam, and Julia Preston. 2000. "Old Ways Die Hard in Mexican Elections Despite Pledges." *New York Times*, May 9.

Domínguez, Jorge. 1999. "The Transformation of Mexico's Electoral and Party System, 1988–1997: An Introduction." In *Toward Mexico's Democratization: Parties, Campaigns, Elections, and Public Opinion*. Edited by J. Domínguez and A. Poiré. New York: Routledge.

———, and Chappell Lawson, eds. 2004. *Mexico's Pivotal Democratic Election: Candidates, Voters, and the Presidential Campaign of 2000*. Palo Alto: Stanford University Press.

Domínguez, Jorge, and Alejandro Poiré, eds. 1999. *Toward Mexico's Democratization: Parties, Campaigns, Elections, and Public Opinion*. New York: Routledge.

Domínguez, Jorge I., and James A. McCann. 1996. *Democratizing Mexico: Public Opinion and Electoral Choices*. Baltimore: Johns Hopkins University Press.

Downs, Anthony. 1957. *An Economic Theory of Democracy*. New York: Harper.

Drake, Paul W., and Eduardo Silva, eds. 1986. *Elections and Democratization in Latin America*. San Diego: Center for Iberian and Latin American Studies and the Center for U.S.–Mexican Studies at the University of California San Diego.

Druckman, James N., and Arthur Lupia. 2000. "Preference Formation." *Annual Review of Political Science* 3: 1–24.

Durand Ponte, Victor Manuel. 1994a. "El papel de los sindicatos en la transición política Mexicana." *Revista mexicana de sociologia* 56 (1): 29–43.

———, ed. 1994b. *La construcción de la democracia en México*. Mexico City: Siglo XXI Editores.

Eckstein, Susan. 1977. *The Poverty of Revolution: The State and the Urban Poor in Mexico*. Princeton: Princeton University Press.

———. 1989a. "Power and Popular Protest in Latin America." In *Power and Popular Protest: Latin American Social Movements*. Edited by S. Eckstein. Berkeley: University of California Press.

Economic Commission for Latin America and the Caribbean (ECLAC). 2006. *Social Panorama of Latin America 2005*. United Nations. Santiago, Chile: ECLAC.

Eisenstadt, S. N., and René Lemarchand, eds. 1981. *Political Clientelism, Patronage, and Development*. London: Sage Publications.

Eisenstadt, S. N., and Luis Roniger. 1980. "Patron-Client Relations as a Model of Structuring Social Exchange." *Comparative Studies in Society and History* 22 (1): 42–77.

Eisenstadt, Todd A. 2004. *Courting Democracy in Mexico: Party Strategies and Electoral Institutions*. Cambridge: Cambridge University Press.

———. 2007. "*Usos y Costumbres* and Postelectoral Conflicts in Oaxaca, Mexico, 1995–2004: An Empirical and Normative Assessment." *Latin American Research Review* 42 (1): 52–77.

Eldersveld, Samuel J., and Bashiruddin Ahmed. 1978. *Citizens and Politics: Mass Political Behavior in India*. Chicago: University of Chicago Press.

Erie, Steven P. 1988. *Rainbow's End*. Berkeley: University of California Press.

Estrada, Luis, and Alejandro Poiré. 2007. "Taught to Protest, Learning to Lose." *Journal of Democracy* 18 (1): 73–86.

Fagen, Richard R., and William S. Tuohy. 1972. *Politics and Privilege in a Mexican City*. Palo Alto: Stanford University Press.

Fairris, David, and Edward Levine. 2004. "Declining Union Density in Mexico: 1984–2000." *Monthly Labor Review* (September): 10–17.

Farrera Araujo, Javier. 1994. "El movimiento urbano popular, la organización de pobladores y la transición política en México." In *La construcción de la democracia en México*. Edited by V. M. Durand Ponte. Mexico City: Siglo XXI.

Ferejohn, John A., and Morris P. Fiorina. 1974. "The Paradox of Not Voting: A Decision Theoretic Analysis." *American Political Science Review* 68: 525–36.

Finkel, Steven. 1985. "Reciprocal Effects of Participation and Political Efficacy: A Panel Analysis." *American Journal of Political Science* 29 (4): 891–913.

———. 1987. "The Effects of Participation on Political Efficacy and Political Support: Evidence from a West German Panel." *Journal of Politics* 49 (2): 441–64.

———, and Edward N. Muller. 1998. "Rational Choice and the Dynamics of Collective Political Action: Evaluating Alternative Models with Panel Data." *American Political Science Review* 92 (1): 37–49.

Fish, M. Steven. 1995. *Democracy from Scratch: Opposition and Regime in the New Russian Revolution*. Princeton: Princeton University Press.

Fitzgerald, David. 2004. "For 118 Million Mexicans: Emigrants and Chicanos in Mexican Politics." In *Dilemmas of Political Change in Mexico*. Edited by Kevin J. Middlebrook, 523–48. London: Institute of Latin American Studies.

Fox, Jonathan. 1993. *The Politics of Food in Mexico: State Power and Mobilization, Food Systems and Agrarian Change*. Ithaca: Cornell University Press.

———. 1994a. "The Difficult Transition from Clientelism to Citizenship: Lessons from Mexico." *World Politics* 46: 151–84.

———. 1994b. "Targeting the Poorest: The Role of the National Indigenous Institute in Mexico's Solidarity Program." In *Transforming State-Society Relations in Mexico: The National Solidarity Strategy*. Edited by W. A. Cornelius, A. L. Craig, and J. Fox, 179–216. San Diego: Center for U.S.–Mexico Studies.

———. 1996. "How Does Civil Society Thicken? The Political Construction of Social Capital in Rural Mexico." *World Development* 24 (6): 1089–1103.

———. 2000. "State-Society Relations in Mexico: Historical Legacies and Contemporary Trends." *Latin American Research Review* 35 (2): 183–203.

———. 2007. *Accountability Politics: Power and Voice in Rural Mexico*. New York: Oxford University Press.

———, Libby Haight, Helena Hofbauer, and Tania Sánchez Andrade, eds. 2007. *Mexico's Right-to-Know Reforms: Civil Society Perspectives*. Washington, D.C.: Woodrow Wilson International Center for Scholars.

Gamson, William, and David Meyer. 1996. "Framing Political Opportunity." In *Comparative Perspectives on Social Movements: Political Opportunities, Mobilizing Structures, and Cultural Framings.* Edited by D. McAdam, J. D. McCarthy, and M. N. Zald, 275–90. Cambridge: Cambridge University Press.

Garretón, Manuel Antonio. 1989. "Popular Mobilization and the Military Regime in Chile: The Complexities of the Invisible Transition." In *Power and Popular Protest: Latin American Social Movements.* Edited by S. Eckstein, 259–77. Berkeley: University of California Press.

Gaventa, John. 1980. *Power and Powerlessness: Quiescence and Rebellion in an Appalachian Valley.* Oxford: Clarendon Press.

Gay, Claudine. 2001. "The Effects of Black Congressional Representation on Political Participation." *American Political Science Review* 95 (3): 589–602.

Gerber, Alan S., and Donald P. Green. 2000. "The Effects of Canvassing, Telephone Calls, and Direct Mail on Voter Turnout: A Field Experiment." *American Political Science Review* 94 (3): 653–63.

Gibson, Edward L. 2005. "Boundary Control: Subnational Authoritarianism in Democratic Countries." *World Politics* 58: 101–32.

Giugale, Marcelo M., Olivier Lafourcade, and Vinh H. Nguyen, eds. 2001. *Mexico: A Comprehensive Development Agenda for the New Era.* Washington D.C.: World Bank.

Gobierno del Estado de Oaxaca. 1998. *Reformas y adiciones a la constitutción política del estado: Ley de derechos de los pueblos y comunidades indígenas.* Oaxaca: Gobierno del Estado de Oaxaca.

Gómez Tagle, Silvia, ed. 1997. *1994: Las elecciones en los estados.* Vols. 1 and 2. Mexico City: Centro de Investigaciones Interdisciplinarias en Ciencias y Humanidades / UNAM.

———. 2004. "Public Institutions and Electoral Transparency." In *Dilemmas of Political Change in Mexico.* Edited by K. J. Middlebrook, 82–107. London: Institute of Latin American Studies / Center for U.S.–Mexican Studies.

González Casanova, Pablo. 1965. *La democracia en México.* Mexico City: Ediciones Era.

———, ed. 1985. *Las elecciones en México: Evolución y perspectivas.* Mexico City: Siglo XXI.

González Casanova, Pablo, and Jorge Cadena Roa, eds. 1994. *La República Mexicana: Modernización y democracia de Aguascalientes a Zacatecas.* Vols. 1–3, *La democracia en México.* Mexico City: La Jornada Ediciones.

Goodwin, Kenneth, and Robert Cameron Mitchell. 1982. "Rational Models, Collective Goods, and Nonelectoral Political Behavior." *Western Political Quarterly* 35 (2): 161–81.

Graham, Carol. 1994. "Mexico's Solidarity Program in Comparative Context: Demand-based Poverty Alleviation Programs in Latin America, Africa, and Eastern Europe." In *Transforming State-Society Relations in Mexico: The National Solidarity Strategy.* Edited by W. A. Cornelius, A. L. Craig, and J. Fox, 309–27. San Diego: Center for U.S.–Mexican Studies at the University of California San Diego.

Greene, Kenneth F. 2007. *Why Dominant Parties Lose: Mexico's Democratization in Comparative Perspective.* New York: Cambridge University Press.

Grindle, Merilee. 1986. *State and Countryside: Development Policy and Agrarian Politics in Latin America.* Baltimore: Johns Hopkins University Press.

———. 1995. "Reforming Land Tenure in Mexico: Peasants, the Market, and the State." In *The Challenge of Institutional Reform in Mexico.* Edited by R. Roett and P. A. Hall, 39–56. Boulder: Lynne Rienner.

Gutmann, Matthew C. 2002. *The Romance of Democracy: Compliant Defiance in Contemporary Mexico*. Berkeley: University of California Press.

Haber, Paul. 1994. "Political Change in Durango: The Role of National Solidarity." In *Transforming State-Society Relations in Mexico: The National Solidarity Strategy*. Edited by W. A. Cornelius, A. L. Craig, and J. Fox, 255–79. San Diego: Center for U.S.–Mexico Studies.

Haggard, Stephan, and Robert R. Kaufman. 1992. *The Politics of Economic Adjustment: International Constraints, Distributive Conflicts, and the State*. Princeton: Princeton University Press.

———. 1995. *The Political Economy of Democratic Transitions*. Princeton: Princeton University Press.

Hamilton, Nora. 1982. *The Limits of State Autonomy: Post-revolutionary Mexico*. Princeton: Princeton University Press.

Harvey, Neil. 1998. *The Chiapas Rebellion: The Struggle for Land and Democracy*. Durham: Duke University Press.

Hellman, Judith Adler. 1994. "Mexican Popular Movements, Clientelism, and the Process of Democratization." *Latin American Perspectives* 21 (2): 124–42.

Herbst, Jeffrey. 1990. "Migration, the Politics of Protest, and State Consolidation in Africa." *African Affairs* 89, no. 355: 183–203.

Hernández-Rodríguez, Rogelio. 2003. "The Renovation of Old Institutions: State Governors and the Political Transition in Mexico." *Latin American Politics and Society* 45 (4): 98–127.

Hilgers, Tina. 2005. "The Nature of Clientelism in Mexico City." Paper presented at the annual meeting of the Canadian Political Science Association, June 2–4, London, Ontario.

Hirschman, Albert O. 1970. *Exit, Voice, and Loyalty: Responses to Decline in Firms, Organizations, and States*. Cambridge: Harvard University Press.

Hiskey, Jonathan T., and Daniel Montalvo. 2008. "Democratization, System Performance, and the 'Exit' Option in Latin America." Paper presented at the annual meeting of the Midwest Political Science Association, April 3–6, Chicago.

Hiskey, Jonathan T., and Shaun Bowler. 2005. "Local Context and Democratization in Mexico." *American Journal of Political Science* 49 (1): 57–71.

Holzner, Claudio A. 2002. "Poverty of Democracy: Political Opportunities and Political Participation of the Poor in Mexico." Ph.D. dissertation, Political Science, University of Michigan, Ann Arbor.

———. 2004. "End of Clientelism? Strong and Weak Networks in a Mexican Squatter Movement." *Mobilization: An International Journal* 9 (3): 223–40.

———. 2007a. "The Poverty of Democracy: Neoliberal Reforms and Political Participation of the Poor in Mexico." *Latin American Politics and Society* 49 (2): 87–122.

———. 2007b. "Voz y voto: Participación política y calidad de la democracia en México." *América Latina Hoy* 45 (April): 17–46.

———. 2009. "Strengths and Weaknesses of Democracy in Mexico." Unpublished manuscript.

Houtzager, Peter, and Marcus J. Kurtz. 2000. "The Institutional Roots of Popular Mobilization." *Comparative Studies of Society and History* 42 (2): 394–424.

Huber, Evelyne, and Fred Solt. 2004. "Successes and Failures of Neoliberalism." *Latin American Research Review* 39 (3): 150–64.

Huckfeldt, R. Robert. 1979. "Political Participation and the Neighborhood Social Context." *American Journal of Political Science* 23 (3): 579–92.

———, and John Sprague. 1992. "Political Parties and Electoral Mobilization: Political Structure, Social Structure, and the Party Canvass." *American Political Science Review* 86: 70–86.

Huntington, Samuel P. , and Joan M. Nelson. 1976. *No Easy Choice: Political Participation in Developing Countries*. Cambridge: Harvard University Press.

Instituto Electoral Estatal (IEE)–Oaxaca. 1995. *Memoria de los procesos electorales de diputados y concejales 1995*. Oaxaca: Instituto Electoral Estatal de Oaxaca.

———. 1998. *Votación por municipio, elección local celebrade el domindo 2 de Agosto de 1998. Elección de gobernador del estado*. Oaxaca: Instituto Electoral Estatal de Oaxaca.

Instituto Federal Electoral (IFE). 1997. *Estadísticas de las elecciones federales y de las elecciones locales en el Distrito Federal de 1997*. Mexico City: IFE.

Jackman, Robert W. 1987. "Political Institutions and Voter Turnout in the Industrial Democracies." *American Political Science Review* 81: 405–23.

Jenkins, J. Craig. 1983. "Resource Mobilization Theory and the Study of Social Movements." *American Review of Sociology* 9: 527–53.

———, and Bert Klandermans, eds. 1995. *The Politics of Protest: Comparative Perspectives on States and Social Movements*. Vol. 3. Minneapolis: University of Minnesota Press.

Jennings, M. Kent, and Richard G. Niemi. 1968. "The Transmission of Political Values from Parent to Child." *American Political Science Review* 62 (1): 169–84.

———. 1975. "Continuities and Change in Political Orientations." *American Political Science Review* 69 (4): 1316–35.

———. 1981. *Generations and Politics*. Princeton, N.J.: Princeton University Press.

Kato, Junko. 1996. "Institutions and Rationality in Politics: Three Varieties of Neo-Institutionalists." *British Journal of Political Science* 26 (4): 553–82.

Key, V. O. 1956. *Politics, Parties, and Pressure Groups*. New York: Crowell.

Klesner, Joseph L. 2005. "Electoral Competition and the New Party System in Mexico." *Latin American Politics and Society* 47 (2): 103–42.

———. 2007. "The 2006 Mexican Elections: Manifestation of a Divided Society?" *PS: Political Science and Politics* 40 (1): 27–32.

———, and Chappell Lawson. 2000. "Adiós to the PRI? Changing Voter Turnout in Mexico's Political Transition." *Mexican Studies/Estudios Mexicanos* 17 (1): 17–39.

Koelble, Thomas A. 1995. "Review: The New Institutionalism in Political Science and Sociology." *Comparative Politics* 27 (2): 231–43.

Kramer, Gerald H. 1970. "The Effects of Precinct-level Canvassing on Voter Behavior." *Public Opinion Quarterly* 34: 560–72.

Kriesi, Hanspeter. 1995. "The Political Opportunity Structure of New Social Movements: Its Impact on Their Mobilization." In *The Politics of Social Protest: Comparative Perspectives on States and Social Movements*. Edited by J. C. Jenkins and B. Klandermans, 167–98. Minneapolis: University of Minnesota Press.

Kurtz, Marcus J. 2004. *Free Market Democracy and the Chilean and Mexican Countryside*. Cambridge: Cambridge University Press.

Lane, Robert. 1959. *Political Life*. New York: Free Press.

Langston, Joy. 2002. "Breaking Out Is Hard To Do: Exit, Voice, and Loyalty in Mexico's One-Party Hegemonic Regime." *Latin American Politics and Society* 44 (3): 61–88.

Langton, Kenneth P., and M. Kent Jennings. 1968. "Political Socialization and the High School Civics Curriculum in the U.S." *American Political Science Review* 62 (3): 852–67.

Langton, Kenneth P., and David A. Karns. 1969. "The Relative Influence of the Family, Peer Group, and School in the Development of Political Efficacy." *Western Political Quarterly* 22 (4): 813–26.

Latin American Public Opinion Project (LAPOP). 2004. "The Americas Barometer by the Latin American Public Opinion Project." Available online at http://www.Lapop-Surveys.org.

———. 2006. "The Americas Barometer by the Latin American Public Opinion Project." Available online at http://www.LapopSurveys.org.

Laurell, Asa Cristina. 2003. "The Transformation of Social Policy in Mexico." In *Confronting Development: Assessing Mexico's Economic and Social Policy*. Edited by K. J. Middlebrook and E. Zepeda, 320–49. Palo Alto: Stanford University Press.

Lawson, Chappell. 2006. "Preliminary Findings from the Mexico 2006 Panel Study: Memo #1: Blue States and Yellow States." Available online at http://web.mit.edu/polisci/research/mexico06/Papers.html.

Lawson, Chappell, and Joseph Klesner. 2004. "Political Reform, Electoral Participation, and the Campaign of 2000." In *Mexico's Pivotal Democratic Election: Candidates, Voters, and the Presidential Campaign of 2000*. Edited by J. Domínguez and C. Lawson. Palo Alto: Stanford University Press.

Leighley, Jan E. 1995. "Attitudes, Opportunities, and Incentives: A Field Essay on Political Participation." *Political Research Quarterly* 48 (1): 181–209.

Leighley, Jan E., and Jonathan Nagler. 2004. "Unions as Mobilizing Institutions in the U.S., 1964–2000." Paper presented at the annual meeting of the American Political Science Association, September 2–5, Chicago.

———. 2007. "Unions, Voter Turnout, and Class Bias in the U.S. Electorate, 1964–2004." *Journal of Politics* 69 (2): 430–41.

Lemarchand, René. 1981. "Comparative Political Clientelism: Structure, Process, and Optic." In *Political Clientelism, Patronage, and Development*. Edited by S. N. Eisenstadt and R. Lemarchand, 7–32. London: Sage Publications.

Levin, Inés, and R. Michael Alvarez. 2009. "Measuring the Effects of Voter Confidence on Political Participation: An Application to the 2006 Mexican Election." Paper presented at the sixty-seventh annual conference of the Midwest Political Science Association.

Levine, Daniel H. 1992. *Popular Voices in Latin American Catholicism*. Princeton: Princeton University Press.

———. 2006. "Civil Society and Political Decay in Venezuela." In *Civil Society and Democracy in Latin America*. Edited by R. Feinberg, L. Zamosc, and C. Waisman, 169–92. New York: Palgrave MacMillan.

———, and Catalina Romero. 2004. "Movimientos urbanos y desempoderamiento en Peru y Venezuela." *America Latina Hoy Revista de Ciencias Sociales* 36 (April): 47–77.

Levine, Daniel H., and José Molina. 2007. "La calidad de la democracia en América Latina: Una visión comparada." *América Latina Hoy* 45 (April): 17–46.

Levy, Daniel, and Gabriel Székely. 1987. *Mexico: Paradoxes of Stability and Change*. Boulder: Westview.

Levy, Santiago. 2006. *Progress against Poverty: Sustaining Mexico's Progresa-Oportunidades Program*. Washington, D.C.: Brookings Institution Press.

Lindbloom, Charles. 1977. *Politics and Markets: The World's Political Economic Systems*. New York: Basic Books.

Lipset, Seymor Martin. 1981 [1960]. *Political Man: The Social Bases of Politics*. Baltimore: Johns Hopkins University Press.

Lupfer, Michael, and David E. Price. 1972. "On the Merits of Face-to-Face Campaigning." *Social Science Quarterly* 53: 534–43.

Lustig, Nora. 1994. "Solidarity as a Strategy of Poverty Alleviation." In *Transforming State Society Relations in Mexico*. Edited by Wayne Cornelius, Ann Craig, and Jonathan Fox.

Macedo, Stephen, Yvette Alex-Assensoh, et al. 2005. *Democracy at Risk: How Political Choices Undermine Citizen Participation, and What We Can Do about It*. Washington, D.C.: Brookings Institution Press.

Magaloni, Beatriz. 2006. *Voting for Autocracy: Hegemonic Party Survival and Its Demise in Mexico*. New York: Cambridge University Press.

———. 1999. "Is the PRI Fading? Economic Performance, Electoral Accountability, and Voting Behavior in the 1994 and 1997 Elections." In *Mexico's Democratization: Parties, Campaigns, Elections, and Public Opinion*. Edited by Jorge I. Domínguez and Alejandro Poiré, 203–36. New York: Routledge.

March, James G., and Johan P. Olsen. 1984. "The New Institutionalism: Organizational Factors in Political Life." *American Political Science Review* 78 (3): 734–49.

———. 1989. *Rediscovering Institutions*. New York: Free Press.

McAdam, Doug. 1982. *Political Process and the Development of Black Insurgency*. Chicago: University of Chicago Press.

———, John D. McCarthy, and Mayer N. Zald, eds. 1996. *Comparative Perspectives on Social Movements: Political Opportunities, Mobilizing Structures, and Cultural Framings*. Cambridge: Cambridge University Press.

McCann, James A., and Chappell Lawson. 2003. "An Electorate Adrift? Public Opinion and the Quality of Democracy in Mexico." *Latin American Research Review* 38 (3): 60–81.

McCann, James A., Wayne A. Cornelius, and David L. Leal. 2006. "Mexico's 2006 *Voto Remoto* and the Potential for Transnational Civic Engagement among Mexican Expatriates." Paper presented at the annual meeting of the American Political Science Association, August 31–September 3, Philadelphia.

McCarthy, John D., and Mayer N. Zald. 1977. "Resource Mobilization and Social Movements: A Partial Theory." *American Journal of Sociology* 82 (6): 1212–41.

Meyer, Jean Francois. 2005. "All along the Watchtower: State-Independent Union Relations in Mexico Under Fox." Paper presented at the annual meeting of the Midwest Political Science Association, April 7–10, Chicago.

Middlebrook, Kevin J. 1986. "Political Liberalization in an Authoritarian Regime: The Case of Mexico." In *Elections and Democratization in Latin America, 1980–1985*. Edited by P. W. Drake and E. Silva, 73-104. La Jolla: Center for Iberian and Latin American Studies at the University of California San Diego.

————. 1995. *The Paradox of Revolution: Labor, the State, and Authoritarianism in Mexico.* Baltimore: Johns Hopkins University Press.

Milbrath, Lester W., and M. L. Goel. 1977. *Political Participation: How and Why Do People Get Involved in Politics?* Second edition. Chicago: Rand McNally.

Miller, Warren E., and J. Merrill Shanks. 1996. *The New American Voter.* Cambridge: Harvard University Press.

Moehler, Devra C. 2008. *Distrusting Democrats: Outcomes of Participatory Constitution Making.* Ann Arbor: University of Michigan Press.

Molinar Horcasitas, Juan. 1987. "Regreso a Chihuahua." *Nexos* 3 (March): 21–32.

Moreno, Alejandro. 2003. *El Votante Mexicano: Democracia, actitudes políticas y conducta electoral.* Mexico City: Fondo de Cultura Económica.

Morrell, Michael E. 2003. "Survey and Experimental Evidence for a Valid and Reliable Measure of Internal Efficacy." *Political Opinion Quarterly* 67: 589–602.

Mostajo, Rossana. 2000. *Gasto social y distribución del ingreso: Caracterización e impacto redistributivo en países seleccionados de América Latina y el Caribe.* ECLAC, 2000. Available online at http://www.eclac.org/publicaciones/xml/9/4589/lc/376e.pdf.

Myhre, David. 1998. "The Achilles' Heel of the Reforms: The Rural Finance System." In *The Transformation of Rural Mexico: Reforming the Ejido Sector.* Edited by W. A. Cornelius and D. Myhre, 39–65. La Jolla: Center for U.S.–Mexican Studies at the University of California at San Diego.

Nelson, Joan M. 1994. "Political Participation." In *Understanding Political Development.* Edited by M. Weiner and S. Huntington, 103–59. Prospect Heights: Waveland Press.

Nie, Norman H., Jr., G. Bingham Powell, and Kenneth Prewitt. 1969a. "Social Structure and Political Participation: Developmental Relationships, Part 1." *American Political Science Review* 63 (2): 361–78.

————. 1969b. "Social Structure and Political Participation: Developmental Relationships, Part 2." *American Political Science Review* 63 (3): 808–32.

Niemi, Richard G., Stephen C. Craig, and Franco Mattei. 1991. "Measuring Political Efficacy in the 1988 National Election Study." *American Political Science Review* 85 (4): 1407–13.

North, Douglass C. 1981. *Structure and Change in Economic History.* New York: W. W. Norton.

Olvera, Alberto J. 2004. "Civil Society in Mexico at Century's End." In *Dilemmas of Political Change in Mexico,* edited by K. J. Middlebrook. London: Institute of Latin American Studies / Center for U.S.–Mexican Studies.

Oxhorn, Philip D. 1991. "The Popular Sector Response to an Authoritarian Regime: Shantytown Organizations since the Military Coup." *Latin American Perspectives* 18 (67): 66–91.

————. 1994. "Understanding Political Change after Authoritarian Rule: The Popular Sectors and Chile's New Democratic Regime." *Journal of Latin American Studies* 26 (3): 737–59.

————. 1995. *Organizing Civil Society.* University Park: Pennsylvania State University Press.

————. 1998. "Is the Century of Corporatism Over? Neoliberalism and the Rise of Neopluralism." In *What Kind of Democracy? What Kind of Market? Latin America in the*

Age of Neoliberalism. Edited by P. D. Oxhorn and G. Ducatenzeiler, 195–217. University Park: Pennsylvania State University Press.

———, and Graciela Ducatenzeiler. 1998a. "Economic Reform and Democratization in Latin America." In *What Kind of Democracy? What Kind of Market? Latin America in the Age of Neoliberalism.* Edited by P. D. Oxhorn and G. Ducatenzeiler, 3–20. University Park: Pennsylvania State University Press.

———, eds. 1998b. *What Kind of Democracy? What Kind of Market? Latin America in the Age of Neoliberalism.* University Park: Pennsylvania State University Press.

Paré Ouellet, Luisa. 1992. "El Estado y los campesinos." In *El Nuevo Estado Mexicano: Estado, Actores y Movimientos Sociales.* Edited by J. Alonso, A. Azis, and J. Tamayo. Mexico City: Nueva Imagen.

Pastor, Manuel, and Carol Wise. 2003. "Picking up the Pieces: Comparing the Social Impacts of Financial Crisis in Mexico and Argentina." Paper presented at the annual meeting of the International Studies Association March 17, 2004, Montreal. Available online at http://www.allacademic.com/meta/p73447_index.html.

Pateman, Carol. 1970. *Participation and Democracy.* Cambridge: Cambridge University Press.

Patterson, Samuel C., and Gregory A. Caldeira. 1983. "Getting out the Vote: Participation in Gubernatorial Elections." *American Political Science Review* 77 (3): 675–89.

Percheron, Annick, and M. Kent Jennings. 1981. "Political Continuities in French Families: A New Perspective on an Old Controversy." *Comparative Politics* 13 (4): 421–36.

Petrocik, John R., and Daron Shaw. 1991. "Nonvoting in America: Attitudes in Context." In *Political Participation and American Democracy.* Edited by Crotty, 67–88.

Piven, Frances Fox, and Richard A. Cloward. 1979. *Poor People's Movements: Why They Succeed, How They Fail.* New York: Vintage Books.

———. 1997a. *The Breaking of the American Social Contract.* New York: The New Press.

———. 1997b. "Low Income People and the Political Process." In *The Breaking of the American Social Compact.* Edited by F. F. Piven and R. A. Cloward, 271–85. New York: The New Press.

———. 2000. *Why Americans Don't Still Don't Vote and Why Politicians Want It That Way.* Boston: Beacon Press.

Pollock III, Philip H. 1982. "Organizations as Agents of Mobilization: How Does Group Activity Affect Political Participation?" *American Journal of Political Science* 26 (3): 485–503.

———. 1983. "The Participatory Consequences of Internal and External Efficacy: A Research Note." *Western Political Quarterly* 36, no. 3: 400–409.

Popkin, Samuel L. 1979. *The Rational Peasant: The Political Economy of Rural Society in Vietnam.* Berkeley: University of California Press.

Portes, Alejandro, and Kelly Hoffman. 2003. "Latin American Class Structures: Their Composition and Change during the Neoliberal Era." *Latin American Research Review* 38 (1): 41–82.

Posner, Paul W. 2008. *State, Market, and Democracy in Chile: The Constraint of Popular Participation.* New York: Palgrave Macmillan.

Powell Jr., G. Bingham. 1986. "American Voter Turnout in Comparative Perspective." *American Political Science Review* 80 (1): 17–43.

———. 1993. "A Cross-national Analysis of Economic Voting: Taking Account of the Political Context." *American Journal of Political Science* 37 (2): 391–414.

Preston, Julia, and Samuel Dillon. 2004. *Opening Mexico: The Making of a Democracy.* New York: Farrar Straus and Giroux.

Przeworski, Adam. 1991. *Democracy and the Market: Political and Economic Reforms in Eastern Europe and Latin America.* Cambridge: Cambridge University Press.

Putnam, Robert D. 1993. *Making Democracy Work.* Princeton: Princeton University Press.

Ramírez Sáiz, Juan Manuel. 1986. *El Movimiento urbano popular en México.* Mexico City: Siglo XXI Editores.

———. 1992. "Entre el corporativismo social y la lógica electoral: El Estado y el movimiento Urbano Popular." In *El Nuevo Estado Mexicano: Estado, actores y movimientos sociales.* Mexico City: Nueva Imágen.

Reygadas Robles Gil, Rafael. 1998. *Abriendo Verebas: Iniciativas Públicas y Sociales de Las Redes de Organizaciones Civiles.* Mexico City: Convergencia de Organismos Civiles Por la Democracia.

Riker, William H., and Peter H. Ordershook. 1969. "A Theory of the Calculus of Voting." *American Political Science Review* 62: 25–43.

Roberts, Kenneth M. 1999. *Deepening Democracy? The Modern Left and Social Movements in Chile and Peru.* Palo Alto: Stanford University Press.

Rodríguez, Victoria Elizabeth. 1997. *Decentralization in Mexico: From Reforma Municipal to Solidaridad to Nuevo Federalismo.* Boulder: Westview Press.

———. 1998. "Opening the Electoral Space in Mexico: The Rise of the Opposition at the State and Local Levels." In *Urban Elections in Democratic Latin America.* Edited by Henry A. Dietz and Gil Shildo, 163–98. Wilmington: Scholarly Resources.

Rodríguez, Victoria E., and Peter M. Ward, eds. 1995. *Opposition Government in Mexico.* Albuquerque: University of New Mexico Press.

Rosenstone, Steven J., and John Mark Hansen. 1993. *Mobilization, Participation, and Democracy in America.* New York: McMillan Publishing Company.

Rosenstone, Steven J., and Raymond E. Wolfinger. 1978. "The Effect of Registration Laws on Voter Turnout." *American Political Science Review* 72: 22–45.

Rubin, Jeffrey W. 1996. "Decentering the Regime: Culture and Regional Politics in Mexico." *Latin American Research Review* 31 (3): 85–126.

———. 1997. *Decentering the Regime: Ethnicity, Radicalism, and Democracy in Juchitán, Mexico.* Durham: Duke University Press.

Rusk, Jerrold G., and John J. Stucker. 1991. "Legal-Institutional Factors and Voting Participation: The Impact of Women's Suffrage on Voter Turnout." In *Political Participation and American Democracy.* Edited by W. Crotty, 113–38. New York: Greenwood Press.

Salas, Carlos, and Eduardo Zepeda. 2003. "Employment and Wages: Enduring the Costs of Liberalization." In *Confronting Development: Assessing Mexico's Economic and Social Policy Challenges.* Edited by K. J. Middlebrook and E. Zepeda, 522–58. Palo Alto: Stanford University Press.

Samstad, James G. 2002. "Corporatism and Democratic Transition: State and Labor during the Salinas and Zedillo Administrations." *Latin American Politics and Society* 44 (2): 1–28.

Schattschneider, E. E. 1960. *The Semi-Sovereign People: A Realist's View of Democracy in America.* New York: Holt, Rinehart, and Winston.

Schedler, Andreas. 1999. "Civil Society and Political Elections: A Culture of Distrust?" *Annals of the American Academy of Political and Social Science* 565: 126–41.

Schlefer, Jonathan. 2008. *Palace Politics: How the Ruling Party Brought Crisis to Mexico.* Austin: University of Texas Press.

Schneider, Cathy. 1991. "Mobilization at the Grassroots: Shantytowns and Resistance in Authoritarian Chile." *Latin American Perspectives* 18 (67): 92–112.

———. 1995. *Shanty Town Protest in Pinochet's Chile.* Philadelphia: Temple University Press.

Scott, James C. 1969. "Corruption, Machine Politics, and Political Change." *American Political Science Review* 63 (4 December): 1142–58.

———. 1972. "Patron-Client Politics and Political Change in Southeast Asia." *American Political Science Review* 66 (1): 91–113.

———. 1977. *The Moral Economy of the Peasant: Rebellion and Subsistence in Southeast Asia.* New Haven: Yale University Press.

———. 1985. *Weapons of the Weak: Everyday Forms of Peasant Resistance.* New Haven: Yale University Press.

Seligson, Mitchell A., and John A. Booth, eds. 1979. *Political Participation in Latin America: Politics and the Poor.* 2 vols. Vol. 2. New York: Holmes and Meier Publishers.

Sen, Amartya. 1999. *Development as Freedom.* New York: Anchor Books.

Shadlen, Kenneth C. 2000. "Neoliberalism, Corporatism, and Small Business Political Activism in Contemporary Mexico." *Latin American Research Review* 35 (2): 73–106.

———. 2002. "Orphaned by Democracy: Small Industry in Contemporary Mexico." *Comparative Politics* 35 (1).

Shefner, Jonathan. 2001. "Coalitions and Clientelism in Mexico." *Theory and Society* 30: 593–628.

———. 2008. *The Illusion of Civil Society: Democratization and Community Mobilization in Low-income Mexico.* University Park: Pennsylvania State University Press.

Shirk, David A. 2005. *Mexico's New Politics: The PAN and Democratic Change.* Boulder: Lynne Rienner Publishers.

Singerman, Diane. 1995. *Avenues of Participation: Family, Politics, and Networks in Urban Quarters of Cairo.* Princeton Studies in Muslim Politics. Princeton: Princeton University Press.

Snow, David E., and Robert Benford. 1992. "Master Frames and Cycles of Protest." In *Frontiers in Social Movement Theory.* Edited by A. Morris and C. M. Mueller. New Haven: Yale University Press.

Snow, David E., Burke Rochford, Steven Worden, and Robert Wenford. 1986. "Frame Alignment Processes, Micromobilization, and Movement Participation." *American Sociological Review* 51: 464–81.

Snyder, Richard. 1999. "After the State Withdraws: Neoliberalism and Subnational Authoritarian Regimes in Mexico." In *Subnational Politics and Democratization in Mexico.* Edited by Cornelius, Eisenstadt, and Hindley, 295–341.

Stephen, Lynn. 1991. *Zapotec Women.* Austin: University of Texas Press.

———. 1997. *Women and Social Movements in Latin America: Power from Below.* Austin: University of Texas Press.

Stokes, Susan C. 1995. *Cultures in Conflict: Social Movements and the State in Peru*. Berkeley: University of California Press.

———. 2001. *Mandates and Democracy: Neoliberalism by Surprise in Latin America*. Cambridge: Cambridge University Press.

———. 2005. "Perverse Accountability: A Formal Model of Machine Politics with Evidence from Argentina." *American Political Science Review* 99 (3): 315–25.

Szélely, Miguel. 2005. "Pobreza y desigualdad en México entre 1950 y el 2004." *Serie documentos de investigación* 24 (Secretaría de Desarrollo Social / SEDESOL). Available online at http://www.sedesol.gob.mx/archivos/801588/file/Docu_24_2003.pdf.

Tamayo, Jaime, and Leonardo Valdés Zurita, eds. 1991. *Movimientos políticos y procesos electorales en México*. Guadalajara: Universidad de Guadalajara.

Tanaka, Martín. 1995. "La participación política de los sectores populares en América Latina." *Revista mexicana de sociologia* 57 (3): 41–65.

Tarrow, Sidney. 1998. *Power in Movement*. Second edition. Cambridge: Cambridge University Press.

Teichman, Judith A. 1997. "Neoliberalism and the Transformation of Mexican Authoritarianism." *Mexican Studies/Estudios Mexicanos* 13 (1): 121–47.

———. 2001. *The Politics of Freeing Markets in Latin America: Chile, Argentina, and Mexico*. Chapel Hill: University of North Carolina Press.

———. 2004. "The World Bank and Policy Reform in Mexico and Argentina." *Latin American Politics and Society* 46 (1): 40–74.

Teixeira, Ruy A. 1992. *The Disappearing American Voter*. Washington, D.C.: Brookings Institution Press.

Tejera Gaona, Héctor. 2002. *"No se olvide de nosotros cuando esté allá arriba": Cultura, ciudadanos y campañas electorales en la Ciudad de México*. Mexico City: Universidad Autónomia Metropolitana (UAM) / Porrúa.

Tilly, Charles. 1978. *From Mobilization to Revolution*. Reading: Addison-Wesley Publishing Company.

Tocqueville, Alexis de. 1961. *Democracy in America*. 2 vols. New York: Schocken Books.

Uhlaner, Carole J. 1989. "Rational Turnout: The Neglected Role of Groups." *American Journal of Political Science* 33 (2): 390–422.

Vélez-Ibañez, Carlos G. 1983. *Rituals of Marginality: Politics, Process, and Culture Change in Urban Central Mexico, 1969–1974*. Berkeley: University of California Press.

Verba, Sidney, Norman H. Nie, and Jae-On Kim. 1971. *The Modes of Political Participation: A Cross-National Comparison*. Beverly Hills: Sage Publications.

———. 1978. *Participation and Political Equality: A Seven Nation Comparison*. Chicago: University of Chicago Press.

Verba, Sidney, Kay Lehman Schlozman, and Henry E. Brady. 1995. *Voice and Equality: Civic Voluntarism in American Politics*. Cambridge: Harvard University Press.

Ward, Peter M. 1998. "From Machine Politics to the Politics of Technocracy: Charting Changes in Governance in the Mexican Municipality." *Bulletin of Latin American Research* 17 (3): 341–65.

Weffort, Francisco C. 1998. "New Democracies and Economic Crisis in Latin America." In *What Kind of Democracy? What Kind of Market? Latin America in the Age of Neoliberalism*. Edited by P. D. Oxhorn and G. Ducatenzeiler, 219–26. University Park: Pennsylvania State University Press.

Weitz-Shapiro, Rebecca. 2008. "The Local Connection: Local Government Performance and Satisfaction with Democracy in Argentina." *Comparative Political Studies* 41 (3): 285–308.

Weyland, Kurt. 1996. *Democracy without Equity: Failures of Reform in Brazil.* Pittsburgh: University of Pittsburgh Press.

———. 2004. "Neoliberalism and Democracy in Latin America: A Mixed Record." *Latin American Politics and Society* 46 (1): 136–57.

Whiteley, Paul F. 1995. "Rational Choice and Political Participation: Evaluating the Debate." *Political Research Quarterly* 48 (1): 211–33.

Wielhouwer, Peter, and Brad Lockerbie. 1996. "Party Contacting and Political Participation." *American Journal of Political Science* 38: 211–29.

Wildavsky, Aaron. 1987. "Choosing Preferences by Constructing Institutions: A Cultural Theory of Preference Formation." *American Political Science Review* 81 (1): 3–22.

Williams, Mark Eric. 2001. "Learning the Limits of Power: Privatization and State-Labor Interactions in Mexico." *Latin American Politics and Society* 43 (4): 91–126.

Wise, Carol. 2003. "Mexico's Democratic Transition: The Search for New Reform Coalitions." In *Post-stabilization Politics in Latin America.* Edited by C. Wise and R. Roett, 159–98. Washington, D.C.: Brookings Institution Press.

Wolfinger, Raymond E. 1972. "Why Political Machines Have Not Withered Away and Other Revisionist Thoughts." *Journal of Politics* 34 (2): 365–98.

———, and Steven J. Rosenstone. 1980. *Who Votes?* New Haven, Conn.: Yale University Press.

World Bank. 2004. *Poverty in Mexico: An Assessment of Conditions, Trends, and Government Strategy.* Washington, D.C.: World Bank.

———. 2005. *Income Generation and Social Protection for the Poor.* Washington, D.C.: World Bank.

World Values Survey Association. *World Values Survey, 1981–2005, Official Data Files.* Aggregate File Producer: ASEP/JDS, Madrid. Available online at http://www.worldvaluessurvey.org.

Wuhs, Steven T. 2006. "Democratization and the Dynamics of Candidate Selection Rule Change in Mexico, 1991–2003." *Mexican Studies/Estudios Mexicanos* 22 (1): 33–55.

———. 2008. *Savage Democracy: Institutional Change and Party Development in Mexico.* University Park: Pennsylvania State University Press.

Ziccardi, Alicia, ed. 1998. *Gobernabilidad y participación ciudadana en la capital.* Mexico City: Miguel Ángel Porrúa.

Index

Note: Figures and tables are indicated by "f" or "t," respectively.

273

Centéotl, 71–74
centralization of government: political
participation discouraged by, 48, 83;
under PRI, 116. *See also* decentralization of government
Chile, 30, 85, 86, 195
The Civic Culture (Almond and Verba), 15
civic voluntarism model, 25
civil society: fragmentation of, 78; income
levels and, 126; organizations and,
75–76, 126; and political participation,
126, 127. *See also* organizations
class. *See* income
clientelism: and authoritarianism, 140;
competitive, 140–45, 150, 168; decentralization and, 79, 141–42; democracy
and, 138; elites and, 5, 80–81, 140, 141,
168; local politics influenced by, 17;
neoliberalism and, 78–81; persistence
of, 17, 79–82, 117, 140–45; petitioning
and, 62; and political participation,
5, 6, 35, 45, 50, 77, 117, 126, 178, 179,
187, 193; political parties and, 79–80,
141–43; and the poor, 80, 142, 156,
178; strategic use of, 45; and voting
practices, 155–57
Cloward, Richard, 30, 34, 36
CNC. *See* Confederación Nacional
Campesina
COCEI, 147
collective action problems, 35, 74
Colombia, 85
Colosio, Luis Donaldo, 105
Comités de Vida Vecinal (COMVIVES),
168–69
community activity, 11, 22, 78, 168–69
community assemblies, 22, 169
Compañía Nacional de Subsistencias
Populares (CONASUPO), 84, 95
comparative research, 208
Comparative Studies of Electoral Systems
(CSES), 7, 18, 111–12
CONAPO, 240n7
CONASUPO. *See* Compañía Nacional de
Subsistencias Populares

Confederación de Trabajadores Mexicanos
(CTM), 66, 235n3
Confederación Nacional Campesina
(CNC), 66–67, 70, 72, 94, 148, 235n3
Confederación Nacional de Organizaciones Populares (CNOP), 66, 235n3
contacting of politicians, 5, 42, 62–63,
125t, 190–91t, 192, 212–13. *See also*
petitions
Convergencia, 143, 151, 158
Converse, Philip, 15
cooperatives, 71
Cornelius, Wayne, 84, 140
corporatism, 45, 64, 67
costs of political participation, 3, 25,
32–33, 35, 37, 43–44, 46, 54–55, 62–63,
73–74, 83, 202, 213
Craig, Ann, 84
customary law. *See* usos y costumbres
cynicism, 3, 98, 99, 109, 157–58, 166, 173

De la Madrid, Miguel, 66, 68
decentralization of government: and
clientelism, 79, 141–42; in Oaxaca,
167–68; outcomes of, 170–71; under
PAN, 117; and political competition, 133;
and political participation, 168–70. *See
also* centralization of government
dedazos (designations of successors), 140,
251n19
democracy: neoliberalism and, 208–9;
quality of, 208–15; satisfaction with,
176, 182, 183
democratic transition: completion of, 1–2;
local vs. national, 154; in 1990s, 128;
origins of, 106; pace of, 154; political
participation during and after, 2, 7–13,
7t, 49–50. *See also* democratization
democratization, 128–53; across Mexico,
175–93; clientelism and, 140–45; electoral competition and, 132–35; electoral
reforms and, 130–32; intragovernment
political competition and, 134–35; key
elements in, 128; in Latin America, 195;
neoliberalism and, 53–54; in Oaxaca,